RURAL SOCIAL WORK IN THE 21ST CENTURY

Advisory Editor
Thomas M. Meenaghan, *New York University*

Related books of interest

New Perspectives on Poverty: Policies, Programs, and Practice
Elissa D. Giffords and Karen R. Garber

Modern Social Work Theory, Fourth Edition
Malcolm Payne

Navigating Human Service Organizations, Third Edition
Rich Furman and Margaret Gibelman

Writing Clearly for Clients and Others: The Human Service Practitioner's Guide
Natalie Ames and Katy FitzGerald

A Practical Guide to Evaluation, Second Edition
Carl F. Brun

The Community Needs Assessment Workbook
Rodney A. Wambeam

Best Practices in Community Mental Health: A Pocket Guide
Vikki L. Vandiver

Surviving Disaster: The Role of Social Networks
Robin L. Ersing and Kathleen A. Kost

Advocacy Practice for Social Justice, Second Edition
Richard Hoefer

The Costs of Courage: Combat Stress, Warriors, and Family Survival
Josephine G. Pryce, Col. David H. Pryce, and Kimberly K. Shackelford

Social Work Practice with Latinos: Key Issues and Emerging Themes
Rich Furman and Nalini Negi

Rural Social Work in the 21st Century

Michael R. Daley

University of South Alabama

Chicago, IL 60637

Published by
LYCEUM BOOKS, INC.
5758 S. Blackstone Avenue
Chicago, Illinois 60637
773-643-1903 fax
773-643-1902 phone
lyceum@lyceumbooks.com
www.lyceumbooks.com

6 5 4 3 2 15 16 17 18

ISBN 978-1-935871-61-3

Printed in the United States of America.

Library of Congress Cataloging-in-Publication Data

Daley, Michael Rex.
Rural social work in the 21st century / Michael R. Daley, University of South Alabama.
pages cm
Includes bibliographical references and index.
ISBN 978-1-935871-61-3
1. Social service, Rural. 2. Rural development. I. Title.
HV67.D35 2014
361.309173'4—dc23

2014013605

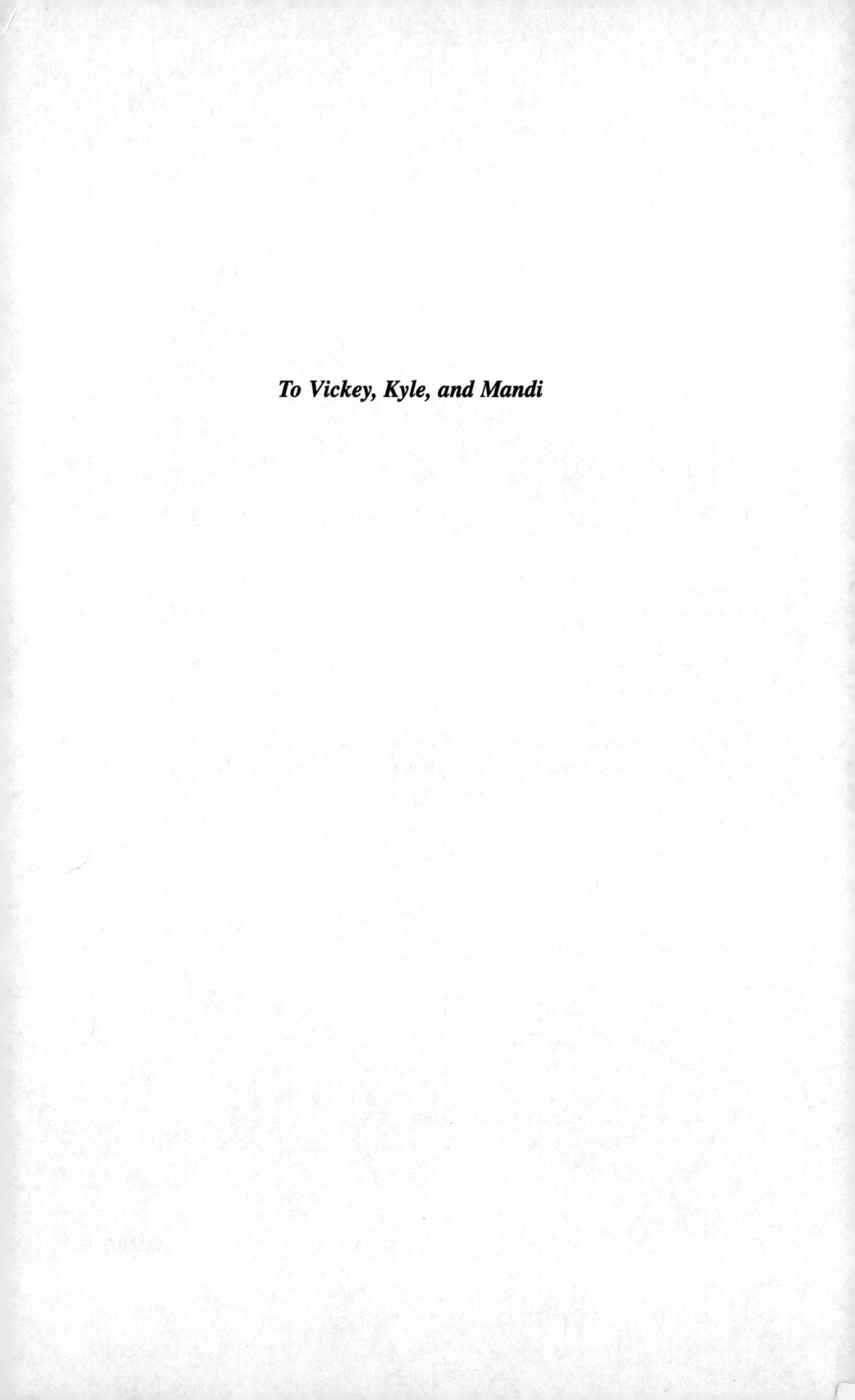

To Vickey, Kyle, and Mandi

Contents

Rural roots: the author's father (left) and siblings in the Arizona Territory 1909.

Preface

Rural social work is an important practice arena that can make a significant and positive difference in the lives of both clients and workers. Popular beliefs to the contrary, the rural population is increasing, and a significant minority of society still lives in smaller communities. Yet rural social work is often overlooked, even by the social work profession. Perhaps this is because of social work's urban roots, which gave the profession a focus on where there is greatest need. Or it may be that it is naively assumed that rural communities are idyllic places with few social problems. And it just could be an "out of sight, out of mind" phenomenon. Indeed, it was many years before the field of social work seriously turned its attention to the needs of rural people and communities.

As the title suggests, this is a book about rural social work as a field of practice. It was written to address what appeared to be a gap in the literature, and it aims to provide an overview of the field to serve as starting point and a resource. Indeed, there are several excellent works about rural social work that currently exist, yet the major resources in this field still consist primarily of collected readings and individual articles. Given the diversity of authors and viewpoints reflected in those, it is sometimes challenging to decide where to start or to get a clear perspective about rural practice. The book provides a survey of the field and is not intended to replace what already exists. Indeed, many existing resources were used in preparing the finished product. But it does provide an overall perspective that incorporates much of the existing literature.

Rural Social Work in the 21st Century does attempt to provide enough specific information to prove useful to students and professionals alike and to guide further study. It is intended for social work students at any level and may be used in a freestanding course on rural social work or as a companion to other courses to add rural content. It can be used as an introduction to the field and can provide a framework for the use of articles and chapters about rural social work. Certainly individual articles and books of collected reading provide more specific detail on selected topics, and the reader is encouraged to explore the many sources used for this book to learn more. But ultimately this book is about the big picture of rural social work, and if it succeeds in providing a foundation for learning more about the field, or in sparking further interest in rural social work, then its primary purpose will have been achieved.

Scholarly work was used as the platform for preparing the material. But the language used here is often informal, direct, and earthy. This may strike some as a little odd or a bit unscholarly. But such is the nature of rural language and rural people, and the book is designed to give a bit of that flavor. This was a conscious decision. In reading drafts of the early chapters, the language did not ring true for a volume on rural social work. In some ways a more formal voice did not get at the true character of rural people. It is my hope that by adding folksy language that the reader's experience is enhanced in terms of giving a better idea of rurality than might otherwise be the case.

Over the past century there have been times when rural social work and the needs of rural people have experienced long periods of neglect. Yet over the past four decades social work has revitalized its interest in rural practice, and as a result the rural literature has expanded considerably in terms of depth and richness. Several good books and articles have been generated to help expand what we know about the field. The logical question, then, is, why another book on rural social work?

The decision to write this work is based on the sum of my experiences over more than thirty years of being involved in the field and trying to teach rural content to students. My first teaching position introduced me, urban born and raised, to living and working in a small rural community. It did not take long for me to learn that I was like a duck out of water. To adapt to this new environment, and especially to teach social work students to effectively work in it, learning about rural practice was essential.

The real question was, where to start? Many fields of practice had a book written by one or more authors that covered the field. Child welfare, school social work, and mental health all had books that surveyed the field and provided a platform for both introduction and further learning. There were books about rural social work, but they were primarily collections of readings around general areas and written by many authors. These were wonderful materials, and very helpful. But they made it challenging to get the big picture.

Moving to the present, the past decade has produced a revival of sorts for rural practice. Several new publications in the field and the emergence of the new journal *Contemporary Rural Social Work* have arrived to provide social workers vital information to strengthen their work. The transformation of rural social work that has occurred as a result of the twenty-first-century resurgence is certainly a positive step, because the work is becoming more challenging as service funding continues to shrink while the rural population continues to grow. Moreover, rural social work is one of the fields of practice in which significantly more social workers are needed. Yet still too few schools of social work provide coursework to prepare graduates for work in rural communities.

To provide an overview of such a broad field of practice was a bit of a challenge in terms of organizing the considerable amount of information. The organizational structure chosen was based on social work competency and content areas. For example, there are chapters on social work practice, human behavior in the rural environment, diversity and culture, policy services, and history. This provided a workable structure for covering the major issues in the field that was flexible enough to address the audiences of students and practitioners.

Throughout this volume several concepts emerge with some frequency. The strengths-assets perspective that has been added to the rural literature is an important concept that offers a more positive approach to practice and is used extensively here. Approaching rural communities in terms of what they lack may be helpful in identifying problems, but it can lead to a negative view that is less helpful in developing solutions. And rural communities do have many assets, which are frequently overlooked.

Rural Social Work in the 21st Century employs the perspective that rural communities and people represent a distinct culture that should be learned and treated with sensitivity. This culture goes with them wherever they go, and rural social work is work with rural people, no matter where they may live. This liberates the field from being constrained by narrow and somewhat arbitrary definitions of rurality based on a specific population figure, thereby considerably expanding the scope of practice. The idea of rural social work as being place bound and confined to small towns, villages, and the countryside has been traditional. Still, it ignores the substantial patterns of migration that have occurred over the past hundred-plus years as rural people have moved to the city in large numbers and congregated in new communities. And substantial numbers of people who have rural backgrounds currently live in the city, where they may come into contact with social workers.

This is a book about rural social work, and rural communities are not static. Indeed, rural populations are in transition; thus, today's rural environment is no longer the rural community that our parents experienced. Better communication; improved transportation networks; and widespread movement of people, goods, and services into rural areas have changed and are changing traditional ways of life. Some of these changes do create additional challenges for rural people.

Another theme is the richness, diversity, and resiliency of rural people. The importance of community and the interactions of individual, family, and community in assessing needs and developing social work interventions is discussed in many contexts. Many rural areas emphasize a more collective, personalized view of social interaction than in an urban context. Another concept discussed here includes the fact that one-size-fits-all does not work for rural communities, as they vary in size, culture, economics, and cultural beliefs and practices. Another important theme relates to the availability of services, which vary locally to create issues of access, adequacy, and specialization for people in the community.

A final theme is social work and social workers in a rural context. Rural social work can be rich and rewarding, and it requires professionals who are flexible, creative, and generalist in their approach. Rural social workers can and do become an important part of the community, and effective intervention requires learning about the culture and people while responding sensitively to them.

Although this book is ultimately my work, it would not have been possible without the contributions of many others. Long associations and frequent conversations with many rural social workers have helped not only in providing important information but also in the formulation of ideas. In this regard, I would like to give special thanks to my rural colleagues who have provided support and given comments on drafts of this work. These include Freddie Avant, Ginny Majewski, Richard Osburn, and Peggy Pittman-Munke. Special thanks to my wife, Vickey, who has provided me with many ideas, insights, and examples, and to my editor, David Follmer, who has encouraged and guided me through the process. I would also like to thank the staff at Lyceum Books, especially Katherine Faydash, whose editing added a great deal to the quality of the text. All of these folks have helped to point me in the right direction and at times have lent a sympathetic ear.

Coauthors who have collaborated with me on prior work have also played an important role in guiding my views of rural social work and deserve thanks as well. They are Freddie Avant, Michael Doughty, Sam Hickman, and Barbara Pierce. Two other colleagues contributed more indirectly over the years, but their influence was important nonetheless. Will Scott and Leon Ginsberg have provided guidance and support that proved extremely valuable. All of these folks are great people and colleagues, and I am lucky to have them. Without the influence and help of them all, this work could not have been completed. At one time or another we all met as members of the Rural Social Work Caucus and discussed rural social work. The caucus is a committed group of professional social workers, without which this work might never have been undertaken.

Capturing the depth and breadth of rural people and rural social work in a way that captures the rich diversity was a formidable task. Rural social work is an important subject that demands an appropriate treatment. It is my hope that to some degree this has been accomplished here. I hope too that readers feel free to embrace the rural experience, and perhaps will develop as much interest in rural social work as I have. Welcome to rural social work in the twenty-first century.

Distance and road conditions are an important feature of rural life and rural social work. Photo of a covered bridge in Indiana.

CHAPTER ONE

Rural Communities and Social Work: An Introduction

RURAL SOCIAL WORK has been with us since the early 1900s and remains a significant and vital part of helping individuals and families, and addressing community problems. Despite the fact that the population of North America has been becoming increasingly urban for more than a century, a significant minority of the population still resides in rural areas. Although we are no longer primarily a rural or agrarian society, rural people, their culture, and their economic contributions remain an important part of our society.

Rural people experience challenges like the rest of society, and sometimes their needs rise to the level of requiring professional help; that is where social workers enter the picture. People from rural communities experience mental health problems; their children need protection from maltreatment; individuals and families are victims of crime or family violence; or people are poor and need assistance in accessing economic resources and health care. But because rural people are a minority and can be less visible because they live outside major urban and media centers, it is often easy to forget their unique needs and wants.

Frankly, even when services may be available, the one-size-fits-all, depersonalized model of service of the twenty-first century, designed to promote efficiency, is likely to alienate rural clients and turn them away from the very assistance they need. Culturally, they expect more personalized relationships, are cautious of outsiders, cling to traditional ways of doing things, and value self-reliance. These characteristics can easily be seen as standoffish, resistant to change and help, and somewhat backward. None of these perceptions is entirely accurate. It is just that the constant change and impersonality that have become so much a part of twenty-first-century urban life really seem unpleasant, depersonalizing, and rude to them.

Social workers are there to help empower—from the elder person who needs a wheel chair, ramp, and caregivers to remain in the home to the toddler who is burned by an angry parent, or the person with an illness needing treatment. Human relationships are important tools that social workers use to effect change in clients' lives (NASW, 2012). But strong relationships with rural clients are difficult to establish if we do not already know them and are reluctant to learn their culture. Developing cultural sensitivity and competence and working to address oppression are basic to social work. Learning to adapt professional helping methods in the context of rural culture is a vital part of building and maintaining the helping relationships needed to work with rural clients and communities. Not all rural communities are alike, and each new context may require some discovery and learning on the part of the social worker. Otherwise, it is more difficult to establish relationships, effectively assess needs, or respond appropriately to the needs of rural people. It is important to understand their worldview and who they really are.

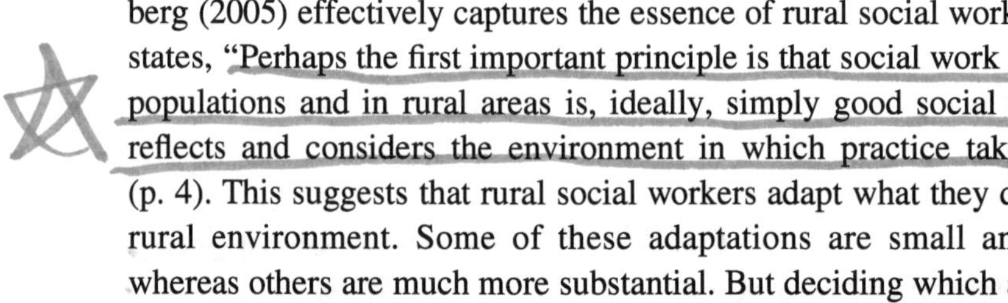

But rural social work, as all social work, is a complex endeavor. Ginsberg (2005) effectively captures the essence of rural social work when he states, "Perhaps the first important principle is that social work with rural populations and in rural areas is, ideally, simply good social work that reflects and considers the environment in which practice takes place" (p. 4). This suggests that rural social workers adapt what they do to each rural environment. Some of these adaptations are small and subtle, whereas others are much more substantial. But deciding which aspects of practice require adapting, understanding the fit between clients and practice, and incorporating all of this into a social worker's skill set are critical and frequently more difficult than they appear.

While there is a rich and growing literature in the field of rural social work, often discovering the kind of information that one may need is challenging, since key knowledge is scattered among journal articles and collections of readings. It has been almost three decades since a book attempted to provide a comprehensive overview of social work with rural populations. The overview of rural practice presented in this book, drawn from several sources, provides the reader with a single source for rural social work. The discussion of topics contained in the chapters is centered on social work competency and content areas.

This chapter begins the journey of discovery about rural social work. It discusses why rural social work is important, how *rural* is defined, the limits of a geographical definition for rural communities, the uniqueness of rural social work, and the potential rewards of being a rural social worker.

WHY RURAL SOCIAL WORK?

Despite our increasingly urban society, people who live in rural areas are a significant minority of the population. According to figures from the 2010 US census, the rural population represented 19.3 percent of the population, or about 59.5 million people (US Census Bureau, n.d.). Canadian statistics for 2006 also indicate a rural population of 20 percent, or 6.3 million people (Statistics Canada, 2011). Census data and Canadian statistical data also both indicate that over the past one hundred years, the percentage of the rural population in the United States and Canada has declined (Statistics Canada, 2011; US Census Bureau, 1995). This trend has led many people to believe that the rural population is in decline in both countries, as they become increasingly urban.

Yet this viewpoint is mistaken, because the absolute numbers of rural people in both the United States and Canada have actually increased. In the United States there are approximately 430,000 more rural residents, and in Canada 150,000, than the previous data collection period, and the rural population continues to grow. This suggests that the percentage decline in the rural population of both countries is more a function of the faster growth in urban areas than an actual decline in rural residents. Indeed, both countries have significant rural populations as well as strong rural traditions. In fact, a majority of the US and Canadian populations lived in rural communities as late as the 1920s.

The 19 or 20 percent of the population living in rural areas today is not an insignificant minority, and this is a minority population that is growing in size, if declining in percentage. But the population that potentially needs rural social work services is actually greater than the official rural figures listed in a census. Rural people do live in the cities, and they could require services as well. Rural people do move to urban areas, and they often do not leave their needs and cultural traditions behind when they do. Many times rural people in cities move into areas where they are most comfortable and form new communities, or rural enclaves, with the larger geographic community. In this sense, rural communities may not be entirely geographic but of the type based on shared interests, social interaction, behavior patterns, trade, or commerce (Meenaghan, Gibbons, & McNutt, 2005). Therefore, rural communities may be found outside of those geographic areas that are typically classified as rural.

Because of significant rural-to-urban migration, and the expansion of urban communities, many country people find themselves outside of their native environment. They may find themselves in an unfamiliar suburban or urban community. Just as in any other segment of society, these rural people may confront a variety of social needs for which they require help. Given their new community context, they may find their traditional rural coping mechanisms ineffective, and so require professional help. Often these are types of needs and challenges that social workers are well prepared to tackle.

Though far from the familiar rural environment in which they may have been raised and socialized, people may still maintain their beliefs and behaviors in their new homes (Daley & Avant, 2004b; Ginsberg, 2005). As they develop problems in living and try to solve those problems, it is important for social workers with whom these people come into contact to recognize the importance and uniqueness of their culture in order to respond in a sensitive way.

So, in a very real sense, urban-based social workers may work with clients who have strong rural beliefs and behaviors, and who live within the boundaries of metropolitan or suburban areas. This scenario is essentially the one portrayed in Harriette Arnow's (1954) book *The Dollmaker*, in which a family faces a series of struggles after moving from rural Kentucky to Detroit. While she is in the city, the heroine, Gertrude Nevils, struggles to keep her family together and to maintain her strong rural values. For rural people, because of their new urban home, their rural culture may be easy to miss, and it could be far too easy for others to view them as dysfunctional. This may not be something an urban social worker is adequately prepared to recognize or incorporate into assessments and services.

Rural communities can also change over time, sometimes involuntarily. As urban areas expand their boundaries, they can surround and absorb traditional rural communities near them. Rural areas can become suburban or bedroom communities for commuters and change the very character of the community. In this case, as urbanites move to the country in large numbers, rural people may view themselves as being invaded or overrun by outsiders. The result is often the displacement of former residents as property values rise and transformation of the community in ways that cause division among residents. New ways are forced onto the community involuntarily and can generate social disruption and problems.

Ultimately, rural communities are communities of people. These communities may be geographic or associational. So, whether rural people live in a rural town or area or form a subgroup in a city or suburb, they can and do form cohesive communities. The issues and problems the different types of rural communities present may vary, but the communality is rural behavior. Although rural communities differ in terms of their norms and culture, there tend to be some common elements. Learning rural behavior and the specific expectations of each community are important parts of any effective social work assessment and of helping empower rural people to meet the challenges facing them.

Rural communities—be they geographic, associational, or neighborhoods—tend to face an increased risk of experiencing several social problems. According to the National Association of Social Workers (2012), the people in rural communities are more likely to have no health coverage or dental care, to smoke and be obese, to suffer from chronic health problems, and to avoid seeing physicians because of the cost. They are also more likely to have low incomes and to be in poverty, and to rely on government forms of economic assistance. Many of these same issues exist for rural people who relocate to suburban or urban areas.

The conditions identified here speak to the need for social workers in rural areas and to provide services for rural people. The National Association of Social Workers' (2012) rural social work policy statement succinctly captures the role of rural social workers as follows: "Social workers practicing in rural areas have historically sought to resolve issues of equity, service availability, and isolation that adversely affect residents. They also work to support and advocate for vulnerable and at-risk people living in rural communities" (p. 296). This is important work and is of significant benefit to both individuals involved and society in general. Social workers who work with rural people who reside in urban and suburban communities face similar issues and have very similar roles.

Unfortunately, there are not enough professional social workers to meet the needs of rural communities (Daley & Avant, 1999; Ginsberg, 2005; NASW, 2012). This is part of a general problem faced by rural communities, and it involves a shortage of service and health-care professionals. For social work the specific concern is that the numbers, distribution, and types of backgrounds of social workers often do not adequately meet the needs of rural communities. Specialized services, such as foster care for special needs children, are an area of especially acute need.

Ginsberg (2011) points out that social workers in rural areas tend to be employed as sole practitioners or in small groups. Daley and Avant (1999) expand on this point by identifying issues with the geographic distribution and specialized and advanced preparation of rural social workers. What these authors suggest is that professional social workers are not available in many rural areas, and when they are, they are frequently isolated or work in very small groups. Even when social workers are available to serve the community, they often do not have the advanced or specialized education or training to address the range of community problems, and they face challenges in terms of getting supervision (Daley & Avant, 2004a; Ginsberg, 2005, 2011; NASW, 2012).

All of this speaks to a basic labor-force issue: more social workers are needed in rural areas, more educational programs need to prepare social workers to work with rural people (Daley & Avant, 1999; Ginsberg, 2011; Lohmann & Lohmann, 2005; NASW, 2012), and there is an even greater need to prepare social workers for advanced rural practice (Daley & Avant, 1999; Daley & Pierce, 2011; Lohmann & Lohmann,

2005; NASW, 2009). The recruitment and retention of social workers in rural communities can be effectively approached by providing social workers with rural content and field placements during their professional education (Daley & Avant, 1999; Lohmann & Lohmann, 2005; Mackie, 2007).

WHAT IS RURAL?

Although it may seem simple, answering the question "Am I working with a rural community?" is a bigger challenge for a social worker than it may appear. The challenge exists not so much because a rural community is difficult to define, but because there are many definitions of *rural*, and this can lead to uncertainty about which definition to use. One can easily get lost or distracted in trying to split hairs over the fine points or technicalities of definitions; it is more important to focus on why it is important for a social worker to determine rurality. Social workers tend to be more focused on how the social environment affects the people than on population figures or density.

There is no one generally accepted definition of rurality (Ginsberg, 2011). There are multiple definitions, each of which is useful for different purposes, so asking, "Is this rural?" may also prove relevant in deciding which definition of the word to use. Some definitions are more useful for research and statistical purposes, whereas others may be more helpful for sociological, economic, or social work purposes. Definitions of rurality can be classified into one of three categories, depending on the core concepts underlying the definition: absolute, relative, or socioeconomic. Each of these is discussed in the following paragraphs.

The absolute method of defining rurality is based on an arbitrarily determined number of residents; this tends to be the most frequently used way to determine whether a community is rural. The advantage of using an absolute method is that communities can be clearly classified as either rural or nonrural. This approach is useful for endeavors that require a clear-cut demarcation between rural and nonrural, as, for example, census data, social policy concerns, and social research. The primary value of the absolute approach is the degree of certainty that it provides in determining what is rural and its ability to convey simply a complex system of social structure and interactions, economics, and special characteristics. However, much valuable information can be lost with this approach, particularly for the purposes of social work services. Absolute definitions tend to either overgeneralize or lose many of the unique characteristics of specific communities. In fact, even at the county or province level, an overall urban classification may cause one to miss rural pockets on the periphery.

Much of the social work literature uses an absolute approach that identifies the rural community as one of geography, place, or locale. As a result, many social workers tend to view *rural* as a synonym for a specific type of physical location that consists of a small town, agricultural region, or ranch. This perspective is further reinforced by the media's portrayal of rural America and Canada, where we find images of a fictional rural Mayberry, North Carolina; Cicely, Alaska; or Dog River, Saskatchewan, to use as a place of reference. These are fictional small towns, and their portrayal is based on the quaint ways of rural people, often used as a vehicle for comedy. Of course, these stereotypes do not begin to capture the richness of diversity that exists in the vast areas of rural North America. Nor do they accurately reflect the complex dimensions of rurality that are important to the practice of social work.

Farley, Griffiths, Skidmore, and Thackeray (1982) indicate that an absolute approach to defining rurality by population may not ultimately be as helpful as it appears. They suggest that rurality and urbanity lie along a continuum and that the various population figures are but points along that continuum. This viewpoint suggests that rurality is much more complex than revealed in a simple population figure and that it is a function of population size, density, and distance from an urban core.

Even with the absolute approach there are at least three discrete population classification systems in use in the United States for deciding whether a community is rural (Daley & Pierce, 2011). The US Census Bureau defines a rural area as having a population of less than 2,500 and as nonadjacent to an urban area. The US Office of Management and Budget classifies communities with a population of less than 50,000 as nonmetropolitan, and the 2000 US Census classified communities as rural areas, urban areas, and urban clusters (Daley & Pierce, 2011; Olaveson, Conway, & Shaver, 2004). This latter classification is a composite definition based on population size and density. Additionally, parts of the

United States with very low population density are often classified as frontier areas.

Canada also uses multiple ways to define rural communities. These include census rural areas and rural and small towns. Census rural areas have a population living outside of places with one thousand or more people or outside of places with a population density of four hundred or more people per square kilometer. Rural and small towns are populations living outside the main commuting zone of larger urban centers of ten thousand or more. Nonmetropolitan areas are communities of people who live outside of major urban settlements of fifty thousand or more (Statistics Canada, 2001).

A second approach to determining rurality is a relative one, which focuses on population density. This type of method compares relative densities of people to reflect the collection of people in a geographic space. Urban areas obviously have a high number of people per square mile or kilometer, whereas the density decreases considerably for small towns and rural areas. These relative densities have some implications for critical masses of people, the institutions that serve them, and the type of economy and social interactions. Thus, a low population density may be attributable to some economic factor like agriculture, ranching, or timber, which require more land to be economically productive than a small business does. Low density may also speak to sparseness of services, a topic frequently discussed in the rural social work literature. Low population densities for rural areas translate into a high cost per unit of service, which is something service providers often try to minimize.

In some sense, the metropolitan and nonmetropolitan dichotomy also loosely reflects the relative concept of population density in both the United States and Canada. The general classification of a metropolitan area also tends to include the idea that population density exceeds one thousand people per square mile. Canada also uses a relative method, defining rural areas as those having fewer than 400 people per square kilometer and rural communities as populations having fewer than 150 people per square kilometer (Statistics Canada, 2001).

Definitions of rurality that focus on absolute population or population density are often not much help to the average social worker, except in a very general sense. The core of social work is about helping individuals, families, and communities to address specific problems and challenges. So, the social, institutional, economic, and cultural characteristics of rurality tend to take on greater significance than geographic components do. Even within rural communities there is considerable variation on these factors, as a rural area may include communities ranging in size from fifty people to forty-five thousand. As a result, the general kind of information that comes from population figures tends to be helpful primarily as background, unless one is engaged in very broad-based community work or social research.

The third approach to defining rurality uses sociocultural characteristics of the community. Daley and Avant (2004b) and Daley and Pierce (2011) suggest using this approach, and Ginsberg (2005) discusses viewing rural communities and services from the perspective of a rural lifestyle. The person-in-environment approach in social work tends to support this way of defining rurality.

The sociocultural method of defining rurality follows the lead of rural sociologists and evaluates the economy, identity, and social interaction within a community. The term *rurality*, designating a community with rural characteristics, has been used by rural sociologists for at least fifty years (Bealer, Willitis, & Kuvlesky, 1965). This sociocultural definition identifies rural communities in terms of institutions and structures, like occupations, ecology, and sociocultural elements. A *sociocultural* approach is a functional way of defining rurality for social workers because it frames rurality in terms of important social systems and issues that affect what social workers do on a daily basis.

There are other advantages to using a sociocultural perspective in rural social work. Definitions of rurality based on population size and/or density do not adequately capture those rural people who have moved to the city and formed communities, rural communities that have been absorbed through urban growth, or rural pockets on the outskirts of metropolitan regions. These communities still have substantial numbers of people who have a rural culture, beliefs, and lifestyle, yet they remain invisible and uncounted in population-based representations of rural community. In many ways there is some substance to the old adage "you can take the kid out of the country, but you can't take the country out of the kid."

The value of the sociocultural approach in defining rurality in a way that is relevant for social work is illustrated by the examples of rural values, behaviors, and institutions that have been consistently identified in the literature. Some of these characteristics are attachment to the land or place, emphasis on a personal style of social interaction, traditionalism or conservatism, importance of faith, use of natural helping networks, and a close-knit community in which people's lives are intertwined (sometimes called "living in a fishbowl") (Daley & Avant, 2004b; Ginsberg, 2005). All of these characteristics have significant influences on individual and collective behavior, as well as on the delivery of social work services—and they tend to be consistent across many rural communities.

So, what does all this mean for the social worker trying to figure out whether a client or community is rural? First and foremost, it is important to consider why one seeks to determine rurality. This has important implications for which approach to the definition is most appropriate. If making decisions that require a dichotomy like rural and not rural is important, then population-based figures may be important. If considering program and service planning, then population density, with its implications for program costs, transportation, and resources, may be important. But in virtually any aspect of social work—from working with an individual client to engaging in community development—rural culture and the self-identification of the people are key elements of practice. This argues for the use of a sociocultural definition of rurality by social workers, perhaps even in conjunction with other methods.

From a practical standpoint, based on what social workers typically do, sociocultural definitions of rurality serve as the best guide for professional practice. This is because the key elements of the human systems with which we work are guided more by culture, beliefs, values, and behavior than they are by the use of the term *rural*. Social workers focus on individualizing the specific situations, and sociocultural characteristics help in that process. This is important because rural social workers often serve multiple communities that differ substantially in culture and characteristics. If people who reside in a community view themselves as rural, then drawing distinctions based on population size is indeed arbitrary.

Perhaps the best advice for determining whether one is working with rural people is that which Daley and Pierce (2011) propose in discussing rural social work education: "The basic questions that social work[ers] . . . must ask . . . are: Do residents of the service area think of themselves as rural and possess rural attributes and behaviors? Do the communities have rural characteristics?" (p. 126). If the answer to these questions is yes, then a social worker is indeed working with rural people, and this should shape the approach to providing services.

IS RURALITY CONFINED TO SMALL TOWNS AND COMMUNITIES?

Rurality does not exist solely in small towns, villages, and the countryside. The presence of rural culture is evident in large cities, medium-size towns, and suburbs. Unfortunately, the use of absolute definitions of rurality suggests a dichotomy of rural and nonrural that is based on a fixed geographic boundary. In our society people move and communities change on the basis of that movement. Social workers who approach their practice as a rural-nonrural dichotomy often overlook the subtle differences in people and behavior essential to effective practice.

Rural communities are collections of people, many of whom share common interests, interact socially, conform to common behavioral norms and expectations, and conduct trade or business with one another. The social worker may find large groups of people, families, or individuals who view themselves as rural in virtually any kind of geographic community. Because of this, rural people and communities cannot always be identified easily just because of the geographic community in which they live, especially for the purposes of professional helping.

Social workers assist people face the challenges of life and adaptation to the surrounding environment. It is not unusual to find rural people in the "big city" in need of help. These people may be out of their cultural element, be far from family support, and have a precarious economic future, and the traditional rural ways of coping with these issues are either nonexistent or not effective in the urban environment.

My own practice experience in a large metropolitan area included numerous examples of rural people who had migrated to the city at various times, primarily to achieve a better economic life. Often they would settle in neighborhoods near a family member, friends, or other people from similar backgrounds. Many of the people needing help faced difficulty because of being separated from their family and community, traditional sources of support. They often faced economic disruption because the jobs they filled either were dangerous or did not offer benefits. Yet these were fundamentally rural people who would, and often did, re-create some elements of their rural home in their new city. For example, they might have looked to live in outlying parts of town where the population density is lower, or have adapted their homes to a more familiar lifestyle. For example, residents in the Southwest may find themselves in neighborhoods that begin to resemble rural Mexican barrios. In effect, the residents from rural areas help these communities become rural islands within a larger urban sphere.

Urbanites and suburbanites may tend to look with contempt upon these neighborhoods and areas. The idea of placing chairs and couches and other furniture on the front porch, or of parking multiple cars or burning trash in the yard, may be viewed as "trashy" within the larger community. Yet in a rural environment having a place to sit on the porch is a way to enjoy the outdoors and an extension of hospitality to friends and neighbors. Many rural homes do not have garages, and trash pickup ranges from less reliable than in the city to nonexistent. So, all of these activities serve useful functions in rural life.

Interestingly, rural communities, whether they are in less populated areas or are islands in the larger urban environment, share some of the same characteristics, which has implications for practice. Most rural areas are not service-rich environments, whether in the country or in the big city. This in turn generates issues of travel to be able to access services, which is not a trivial issue for people without reliable cars and trucks.

WHAT IS UNIQUE ABOUT RURAL SOCIAL WORK?

The unique aspect of social work with rural people is the context, as rural culture tends to shape a lot of individual and collective behavior. In a broad sense people are people, and the basic principles of social work practice do not fundamentally change in rural areas. But ideas, perceptions, belief systems, and behavior are unquestionably shaped by the rural experience. To effectively engage and work with rural people, it is essential to understand their background and worldview. This, of course, is basic good social work in any context, but it is still significant to keep it in mind for rural work. As an example of this, consider that in social work, as in other professions, the social worker is expected to maintain a distinction between the personal and the professional relationship. This is done to maintain objectivity and fairness, and to ensure that each client receives similar-quality service. If personal and professional relationships are not distinct, this may create confusion for the client about the nature of the relationship. But in the rural community, personal relationships are the norm and are expected. Moreover, the impartiality associated with professional help can be seen as standoffish or rude. If clients develop this perception, they may be distant or mistrustful of the social worker. Successful rural social workers must learn to adapt their practice methods to account for the informality of the rural context by finding more personal ways of connecting with clients while still maintaining appropriate professional boundaries. An ability to discuss people whom they know in common, community activities, and events like football games are more informal ways of establishing a relationship without being unprofessional.

Even delivering a basic service in the rural setting may evoke a need for creativity (Riebschleger, 2007). For example, a person who needs a basic mental health service may need a referral to the local mental health or health center. But the client may balk at going to that center because he or she—or his or her car or truck—might be readily recognized by others in the community. In this context, driving into a mental health or health-care center is perceived as advertising to the community that a person is "crazy" or "sick"; it's something a person does not want everyone to know. Providing alternative means of service delivery, such as in another nearby community, might be a creative solution that a rural social worker could use.

Rural social workers may also have to spend extra time in community-based work, hence the need for them to be generalists. They may need to develop or bundle the services a client needs if a specific type of service or agency does not exist in the community. In this sense, rural social workers may need to work with more than just individuals and families to get the job done.

Rural social workers are also more visible in the community, both as professionals and as individuals. Secrets don't last very long in a small town, so what a social worker does either professionally or personally ends up as part of a general perception about who he or she is. Consequently, rural social workers have to be careful about how they act. For example, drinking or partying will be noticed in a small town, whereas this would be unlikely in the more anonymous environment of a large city. Rural towns may be located in dry counties or in areas where drinking is frowned upon. Even though adults can consume alcohol on their own time, if people in a community notice, it might affect their perception of the social worker.

REWARDS AND CHALLENGES OF RURAL SOCIAL WORK

Being a social worker in a rural community can be quite a rewarding experience and a fulfilling career choice. Indeed, there are both rewards and challenges to this field of practice, but for the social worker who is prepared and who adapts well to the rural environment, the rewards tend to outweigh the challenges. But rural practice is not for everyone. Consequently, it is important for social workers to understand the structural environment in which social workers carry out their responsibilities, as well as the potential rewards and challenges of the work.

It seems clear that many social workers in rural communities already have rural backgrounds (Mackie, 2007, 2012), as they are from or have prior work or field placement experiences in rural communities. The advantage they have is that they already have some understanding of the environment, and they have demonstrated some ability to adapt to it—as a result, they are probably more comfortable working in and with a rural community. Given this, these social workers are also more apt to remain in rural areas over the long term.

Yet if rural residents do not already have professional credentials in social work, they must often go to urban centers to get their education, especially advanced education. Some do not return, and others find that there is not much in the way of rural content to support their practice. Advocates for rural social work suggest that rural communities would be better served if social work education were to add more rural content and extend programs to rural areas (Daley & Avant, 1999; Mackie, 2007; NASW, 2012). The expansion of online and other forms of distance education in recent years may eventually serve to deliver social work programs to more outlying areas, but the extent to which rural content may be added is still not known.

What are the potential rewards of being a rural social worker? Ginsberg (1998, 2005) identifies five positive aspects of rural social work: (1) autonomy and independence, (2) opportunity and promotion, (3) the ability to see the results of one's intervention, (4) personal rewards, and (5) recognition. To this list one can also add quality of lifestyle and work environments. Each of these benefits offers a potentially attractive opportunity to social workers.

Rural social welfare services and agencies operate on a smaller scale than is generally the case in urban centers. The smaller and simpler structure of the rural agency allows the social worker a higher degree of independence and autonomy than in many other settings (Ginsberg, 2005; Riebschleger, 2007). Rural communities generally have smaller agencies, employing fewer staff, which reduces the need for a complex, flatter administrative structure. As a result, rural social welfare organizations tend to have less distance and formality between administrators and workers. Having fewer supervisors and administrators, especially on-site, often frees up social workers to take more initiative to do what needs to be done. Simply put, superiors may be harder to reach or ask questions of, there are fewer people to look over one's shoulder, and the relationships that exist with administrators and supervisors tend to be less formal. To deal with pressing issues, workers must develop autonomy to act, and they commonly seek approval after the fact. So, the rural environment leads to increased opportunity to demonstrate initiative and act autonomously.

The smaller professional staffs in rural communities also create increased opportunities for visibility, responsibility, and promotion. In many rural areas there are proportionately fewer professionals of any kind to serve the needs of the community. Physicians, nurses, and social workers all tend to be in short supply. For social workers this means that there may be only one per county or one for several counties. A social worker may often work with coworkers who are caseworkers, people who are not necessarily professionally educated in providing human services but have learned to be caseworkers by experience. There also tend to be proportionately fewer social workers with specialized and advanced professional skills in rural communities (Daley & Avant, 1999).

All of this creates a work environment in which the rural social worker is likely to be more visible and given increased responsibility much more quickly, because there may be no one else adequately prepared to do the work. The responsibility may include some supervisory or administrative duties, or the opportunity to provide advanced services. This opportunity is a bit of a double-edged sword, because licensing laws and professional protocols often limit what a social worker can do—depending on education, license, and experience—and social workers must be careful not to violate those limitations. But having additional responsibility can provide one with valuable experience that can lead to expanded opportunities and professional growth. The increased visibility of the social worker in a rural community also creates an opportunity to be noticed, particularly when the social worker does a good job (Ginsberg, 2005; Riebschleger, 2007).

Small agency size and increased involvement in the community often lead to quicker, more visible results for interventions (Ginsberg, 2005; Riebschleger, 2007). In rural communities there may be fewer obstacles or red tape that delay the implementation of interventions. The closeness of a rural community may make it easier to engage individuals and services in the helping process. In any event, because there are fewer secrets and less anonymity in the rural community, results may be easier to see, which can be very rewarding for the social worker, particularly if interventions are successful.

Rural social workers are usually closer to clients and coworkers and maintain closer connections to the broader community than their urban counterparts. This can provide a strong sense of personal reward, as the social worker can see his or her contribution to the community. Work with rural people, many of whom are down to earth and very resilient, have strong family connections, and attempt to be self-reliant even in the face of adversity, can be very uplifting as well. Because of this, the social worker may feel a strong sense of personal reward.

Social work jobs tend to carry a greater chance of recognition and to convey greater status in rural communities than they do in many other settings. The position one holds is commonly known in the rural community, and because social workers are professionals and help solve problems, community members tend to know and respect both the person and the position. As a result, the social worker is frequently seen as a person of some importance and is accorded respect. In a very real sense, the rural social worker is "somebody." Having an understanding that people in the community know not only who you are but also what you do can be a great source of gratification.

A final potential reward is that social work jobs can be good jobs in a community's economic structure. Social work positions are often reasonably stable and have benefits. This may not be true of many jobs in a rural community, where lack of economic diversity may lead to unstable employment or periodic declines in earnings. Many other jobs may be of low pay or not offer benefits. Social work positions, especially those funded by public dollars, can be less subject to local fluctuations. The types of benefits that social workers can receive, including retirement plans, health insurance, and paid leave, may be unavailable to hourly or agricultural workers. So, in the context of the local rural economy, social work positions may be seen as conveying some status.

Despite the rewards, rural social workers do face some challenges in professional practice, including professional isolation, difficulty in getting supervision, fewer professional development opportunities, less availability of services and funding, and transportation barriers. Addressing these challenges requires adaptability and creativity, and successful rural social workers are able to take these challenges in stride and overcome them, but such challenges may also deter others from rural practice.

Rural social workers sometimes feel slighted by their own profession and by society at large. One has to look only at rural content in professional education, as well as the resources and array of services in rural areas, to perceive that more attention, status, and resources are given to urban areas. At times rural social workers experience envy, frustration, disappointment, feelings of inferiority, and a sense of challenge over this perceived disparity between rural and urban social work. Rural social workers may even face bias against the importance of rural work from members of their own profession who do not fully understand the needs of rural communities.

The scarcity of professionals in the rural community can also tend to isolate the social worker (Ginsberg, 2005; Riebschleger, 2007). Much of what social workers do involves collaborative work and consultation with colleagues, yet rural social workers may find that their colleagues are miles away, which can create barriers to frequent or easy means of consultation and collaboration. In some areas, rural social workers might find that they have no social work colleagues for many miles. So when one struggles with a difficult or perplexing case or is considering an ethical issue, peer help is not just a trip down the hall or a quick lunch away. As a result, the consultation and peer support that social workers routinely seek out may need to be more carefully planned, which may postpone a social worker's actions or decisions, or may be frustrating. The challenges of finding appropriate professional support should not be underestimated, because isolation can create negative effects on the services delivered and can deny one a sense of reward from successful work. These challenges may also lead to feelings of being alone, and/or that no one else understands, knows, or cares about what the social worker is doing. Professional isolation can produce professional burnout. This isolation can be effectively addressed and overcome, but it does require awareness and planning.

As is the case with consultation, rural social workers have to be aware about getting an appropriate level of professional supervision. In rural offices, supervisors may not be on-site, because they are responsible for work groups spread across a wide geographic area. In addition, the worker's supervisor is less likely to have a professional education in either supervision or social work, and this may affect the quality of professional support the social worker receives (Daley & Avant, 1999). Given this type of administrative arrangement, the worker may not have on-site access to his or her supervisor on a regular basis. When this is the case, then the worker must plan for supervision. Once again, this is not a simple drop down the hall or asking, "Do you have a minute?" The supervisor responsible for workers across several counties may not be readily available when needed. Even communication may be spotty, as many rural areas have large dead zones for cellular phones and Internet, so rapid communication may be a problem.

Failure to get appropriate supervision or consultation can be problematic, as social workers may face situations that are beyond their expertise.

Professional supervision and consultation can also include components of support and education for the social worker. Since the rural social worker may be the only help available in the immediate area, there is some pressure to provide helping services. Yet moving beyond one's professional expertise runs the risk of running afoul of ethical or licensing issues. As Daley and Doughty (2006) found in their study of licensing violations, practice outside of one's recognized area of competence was a major source of ethical code violations for rural social workers. They concluded that this may be a particularly difficult problem for rural social workers, who feel the need to help as best they can. The effective use of supervision and peer consultation is a good way to reduce this risk, but in rural work, the development of communication links may require extra work and planning.

Ongoing professional development is essential to any social worker. Continuing to learn and improve one's skills and incorporating new knowledge are basic professional and ethical responsibilities. Licensing laws institutionalize this idea by requiring minimum numbers of continuing education hours for license renewal. But continuing education for social workers may not be offered locally in a rural community. To get continuing education, the worker may have to take time away from the office and incur extra expense. Recent innovations in the delivery of continuing education through the Internet and video have made continuing education more available to rural social workers, but workers may still need some face-to-face hours to meet agency and licensing requirements.

One does not have to read much social work literature to discover that rural communities do not have the rich array of social welfare services that are typically found in larger communities. Indeed, much has been written about the lack of rural services and the scarcity of funds to create and run them. In many cases, one of the biggest challenges a rural social worker faces is assembling an appropriate group of services that are accessible to their clients. For example, day care might not be generally available in the community, but acceptable arrangements could be developed by the social worker with neighbors, family members, or churches to provide such a service. Rural communities do not entirely lack services, as some would have us believe, but they usually do not have the breadth and depth of services of larger communities. Rural social workers must be creative in bundling, developing services, and using natural networks in the community to provide what clients need. This kind of creativity for service delivery might not be appealing to every social worker.

People in rural areas are less densely grouped than in other types of communities, so when people need help, some travel is required. Yet mass transit and public transit in rural areas are rare, and the cars and trucks of people with limited incomes can be less than reliable. Because people need to get to services, there are frequently transportation barriers. Even the best-designed services cannot work if people cannot access them. Rural social workers commonly face the task of overcoming transportation barriers for their clients by finding transportation for them. This might not be easy, and it might involve finding a family member, working with a church, or getting community funding to address transportation. It might not be glamorous work, but it is often essential for rural practice to work.

A social worker should weigh the benefits and challenges of working in a rural community to evaluate whether rural social work is the right choice for practice. If independence and autonomy, being known in the community, being able to see results, having more responsibility and better opportunities for promotion, and living and working with rural people are appealing, then rural social work may be a good choice for a social worker. If being required to have professional creativity, having less frequent contact with peers and supervisors, facing more challenges for professional development, living and working in a smaller community, developing resources, and finding transportation do not seem interesting, then rural social work may not be the best choice.

CONCLUSION

Most of the land area of North America can be classified as rural, and while these areas have low population density, rural people still represent a significant minority of society. But beyond mere geography, there is a significant rural population in areas that are not typically classified as rural. Rural people are in urban and suburban areas either because they have moved there or because urban expansion has reached out to transform their home communities.

All too commonly, the need for rural services and the culture of rural people are overlooked. Modern stereotypes sometimes suggest that rural areas are unimportant because they are dying or because rural people are simply backward. Rural people who live in urban areas are easy to overlook, because they may not be recognized or people assume that they have been assimilated into the urban culture.

In any group of people, a certain percentage of them will need social welfare services and the assistance of social workers. This certainly holds true for rural people, as they often live in areas where the economy is not diverse, they tend to have lower incomes and fewer services readily accessible to them, and they may experience difficulty in adapting when they do move to urban centers. Social workers with a rural knowledge base can help empower them to access the help they need.

Yet rural communities have too few social workers to meet their needs. More social workers with a background in understanding and addressing rurality are needed to respond to the needs of such communities. There are multiple definitions of rurality that are based on different ideas about what constitutes a rural community, and many of these are not particularly informative for practice. For social work purposes, if people think of themselves as rural, then they probably are, no matter where they live. The importance of rurality for social work is the way in which it influences the characteristics and behaviors of the people and communities. For the social worker, it is most important to understand how people view themselves and how that influences their situations.

Rurality is not and cannot be narrowly confined to small towns and geographically rural communities, given the significant numbers of people who move into cities, often in search of work and economic opportunity. Whether they were raised in a rural community or have a rural heritage, rurality is an important part of these people's worldview, decision making, actions, and relationships. When this rural belief system is not entirely compatible with the urban environment, a social worker may need to assist a person. To neglect the culture and beliefs of rural people, even through a lack of awareness, would be a serious error for any social worker.

One of the most important factors in rural social work is the context in which one practices. Whether working in a rural geographic area or an associational community that identifies as rural, social context affects the nature of social work in many ways. Sometimes friends, family, and local groups, though not professional, are the most important sources of help.

Rural social work is an important field of practice that offers many potential rewards and some challenges to social workers. Rural social workers tend to have more independence and influence, yet they are commonly isolated from peers and supervisors to some degree. They are well known in the community and often able to implement interventions more quickly. But they live their lives in a bit of a fishbowl, and even their private lives can become part of everyday conversation, affecting how community members view them professionally. Rural practitioners must be creative and flexible and work across all social systems to be effective.

The lifestyle in a rural community offers a slower pace of living, but the number and diversity of stores and services available in larger communities may be absent. Social work jobs may tend to be attractive and carry some prestige in a local rural community, as they have stability, pay relatively well, and offer benefits when many jobs do not. Rural social work can be attractive, but it might not be the ideal field of practice for everyone. It is undoubtedly important, though, particularly for the rural people who need professional assistance.

REFERENCES

Arnow, H. L. S. (1954). *The Dollmaker*. New York, NY: Macmillan.

Bealer, R. C., Willitis, F. K., & Kuvlesky, W. P. (1965). The meaning of "rurality." *Rural Sociology*, *30*(3), 255–266.

Daley, M. R., & Avant, F. (1999). Attracting and retaining professionals for social work practice in rural areas: An example from East Texas. In I. B. Carlton-La Ney, R. L. Edwards, & P. N. Reid (Eds.), *Preserving and strengthening small towns and rural communities* (pp. 335–345). Washington, DC: NASW Press.

Daley, M. R., & Avant, F. (2004a). Advanced generalist for rural practice. In A. Roy & F. Vecchiola (Eds.), *Advanced generalist practice: Models, readings, and essays* (pp. 37–57). Peosta, IA: Bowers.

Daley, M., & Avant, F. (2004b). Reconceptualizing the framework for practice. In T. L. Scales & C. L. Streeter (Eds.), *Rural social work:*

Building and sustaining community assets (pp. 34–42). Belmont, CA: Thomson

Daley, M. R., & Doughty, M. O. (2006). Ethics complaints in social work practice: A rural-urban comparison. *Journal of Social Work Values and Ethics*, *3*(1). Retrieved from http://www.socialworker.com/jswve/content/blogcategory/12/44/.

Daley, M. R., & Pierce, B. (2011). Educating for rural competence: Curriculum concepts, models and course content. In L. H. Ginsberg (Ed.), *Social work in rural communities* (5th ed., pp. 125–140). Alexandria, VA: Council on Social Work Education.

Farley, O. W., Griffiths, K. A., Skidmore, R. A., & Thackeray, M. G. (1982). *Rural social work practice*. New York: Free Press.

Ginsberg, L. H. (1998). Introduction: An overview of rural social work. In L. H. Ginsberg (Ed.), *Social work in rural communities* (3rd ed., pp. 3–22). Alexandria, VA: Council on Social Work Education.

Ginsberg, L. H. (2005). The overall context of rural practice. In L. H. Ginsberg (Ed.), *Social work in rural communities* (4th ed., pp. 4–7). Alexandria, VA: Council on Social Work Education.

Ginsberg, L. H. (2011). Introduction to basics of rural social work. In L. H. Ginsberg (Ed.), *Social work in rural communities* (5th ed., pp. 5–20). Alexandria, VA: Council on Social Work Education.

Lohmann, N., & Lohmann, R. A. (2005). Introduction. In N. Lohmann & R. A. Lohmann (Eds.), *Rural social work practice* (pp. ix–xxvii). New York, NY: Columbia University Press.

Mackie, P. F. E. (2007). Understanding educational and demographic differences between rural and urban social workers. *Journal of Baccalaureate Social Work*, *12*(3), 114–128.

Mackie, P. F. E. (2012). Social work in a very rural place: A study of practitioners in the upper peninsula of Michigan. *Contemporary Rural Social Work*, *4*, 63–90. Retrieved from http://journal.und.edu/crsw/article/view/445/164.

Meenaghan, T. M., Gibbons, W. E., & McNutt, J. G. (2005). *Generalist practice in larger settings* (2nd ed.). Chicago: Lyceum Books.

National Association of Social Workers. (2009). Rural social work. In *Social work speaks: National Association of Social Workers policy statements* (8th ed., pp. 297–302). Washington, DC: NASW Press.

National Association of Social Workers. (2012). Rural social work. In *Social work speaks: National Association of Social Workers policy statements* (9th ed., pp. 296–300, 379). Washington, DC: NASW Press.

Olaveson, J., Conway, P., & Shaver, C. (2004). Defining rural for social work practice and research. In T. L. Scales & C. L. Streeter (Eds.), *Asset building to sustain rural communities* (pp. 9–20). Belmont, CA: Thomson.

Riebschleger, J. (2007). Social workers' suggestions for effective rural practice. *Families in Society*, *88*(2), 203–213.

Statistics Canada. (2001). *Rural and small town Canada analysis bulletin.* Retrieved from http://www.theruralcentre.com/doc/RST-Def_Rural.pdf.

Statistics Canada. (2011). *Population, urban and rural by province and territory*. Retrieved from http://www.statcan.gc.ca/tables-tableaux/sum-som/l01/cst01/demo62a-eng.htm.

US Census Bureau. (1995). *Urban and rural population 1900 to 1990.* Retrieved from http://www.census.gov/population/censusdata/urpop0090.txt.

US Census Bureau. (n.d.). *2010 Census urban and rural classification and urban area criteria.* Retrieved from http://www.census.gov/geo/www/ua/2010urbanruralclass.html.

Teaching children about the use of firearms has been an important part of rural culture for a long time (taken in Texas about 1910).

CHAPTER TWO

Rural Culture and Behavior

THE HEART AND SOUL of rural work is the relationship that a social worker builds with clients and members of the community (Locke & Winship, 2005). The social work relationship as a vehicle for change and for helping empower people is so important that it is one of the ethical principles identified in the National Association of Social Workers' (2008) Code of Ethics. Yet in some ways, rural communities and people are a bit of a mystery to those who do not learn the rural culture. And rural communities are often wary of dealing with outsiders.

Rural communities are often deceptive in external appearance. In rural society the people, stores, schools, churches, and other institutions outwardly appear and often act like their urban counterparts. To some degree, a Walmart is a Walmart, and all Walmarts follow similar operating procedures no matter where they are. But on more subtle levels, the culture of rural communities is different. Given the urban orientation of most social work models and education, practitioners are not typically thinking about rural culture as they engage clients in the helping relationship. Social workers who grew up in rural communities may have a bit of an advantage in working with rural people, but then even rural people usually do not think much about their culture—it is just how they were raised.

In recent years the literature on rural social work has begun to refer to rurality as a form of diversity with which social workers should be familiar (Daley & Avant, 2004b; Ginsberg, 2011). Of course, social workers are used to learning about diversity in clients, but they traditionally think of factors like race, ethnicity, age, gender, disability, and religion—they rarely consider rurality. Unless one consciously makes an attempt to understand and learn the rural culture, it will be more difficult to form the kinds of client relationships that lead to successful outcomes.

Developing competency in working with rural communities is an ongoing learning experience because not all rural communities are the same, and people differ even within communities. But there are common characteristics and norms that occur across many rural communities that can serve as a basis for further learning. The ongoing learning of rural culture is critical to rural practice because it is the community that expects the worker to adapt to it instead of adapting to the worker, especially if the worker is viewed as an outsider.

Rural communities distrust outsiders, and social workers have to gain acceptance to work effectively. Just because a social worker holds a professional or official position does not make it likely that he or she will receive the level of acceptance needed to form strong helping relationships. Rural people have a number of folksy colloquialisms to refer to people who cannot adapt and who just do not get it. Expressions like "ain't got the sense God gave a goose" or "doesn't know his butt from a hole in the ground" are stinging assessments that show people do not have good sense or know what is going on. If the word is out that a social worker doesn't know what's going on, then building a trusting professional relationship with someone is not an easy proposition.

But where and how to best adapt to local rural culture is the key question. The concept of culture is a broad one that encompasses many aspects of life. The definition of culture used here is as follows: The customs, habits, skills, technology, arts, values, ideology, science, and religious and political behavior of a group of people in a specific time period (Barker, 2014). Rural culture in this sense refers to the behavioral expectations and living environment of those in a rural community, whether it is geographic or associational.

All social workers receive content and develop skills in working with diversity as part of their professional education, but that content infrequently includes rurality. There is also much literature in social work that deals with diversity—race, gender, ethnicity, religion, sexual identity—but there are few sources that directly address rural culture. To be successful, the rural social worker has to mine the existing books and articles for relevant content on rurality. This can be a challenging task, since much of this material is scattered across several sources. Still, it is a manageable job for the serious social worker wanting to develop good practice skills. Additional effort is required to learn the specifics of individual communities and their unique characteristics and expectations. This may be done, at least in part, by listening to the residents' narratives, which likely contain strong elements of their cultural context (Carawan, Bass, & Bunch, 1999).

In addition to all the basic practice skills that social workers bring to the community, they have to become part ethnologists too and be willing to both study and learn from the culture. Good rural social workers do these things and learn their communities, and arguably this is more important in the rural context than it is in the cities. This chapter can only begin to scratch the surface of the richness and range of rural culture, but it does give a starting point for learning about communalities across rural areas.

RURAL VALUES

Considering rural culture as a whole is a formidable undertaking. As one moves from one context and region to another, there are clear differences: population density, ethnic diversity based on settlement patterns, historical traditions, and a variety of other characteristics that affect the ethos of a community. For example, frontier areas with wide open spaces and few people tend to be different from rural communities. Small towns settled by Scandinavians in the Midwest are distinct from those settled by the Scots-Irish in the South. The economic base of an area may create differences between communities separated by too many miles. Consider four different communities, one with an economy based on logging, one based on a sawmill and distribution hub, one based on mining, and another based on agriculture. These communities could be very different indeed.

Given all the possibilities that could create such differences, perhaps the best place to begin discussing rural culture is in highlighting characteristics of rural communities identified in the social work literature. While the following list may not be exhaustive, the themes seem to be consistent across sources.

ATTACHMENT TO THE LAND

Country people feel a close connection to the land and to place that is deeply ingrained in them (Locke & Winship, 2005; Tice, 2005; White & Marks, 1999). Gumpert, Saltman, and Sauer-Jones (2000) refer to the importance of the rhythms of nature in rural work as a cultural characteristic that many social workers often use in their practice. The connection to the land, place, and rhythms of nature—and behaviors related to these things—may be because rural people tend to see the land as a source of birth, sustenance, social relationships, and/or economic livelihood. These beliefs and behaviors may have developed due to long residence in the area where generations may have lived and been born. As a result, rural people may be more resistant to development, particularly if old meaningful places are destroyed in the process. And country people may be more reluctant to leave the land even after conditions make life in a small community more challenging. As a result, they may be seen as stubborn, resistant to change, opposed to progress, or even just plain foolish.

Importance of Family

The family is a basic unit of society and assumes a central role in people's lives, especially in a rural community (Carlton-LaNey, Edwards, & Reid, 1999a; Daley & Avant, 2004a; Farley, Griffiths, Skidmore & Thackeray, 1982; Locke & Winship, 2005; NASW, 2009). Rural families tend to be traditional, close knit, spend a great deal of time together, and rely on one another for support. For example, relatives may tend to young children during the day as an alternative to day care, and family members often belong to the same church and social groups, jointly participating in civic activities. One often finds more than one generation of a family living with or near one another, and it is not unusual to find that a family has roots in the community that extend back for many years. A family member who leaves the community for better opportunities has to consider the loss of close family connections, of social relationships and informal support systems. This may influence a person's decision to remain in the rural community. But those close connections may also mean that those who leave and find success in larger communities could find their family members moving into nearby neighborhoods.

Importance of Church and Schools

Churches and schools can be important institutions in any community, but in a rural area they take on extra significance (Farley et al., 1982; Hartley, Savage, & Kaplan, 2005; Johnson & Dunbar, 2005; Locke & Winship, 2005; Waltman, 1986; Weber, 1980). Small communities have few institutions that serve as focal points for residents, and because churches and schools are often found in small communities, they can become those focal points. As village institutions, churches take on significance beyond their religious function and the importance of schools transcends just education, as schools provide the community with gathering places and sources of identification and pride. These institutions play key roles in community identification and pride, and they provide places where people can meet and organize for collective action. They may also serve as resource centers for informal helping activities in the community. As a result, local ministers and school administrators can wield considerable influence.

Informal Helping Networks

For a long time social workers have noted the scarcity of formal social welfare resources in rural communities (Daley & Avant, 2004b; Daley & Pierce, 2011; Ginsberg, 2011; Gumpert & Saltman, 1998; Gumpert et al., 2000; Patterson, Memmott, Brennan, & Germain, 1998; Riebschleger, 2007; Waltman, 1986; Watkins, 2004). Yet these communities have developed a way of coping with social needs and problems through community spirit and a sense of self-help. Rural people often rely on informal networks of people to provide for the social welfare needs of their community. Often, these are neighbors helping their neighbors who are in need. People work as individuals, small groups, civic organizations, and through existing institutions to develop responses to need. For example, when a family's house is wiped out by fire, friends, neighbors, and civic groups collect money and supplies, and they may even provide temporary housing to see the family through. This type of response occurs through an informal network of helpers who step in to meet a need in the absence of the formal services that might exist in a larger city.

The Personal Nature of Relationships

Rural social relationships tend to be personal in nature, and at least part of the purpose of social exchanges is not just social interaction but also often to address daily living (Daley & Avant, 1999; Ginsberg, 2005, 2011; Gumpert & Saltman, 1998; Locke & Winship, 2005; Martinez-Brawley, 1990, 2000; NASW 2009, 2012). This is distinctly different from urban environments, where exchanges between people tend to be more anonymous and formal, and aimed at transacting business. In some ways this makes sense because in small communities people often know or know of the people with whom they are dealing and need to maintain good relationships for the future. This results in the idea that a person's word is his or her bond, or that a handshake is a form of social contract. In urban communities many times inhabitants interact with people they do not know and may never see again. So more formal written relationships like contracts are developed as a matter of course. Writers on rural culture frame this in terms of *Gemeinschaft* and *Gesselschaft* communities. *Gemeinschaft* communities are those in which social interactions are personal, enduring, and based on knowledge of where a person stands in society. In *Gesselschaft* communities most social interactions are impersonal and contractual (Martinez-Brawley, 2000). Rural communities are often considered examples of *Gemeinschaft*, whereas urban communities are viewed as examples of *Gesselschaft.* This distinction is helpful in understanding rural values, social exchanges, and behavior, particularly for social workers. The formal distance associated with professional relationships can prove problematic in working with country people who expect a more personal connection. Engaging clients appropriately while working within the community's norms is one of the challenges of rural practice.

Closeness of the Community

Small communities are apt to be ones in which people know many other members of the community (Ginsberg, 2005; Gumpert et al., 2000; Johnson & Dunbar, 2005; NASW, 2009, 2012; Riebschleger, 2007). Obviously, they know some people better than others, but in rural communities it is easy to get information about someone. Community members grow up together and learn about people through their friends and acquaintances. Family members extend the network of learning about other people, and it is often easy to learn about whom someone is related to or some other fact about a person. People in small towns recognize others on sight, and they recognize their cars. Since individuals are constantly in the public view, there are few secrets in a rural community. This knowledge leads rural people to be more trusting of those they know, and many households still leave their doors unlocked. People in a rural community also tend to be more circumspect with their actions, because they know what they do will be seen and judged by others in the community. For example, children who misbehave can often be brought into line with a simple "I know your mama." Some homes, especially in the Southern United States have furniture on the front porch, and during good weather residents may sit outside and interact with their neighbors. In this sense, the front porch is an extension of the living room and way of social interaction. Given this, outsiders can represent an enigma in a small community. There may be little background about them available and so people may distrust outsiders, even if those "outsiders" grew up only a few miles away. Sometimes this distrust, and even efforts to keep outsiders away, is formalized through signs that say POSTED NO TRESPASSING. Any attempts by outsiders to blend in are subject to harsh criticism if those attempts are not perceived as genuine. *Drugstore cowboy* and *greenhorn* are not terms of endearment; they are used to refer to clumsy or insincere attempts to blend in. After arriving in the community it may take someone several years to gain acceptance, and newcomers may hear the question, "You're not from here, are you?" for a long time. Some distrust of outsiders is for good cause. For example, oil companies were very good at convincing country people to sell them mineral rights to the land by promising owners that they could keep the surface for their own use. Only later did landowners find ecological disasters from dumped or improperly stored crude oil, abandoned oil derricks and tanks, and access roads that cut into the property. Moreover, rural communities found that oil and gas production created boom and bust cycles in their local economy, which resulted in the need for additional social welfare services (Weber, Geigle, & Barkdull, 2014). The modern practice of hydraulic fracturing, known as "fracking," is repeating this process today for a new generation of rural people.

Open Communication

Before there was Facebook, rural people established their own local version of social media (Daley & Avant, 2004b; Farley et al., 1982; Ginsberg, 2005; Gumpert et al., 2000; Johnson, 1980; Riebschleger, 2007). In a rural community, most everything is connected—clients, community members, families and organizations—and there are few secrets. Given the closeness of the community, people know about others and see what they do, and anything interesting is newsworthy. Country people do not need a computer, the Internet, or a smartphone to send such information, and the community grapevine spreads information widely. The grapevine consists of beauty and barber shops, schools, local restaurants, churches, the feed store, and almost anywhere else people routinely gather to talk. Thus, it is easy to learn about who is new to the community; about successes and failures, marriages, births, and deaths; about who was arrested and what for; about who was drinking too much and who was doing something he or she shouldn't be doing. Interestingly, the Rural Social Work Caucus has adopted the close community and open communication style of rural people, so much so that the organization exists without much formal structure and has even been said to exist by rumor (Hickman, 2004, 2014).

Reliance on Tradition

Rural communities are traditional and often try to retain the older ways of doing things, making it slow for the newest trends to catch on (Carlton-LaNey, Edwards, & Reid, 1999b; Daley & Avant, 2004a; Gumpert & Saltman, 1998; Gumpert et al., 2000; NASW, 2009, 2012; Riebschleger, 2005, 2007; Watkins, 2004). They are not too interested in change for the sake of change. Small towns and villages often retain their stories and traditions to remind them of their past. For example, I once visited a town in rural Mississippi where the stories were of the damages caused and outrages perpetrated by one General Sherman during "the War." Of course, those events were from 150 years earlier, but the anger was as fresh and the stories as vivid as if it had happened last month. Part of the reliance on tradition comes from the viewpoint that patterns of doing things in the past have proved successful, and there is less certainty about newer approaches. This is the "if it ain't broke, don't fix it" perspective. Curiously, this traditionalism has resulted in an unexpected financial boon for some rural communities, as outsiders come to purchase folk arts and crafts like quilts and woodcarving, listen to traditional music, and see the pristine beauty of the outdoors not yet spoiled by urban development. But traditionalism goes beyond this too. People respect the land, their ancestors, their heritage, and their stories. Traditions give them a sense of community. One way tradition may appear is through what seems to be a slower pace of life. Many rural people follow the old adage "early to bed and early to rise," and unless they work for an hourly wage, they are less governed by the clock. Modern society has made the clock more influential than the traditional sunrise, midday, and sunset of rural culture, but many agree that rural people often move at a slower pace, not as driven by the tick of the clock as people in a city.

Sense of Self-Reliance

Country people have a strong sense of individualism and self-reliance (Farley et al., 1982; Gumpert & Saltman, 1998; Gumpert et al., 2000; Osgood, 1980; Riebschleger, 2005; Waltman, 1986), which some call rugged individualism. This kind of self-reliance may stem from a deeply instilled work ethic that leads people to look to the fruits of their own labor to meet their needs and those of their family. Everyone understands that the rewards from such labor may not be great and are sometimes uncertain, but still, there is value in the labor. A strong work ethic is very important for the kind of economy that has traditionally been prevalent in rural communities. Farming, logging, ranching, and mining take hard work to be successful in them, and rural areas are often not rich in surplus income to provide for those who cannot support themselves. It is not surprising that rural culture values self-reliance, taking care of one's family, and being frugal. Self-reliance is demonstrated, for example, in households making their own goods instead of buying them at the store, such as by sewing, quilting, and canning surplus food. There is also an inherent frugality in this approach to life. Having old shoes and boots resoled instead of buying new ones, repairing old equipment, and using fatback and old bacon drippings for cooking illustrate frugality. Self-reliance and support of the family is a source of pride for many rural people, and the acceptance of outside help, particularly from those whom they do not know, is widely viewed as a mark of failure, which conveys a sense of shame. Country people often sum up this complex idea in just a few words: "poor but proud." When faced with adversity, the rural attitude is to face it head on and overcome it. In the American West the saying is to just "cowboy up" and go on. This is admirable, but from a social work perspective, it can mean that country folk can have difficulty asking for and even receiving help.

Despite the communalities among them, each rural community has unique qualities that make it special to its residents. Perceptive social workers will attempt to learn as much as they can about what the residents believe makes their community special. That will enhance the social worker's ability to connect with community members, gain acceptance, and build relationships with the people. This will take a keen sense of observation and a desire to learn how the community works.

Social workers who were not born or raised in the community may be perceived as outsiders. Rural people use subtle means to assess someone they do not know personally, and small nuances in dress, speech, or social interaction can promote distrust and caution in dealing with social workers (Johnson & Dunbar, 2005). Gaining acceptance and trust may be a slow process, but it is an ultimately manageable one. To build acceptance, social workers have to establish personal connections, and that requires having some understanding of the culture. But what is it the social worker needs to understand?

MICRO SYSTEMS

Language

Rural people develop their own language, which is best understood by those who live or have lived in the area (Bowman, 1995; Mohr, 1987). This is not to say that the way rural people talk is completely arcane or unintelligible. Rather, communication is developed locally and regionally using collections of common terms, ethnic-based words and phrases, and descriptive idioms, and these are often topped off with a distinctive accent. In many rural areas idiomatic expressions are used to convey complex ideas simply, in a way all can understand.

Learning the "language" is essential for acceptance, but social workers raised and educated in urban areas may not know or understand the words or phrases country people use. And rural people may not fully understand the urban language either. The journal *Rural America* (1980) indicates that IQ tests use language that is biased against and disadvantages rural children.

If social workers do not understand the local language, then they are quickly identified as outsiders, and this may lead people to discount by saying things like "his pilot light isn't lit" (he's stupid) or "she is one brick short of a load" (she is not mentally sound). An urban social worker may not understand the Canadian expression "I'll tow that alongside for a bit before I bring it aboard," used to express skepticism (Cassleman, 1995). The social worker who cannot tune in to the local language may be the target of some rough country humor or be the butt of jokes and pranks. For example, social workers need to know that a "meadow muffin" (cow excrement) is not a pastry that one serves at brunch, a "donkey puncher" (rural Canadian saying, for "operator of a small engine," such as a log puller) does not assault animals, and "going snipe hunting" (practical joke involving an impossible task) is not a local sport. Or the community may use ethnic or regional expressions that may not be familiar to outsiders, such as *uff da* (surprise, relief, or dismay) in the US Midwest, the Southern *y'all* (more than two of you), and the US and Canadian *doohickey* (unspecified type of gadget).

In many ways, until a social worker learns the language and the community, it is best to be humble or have one's "hat in hand" with respect to learning about the new community. There is no substitute for honesty with people about the fact one is learning about the community and about asking for help when needed. Rural relationships are overwhelmingly personalized, and if community members do not think social workers speak their language and are not sincere about learning it, then they are likely to keep social workers at arm's length.

Recreation

Rural and urban lives differ markedly in the types of recreation available to people. Many recreational pursuits in rural communities tend to center on outdoor activities, whereas urban residents may have to travel to the country to engage in outdoor pursuits. In a rural community, the theater is more likely a community group, and although community-based theater may exist in an urban setting, cities offer the option of professional theater. Cities usually also have several multiplex cinemas with state-of-the-art equipment showing the most current films, whereas rural areas have older facilities with few screens, if they have a movie theater at all. Cities may have a symphony orchestra, whereas in a rural community concerts may be held by the school band.

The big advantage in recreational activities that rural areas have is access to the outdoors. As a result, hunting and fishing are popular pursuits, as are other activities like skiing, horseback riding, mud racing, and rodeo. Some of these recreational activities cross over from work to recreation, as horses and four-wheelers are used both to get around off-road for work and for recreation.

Some rural communities have been able to translate their land into a destination for tourists, creating a source of employment for the local economy. In many cases, tourists and the income they bring are seasonal, and the area must rely on other sources of income for the remainder of the year. Areas with great natural beauty attract hikers, campers, and sightseers, and places that have significant wildlife attract hunters. Regions with good lakes, streams, or coastline attract both recreational fishing and tourism. Rural communities with a significant connection to history and historical events also attract tourists.

Rural people tend to enjoy their natural recreational advantages and their space. Many are hunters or enjoy fishing. Wild game or fish may be a supplement to the regular diet, but often it is a type of food that people have grown to like. Venison, possum, raccoon, squirrel, dove, wild duck, and goose are not for sale in most grocery stores, and recipes for preparing them are not found in many cookbooks. Also, hunting and fishing are often the source of much social interaction among rural people. The ritual of the annual deer or duck hunt, and the opening of the "season," is a subject of much planning and anticipation during the year. There is much discussion of the catch, the one that got away, or how one bagged the eight-point buck—these things are a source of much pride to the storyteller and the subject of much conversation.

It is common for rural people to own guns and have some attachment to them, and firearms are often a symbol of independence. Firearms often are the embodiment of a broad set of fervently held values that are important to the rural way of life, including self-reliance, freedom from outside interference, and a connection to the past. Guns may be reverently passed down through generations, as they are treasured possessions that often provide a link to previous generations. As they grow up, many children are taught about the care and use of firearms by members of their family. They are also taught about hunting, as well as preparing and cooking fish and game, as a rite of passage. Many are also taught a grassroots variety of conservationism: "you kill it, you clean it, you eat it." The lore and customs of the hunt and fishing are extensive and intricate, and they are usually passed on as treasured information. Guns are used for hunting, as a form of recreation, as a link to family history, and for putting food on the table.

Observant people might see the results of gun use that went a little out of bounds. The shiny silver circles on road signs indicate that someone was overly bored (and perhaps induced by a little alcohol) to drive down the road and shoot those signs with a shotgun. While this is illegal, locally it may be considered all in good fun.

Guns also serve another purpose—protection. In many rural areas law enforcement's response time may be an hour or more. Thus, if there is a threatening situation, there may not be time to wait. Moreover, deer and wild hogs can destroy crops and gardens, and some animals pose potential threats. People who live in the country may have occasion to deal with a bear trying to get into the house, a coyote killing their livestock, a wild hog running around, or an alligator in the pond. When confronted by these kinds of situations, a firearm provides some degree of security.

So, it is not unusual to see trucks around a small town with a rack in the rear window that holds a rifle or shotgun. This is just a part of the local culture, and most people think little of it. Of course, this practice may seem strange to those from the city, where firearms serve a different purpose and guns are rarely carried openly except by law enforcement. To those with urban backgrounds, the presence of guns may speak to a culture of violence and make them uncomfortable. The idea of children and adolescents learning to kill and skin game may seem even less appealing, even barbaric. Yet for most rural people, guns are a symbol of independence and a means of self-protection, not instruments for doing violence to other people. Guns are an important piece of rural culture, one that many rural residents value.

Social workers who do not grasp the role that guns, hunting, and fishing play in rural life may have difficulty relating to rural people. Conversely, being able to talk about topics related to hunting, fishing, and guns is an excellent way to establish relationships.

Food

Food in its various forms is a significant aspect of rural culture. Preparing food and eating meals together has traditionally been a way that country people were able to connect to one another. It is likely that this tradition is an extension of when family members worked together in preparing food and family and friends came together over a shared meal at the dinner table. Shared food preparation included canning fruit and vegetables, shelling peas, baking pies, and making jelly. Shared meals often are an expression of gratitude for lending a helping hand with chores or of renewal of the bonds of relationships.

Indeed, many rural people use food as means of social exchange and interaction. It is not uncommon for friends, neighbors, and clients to offer a social worker something to eat or a jar of pickles as a token of acceptance. Yet traditional professional models of practice encourage social workers to shun gifts of this kind for fear that they may unduly influence their practice or drive them to engage in behavior that may be exploitive of clients. In this sense, accepting small gifts, especially of food, may not only be prudent; failure to do so may be considered rude and a major faux pas in working with rural people.

Some foods evolve to be local favorites and can become a source of local or regional identification and pride. Local and regional dishes may be distinctive and based on local products, providing a connection with home even after someone has moved away. Since foods and meals are a big part of everyone's life from youth to old age, memories of favorite foods and dishes become a part of one's memories and self-identification. In many ways, the memories of food experiences take people back to places, times, and people of the past, and there is real significance to the phrase "just like mama used to make." For example, a person from the US Southwest who relocates may have a yen for tamales and chili, yet in new surroundings, even the ingredients to make tamales may be hard to find, and tamales from a jar just will not do. Even moonshine is an example of this.

Rural foods were traditionally made from scratch and by hand, sometimes without a recipe. The twentieth century spawned fast food and frozen meals, in the name of convenience. Yet the "made from scratch" appeal to taste that many restaurants use does not re-create personal experiences with food. The appeal of capturing the "old country" atmosphere and the taste of food from rural roots has commercial appeal but cannot capture the experiences of home.

Of course, regional foods in rural areas vary considerably: grits and chicken-fried meats of the South, the hotdish of the Upper Midwest, fish and seafood dishes of the coastal Northeast, fry bread and chili of the Southwest, and beef and potatoes of the West. Some of these foods require special preparation not often found in general-purpose cookbooks. Meats like possum and raccoon take a little extra care for them to come out right, and food like poke salad and rhubarb have potentially toxic components if used improperly. The care and instruction of family members in preparing these and other local favorites is typically part of growing up and the enculturation process of many rural people.

In some sense, many country diets often tended to reflect the hard physical labor people did. As a result, there were large family meals, and heavy eating was encouraged. Some of these diets were high in fats, carbohydrates, and calories, to provide fuel for the work. Such diets tend to be less functional in modern society, when people burn far fewer calories. People today drive instead of walk, and sitting astride a tractor requires less energy than plowing behind a mule. So keeping old eating habits may lead to increased obesity and health problems. For example, the Southern staples of fried meat, vegetables flavored with pork fat, and heavy doses of starches may not be healthy for a person who uses a forklift to load hay instead of lifting the bales by hand. The health problems that result from these kinds of diets and the need to find healthier ways of eating may fall directly into the realm of services that social workers might help coordinate.

Music and Arts

Many aspects of rural culture are conveyed in music, arts, and crafts (Tice, 2005). Rural music presents songs that convey values, work, day-to-day life, and traditions—it is based on the people's heritage and spiritual beliefs. Traditional rural music takes many forms, including blues, zydeco, bluegrass, country, and folk music, all of which have their roots in rural society. These songs convey information about historical events and about the hopes, disappointments, and aspirations.

In the days before literacy was widespread, music served an important function in rural communities by communicating important ideas, experiences, and values. Songs represented a sort of collective narrative for the community and became popular because many people connected with their messages. These personal and collective narratives can be helpful in enabling social workers to understand rural people (Tice, 2005). Today music still helps to reinforce ideas, values, and heritage for members of a community.

Music helped bring people together in rural communities and provided entertainment, allowing people to take a brief break from their hard work. Television and radio were slow to reach the country, and so most music was performed live by talented local residents who held other jobs during the day. Before rural areas had electricity, some used battery-powered radios and rigged up antennas for a signal to come through. Television signals were weak in many areas, and it was not until the advent of cable and satellite dishes that families had much variety in programming. Music often filled the void in entertainment while bringing people together. Interestingly, the modern Rural Social Work Caucus, in a true rural tradition, has an official caucus song (Hickman, 2004; Locke, 2009), and it may be the only social work organization to celebrate membership in this way.

Rural musicians developed and adapted instruments to their style of music. For example, the violin was an instrument traditionally used in classical music. Yet in rural music, this instrument became the fiddle. But a violin and the fiddle deliver very different styles of music. An old rural saying is that the difference between a violin and a fiddle is that a violin is carried in a case and a fiddle is carried in a sack. Other instruments were either developed or adapted for music played in the country. Examples of these instruments include the mandolin, dobro, banjo, dulcimer, washboard, and string bass. Some of these instruments were handmade by local craftspeople.

Music is an element of culture that appears to be deeply ingrained in people, as it creates a sense of identity and conjures images and feelings of one's home environment. The rhythms and familiar words remind people of home and community, and many people maintain a connection to traditional music even when they move away. This helps account for some of the popularity of country music and blues in urban settings. Urbanites enjoy the music as well, though, as they are able to connect with the values the music conveys.

Many people highly prize rural arts and crafts. Hand-worked quilts and woven blankets can fetch high prices because of their beauty, the skill required in making them, and the fact that so few are made by hand anymore. Other types of collectible arts include handmade furniture, metalwork like weathervanes, wood carvings, and paintings. Rural arts and crafts are admired for their rustic qualities, skills involved, and uniqueness of their production. Rural arts and crafts exemplify a more traditional way of doing things based on craftsmanship. Rural arts and crafts are not only forms of expression; they have been a way to earn extra income in places where cash has traditionally been less plentiful.

Folk arts and crafts are undergoing somewhat of a renaissance with attempts to recapture many of the old folkways before the skills die out, perhaps to be lost to posterity. Rural families tended to be fairly self-sufficient in producing much of what they needed to live. But today few families make their own clothes, much less produce their own cloth. In the past, country people would shear sheep, clean and card wool, spin thread, weave cloth, and sew garments. But today it is easier, and often cheaper, to buy clothing at the store. Rural families saved things like fat and ashes to make soap, but these skills are lost to many modern families. Much metalwork in the country was done by local blacksmiths, yet today there are fewer and fewer practicing blacksmiths. Historical villages and museums try to keep some of these old ways alive for subsequent generations.

Yet while many rural families have shifted from producing most of what they need on their own, the values of self-sufficiency and frugality that are part of home-based production remain strong in rural communities. The narratives and themes of the music, the expressions of folk culture, and the everyday life skills are important parts of community identity and are something in which individuals as well as families take pride. Learning about these things will help social workers fit into a community and understand the people with whom they work.

Health and Wellness

Some of the traditional practices of rural people may extend into the practice of health care. In an environment where physicians, and the resources to pay them, were scarce, folk medicine was practiced as a form of healing. Folk medicine practices developed from the knowledge that people brought to and developed in the lands they settled, and they continued relatively unchanged until World War II (Cavender, 2003). Some folk medicine practices persist today, although they are often used in conjunction with traditional medicine. Although folk medicine may seem strange or archaic to some, many remedies were effective, and some are not terribly different from those of the modern herbalist.

Among folk medical practices are burn doctors, who reputedly "talked the fire out of burns." Many families also use hot tea or a hot toddy as a cold remedy, and castor oil for stomach ailments (Cavender, 2003). These remedies sometimes included stylized sayings and appeals to God. There is also the practice of folk healing among African Americans and Native Americans, which includes spiritual elements, as well as ritual, words, and dreams (Mitchem, 2007). Such practices are also common among traditional Latino people. The point is that some of these practices persist today and are culturally part of rural people. The context of their use and their effectiveness may need to be incorporated into social work with country people.

MEZZO SYSTEMS

Whoever decided that rural people were "simple folk" surely got it wrong. Rural people and their social relationships are every bit as complex as those found in a city, if not even more so (Ginsberg, 1976). Rural communities have been compared to very large extended families because almost everyone knows something about everyone else. Obviously, some relationships are closer than others, and people know more about those with whom they are close. But the old saying is, "The nice part of living in a small town is that when I don't know what I'm doing, someone else does."

But some relationships are even more complex than they appear on the surface. Families sometimes have relationships, good and bad, that go back generations. The nature of these relationships is communicated to family members, and while individuals may be operating in the present, they might also be addressing past favors owed or trying to redress old wrongs done.

Country people tend to understand relationships and are good at sizing up a person, in terms of character and background. A criterion they use is to place someone on a citified-countrified continuum. This helps them predict the behavior of someone they do not know that well. There is even a rough classification scheme for being rural. Folk expressions of how rural someone is are often framed in terms of being countrified, and one person can be more "country" than another. Examples of sayings describing a person as very rural include the following: "He lived so far back in the country that he had to walk toward town to hunt squirrels," "He lived so far back in the country that he had to grease the wagon twice to go to town," "Those folks use owls for roosters and possum for yard dogs," "He's as country as homemade soap," and "She saucers and blows her coffee" (Bowman, 1995, p. 39). All of these sayings conjure images of people with quaint, unsophisticated ways who live in very out-of-the-way places. So even to country people, some people are more country than others, which is just one indication that the social structure of a small town is much more complex than it appears.

MACRO SYSTEMS

Power Structure

A key part of knowing the community is developing an understanding of its power structure. This is especially important for rural social workers who must frequently work with and get the assistance of community decision makers (Ginsberg, 1998; Locke & Winship, 2005, Martinez-Brawley, 2000). Rural communities are close, and people are interconnected, so whatever a social worker is doing will be known before long. Community decision makers are in a position to help or to impede the process, but ideally social workers can enlist their assistance.

The most important task for the social worker is to identify who has major influence in key decisions. This isn't always easy, because in rural areas decision makers are in formal and informal positions. Decision makers in formal positions may be easy enough to spot: mayors, county judges, council members, commissioners, sheriffs, police chiefs, county directors, and more. All of these are positions in which people can potentially make things happen if they are approached in the right way. It is easy to lose sight of the fact that everyone answers to someone, and that some people can get a person's ear better than others. Of course, in a rural community much of the influence on decision making, as with many other things, is handled informally and not easily observed unless one knows about the relationships between people.

Many decision makers remain in the background, often out of public view. These are the informal decision makers: ministers, business owners, large landholders, members of important families, and those with earned influence in the community. These people may have the respect of others because of their past achievements, their skills, and the fact that they hold key positions or have personal influence, and they may be consulted about matters within their expertise. Indeed, the influence of informal decision makers can be stronger than that of those in formal positions, and if someone's influence is strong enough, it will be difficult to convince anyone in a formal position to go against that person's wishes. In fact, real decisions may not be made in formal commission meetings at the county courthouse; instead, they may be made over coffee and breakfast at a local restaurant where a group of leading influential people routinely meet.

Members of the power structure must be engaged for much of the substantial work to be done in a rural community. In a very real sense, social workers may need to get a tacit endorsement from the community powers that be in order to get much support in their work. This is certainly the case with respect to community and resource development. Not much will escape the notice of community decision makers—even case management and work with individual families—and if a social worker's activities are viewed as having some significance, then getting much done without some kind of approval can be difficult. Failure to ask for approval may be viewed as an insult and generate opposition. As the rural sayings go, people may perceive that the social worker "did them dirt" (insulted them), and so after that, the social worker would be "sawing against the grain" (pushing uphill).

The role of the power structure in social work in a smaller community can be more critical than it is in the city. It is harder for what social workers do to escape notice, and there are fewer degrees of separation between social workers and community decision makers. There also tend to be fewer decision makers, and they know the powerful people, so the reach of some of them into many facets of life may be greater than in a city. Of course, there may be social work activities that make little or no difference to the power structure, and so workers would face no difficulty in proceeding. But it is helpful to have an idea of what differentiates important from unimportant activities.

A useful approach to identifying members of a community's power structure is to use a reputational approach (Martinez-Brawley, 2000). This is done by working with a list of key informants, people knowledgeable about the community. A list of names of influential people can be collected and their areas of influence identified. Another way to identify important decision makers is to establish a list of people in positions of influence, especially those of relevance to social welfare issues. The social worker may then seek to understand which decision makers have more influence than others. This may help rural social workers develop an understanding of the community power structure to be able to better work with it.

The Community's Identity

Every community has some important features by which it frames its identity. To really understand a community and connect with the people, it is essential to know what those attributes are and how they are significant to community members. Examples of these attributes are sometimes included in slogans that reflect the spirit of the area: "Where the West begins," "State AAA football champions, 1994," or with phrases like "oldest town in . . . ," "capital of . . . ," or "heartland of . . ." Even Garrison Keillor's fictional Lake Wobegon has an identity: "where all the women are strong, all of the men good looking, and all the children above average."

These points of identity are something community members know, understand, and—to some degree—come together around. They serve to build social capital in the community, are often points of pride, and celebrate what a community values (Carlton-LaNey & Burwell, 2011). For example, if the high school football or softball team is a source of community pride, then game-day events may be well attended and give a sense of community solidarity. If one of the local agricultural products is strawberries, then there may be a strawberry festival, or if an area was settled by Germans, Oktoberfest might be a big event.

The nature of a community event can give a strong indication of the origins of the community's identity: Mardi Gras in the French-settled United States, a blessing of a maritime fleet can show a fishing identity, and an apple festival shows agricultural roots. These may be very different types of communities, and learning about the activities and events that impart local identity helps social workers develop working knowledge of how people think of themselves and shows an effort to understand the people and their beliefs. This can be a start for building trust for professional relationships.

Heritage

Rural communities tend to be traditional in outlook (Riebschleger, 2005). Some may describe this as conservative or even backward. Small towns and rural areas do tend to resist change and follow old, established ways. Some people may see this as resistance to progress. Yet rural communities tend to focus on embracing customs and patterns of behavior that have served people well in the past, and "progress" can be viewed as the intrusion of outsiders who may not understand the local people or the community. Since many ideas about change tend to originate in urban areas, it is small wonder that rural people are less enthusiastic about change.

A community's traditions, norms, and behavior are influenced by the historical and cultural heritage of past generations, and rural communities exhibit this with great pride (Johnson & Dunbar, 2005; Morris & Morris, 1999; Tice, 2005). Often, this kind of information passes from generation to generation verbally as part of the socialization process, which helps provide stability for the community. Some traditions and heritage are so strong that in some places, events and settlement patterns from more than two centuries ago still affect the way community members view themselves and act. For example, in much of the US West, traditions of the frontier and cowboys are often part of local culture. The period of frontier settlement and the cowboy's heyday were brief, and the reality of living conditions in those times often has only a loose connection to our modern myths about them, but the spirit of the frontier and of the cowboy are still part of rural lore and tradition. To be sure, there are modern cowboys, but their methods and lives are somewhat different from those of the past.

Who settled a rural area can also make a difference in the cultural tradition of a small town or village. Areas where Native Americans or First Nations people settled tend to have very different community norms and structure from those in the areas settled by Europeans. Areas settled by Spanish, French, Germans, Scandinavians, and Dutch tend to differ socially, economically, culturally, and religiously. Indeed, these communities may differ in significant ways from those settled by those of English, Irish, Scottish, Welsh, and Scots-Irish descent. The traditions that these varied groups of settlers brought with them ultimately found their way into the community's overall philosophy, particularly how social welfare issues are addressed.

Ultimately, traditions are an important part of who rural people are, and it can be difficult to understand or connect with them well without learning about their traditions. Learning about the heritage of traditional people shows an interest in understanding them and a way of creating a personal connection that can be very helpful in gaining acceptance from members of the community.

Work

As a rule, the rural economy is not nearly as diverse as that of a city (Ginsberg, 1998, 2011; NASW, 2009; Schott, 1980). In other words, in the country many people share common or related occupations, which become a further source of social interaction. They share similar labor or use of their time, and they frequently discuss the work they do. The common view of a rural community is one of an economy based primarily on agriculture, which is only one type of economic enterprise in rural areas and is no longer as central to rural life as it was even forty years ago.

In farming communities there tends to be a limited number of agricultural activities and crops. For example, in one area the major crops might be grain and soybeans. Related local industries might include farm implements, grain silos, and agricultural supplies. There might also be services like grocery stores, restaurants, banks, and churches, but in the community a high percentage of the people would have working knowledge of the agriculture predominant in the region.

Farming, especially family farming, has declined in importance even in rural areas. Some in agriculture now maintain farms but work for large agricultural corporations. For example, chicken farmers may have their own land and chicken houses but buy their chicks and feed from a large meat products company. Farmers may then be obligated to sell the grown chickens to that corporation. Davenport and Davenport (1999) point out the potential loss of agricultural jobs and the environmental dangers of corporate agribusiness like hog farming, and they suggest that, ultimately, rural areas may suffer from this form of economic enterprise.

Some rural areas that once depended on farming, logging, or fishing have transitioned to an economy based on recreation, camping, and tourism. Often, this is primarily a seasonal economy that offers more economic rewards. A significant drawback is that employment and incomes may not be stable, and they may be at the mercy of the weather. For example, a very dry or wet season may make fishing or camping unappealing. Another disadvantage is the number of outsiders who enter the community and have little stake in it. Tourists spend their money and leave, or if they remain for at least part of the year, they might push up land prices and press for additional services to which they are accustomed.

Rural areas may have many kinds of economic enterprises other than farming that employ large sections of the community. In some areas, extractors of natural resources are the leading employers. Mining, oil and gas production, timber production, and even hunting and fishing are examples of these types of work. Many extraction industries carry environmental hazards or create boom and bust cycles that are very harmful to rural communities (Davenport & Davenport, 2005). Even the boom cycles, while good for the community, present major transitional problems for community members, who must cope with the growth and influx of outsiders (Davenport & Davenport, 1998). For example, the new method of extracting natural gas by fracking was at first touted as an economic boom for rural areas. Yet there is evidence of polluted groundwater (Peeples, 2012) and earthquakes (King, 2013) that have harmful effects on rural communities. While the extraction of resources provides employment for the area, some industries affect the environment in ways that are harmful to both the environment and the area residents. Oil and gas can leak killing wildlife and polluting water supplies and clear-cut lands may be subject to deep erosion.

Work in extraction industries is often hard, poorly paid, and dangerous (Riebschleger, 2005). According to a CNNMoney (n.d.) report, four of the five most dangerous jobs in the United States are primarily rural occupations: fisherman, logger, farmer and rancher, and mining machine operator. The danger of this work is evident enough to attract the attention of the audiences who watch current reality television shows that deal with logging, commercial fishing, and alligator hunting. While this activity is exciting to television audiences, it is hard, dangerous work, and workers can be killed or become disabled easily, meaning that families can experience a significant loss in income, perhaps permanently.

Some extraction industries coexist near farms or ranches. But in a rural area one source of employment may dominate, and people in surrounding communities will know many of the ins and outs of the business, just as they would know about farming in an agricultural area. For example, where logging is practiced, some people cut the timber, others drive the log trucks, and others work for the sawmills.

Some companies have located manufacturing plants in rural areas to take advantage of the availability of a relatively cheap labor supply and more tax advantages than might be found in urban areas. Where rural manufacturing is located, many in the community will have knowledge of "the plant" because they work there, have worked there, or have relatives or friends who work or have worked there. These plants can contribute to the local economy in a significant way, and they can also attract workers from outside the area, creating social stress and resentment toward newcomers. The plants may also bring management in from outside the area, and management's higher income and education may be another source of tension in the community.

Some rural areas experience growth through migration from urban areas. Often, this migration flows into or near "micropolitan" cities that serve the region. Micropolitan areas have a core large town or city, with ten thousand to fifty thousand residents, that serves one or more counties (US Census Bureau, n.d.). Many of the urban transplants are looking for better living conditions in terms of less congestion and safer environments. But whether the urban transplants are retirees, commuters, or those who want a lifestyle change, they often are better off economically and have higher education levels than the average community resident. This influx of outsiders can create friction in the community.

Large merchant chains from outside the area have moved to rural areas, changing the nature of the economy and the community. For example, Walmart (n.d.), which began as a retailer in the small town of Rogers, Arkansas, in 1962, is a multinational corporation with stores in many rural communities. Walmart provides employment and a wide array of goods for many small towns. Yet the effect of large corporations like Walmart and McDonald's has also been the loss of many locally owned businesses. The large, corporate stores and restaurants keep less of the money and profits locally than community-run businesses, have less of a stake in small towns, and tend to give back less to an area—all of which ultimately serve to weaken rural areas.

Because rural economies are not as diverse as those of larger cities, disruptions in the primary industry or occupation can significantly affect the local people. When a plant closes or relocates, or when the oil plays out, or the price of coal drops, or the timber is cut, an area can be hit hard because there are few jobs in other industries to pick up the slack. Residents are then forced to choose between moving from a community where they may have significant connections and family, and remaining there and trying to find some new way of making a living. The decision to move on is not an easy one.

For rural social workers, understanding the major types of employment, wages, benefits, and possible physically disabling conditions of the work offers a way to connect with local people about something central to their lives. It also helps in understanding people themselves, because the work one does is a significant part of that person's self-identification. Knowledge of a person's work environment can also help social workers understand how some problems develop, help assist in identifying strengths and assets, and explore potential resources to address individual and community problems.

CHANGE IN THE TWENTY-FIRST CENTURY

Despite a reliance on traditions to guide them, rural people and rural life have changed considerably over the past century. Most of what has been written about rural social work has suggested that rural communities are underserved by social welfare services. This is generally true, but the scarcity of services is relative. In the early twentieth century social workers often talked about convincing a community of the need for services and then developing them. Today, social welfare services are much more widely distributed, and scarcity relates to accessibility, with respect to distance and travel required to access services, as well as the availability of specialized services. There is still a need for community and service development, but with existing rural assets, rarely are social workers starting from scratch, as they were a century ago.

Many other aspects of country life have changed as well. Work has shifted from agriculture as the primary occupation to wage work. Two-income families are more common than they were in the past, and often at least one wage earner has to commute a considerable distance to a job. The preparation of food has changed, as well. For example, as one former rural resident told me: "My grandmother used to kill it, cook it, and clean it. My mother would clean it and cook it, and I [would] clean it sometimes, but I often just microwave prepared food." So while fresh vegetables and meats are still eaten in small towns and rural areas, prepared food, canned goods, and frozen foods are much more a part of modern life.

More elements of urban or modern life have crept into the rural community, despite the tendency to retain traditional ways. Transportation outside of the area is much better than it was even fifty years ago. More and better roads and highways have decreased the time it takes to get to other communities, provided that one has reliable personal transportation. No longer is it common, as it was at the start of the twentieth century, for rural residents to have never left their county of residence. Radio, television, and the Internet have reached most, but not all, areas of the country, and with them came new ideas and new ways of doing things. All of this tends to push rural communities in the direction of the bigger cities. Of course, the lure of the cities, particularly in terms of drawing young people away, which has confronted rural areas for more than a century, remains even today.

Churches, schools, and other local institutions remain an important part of rural communities. Communities are still close knit, with an emphasis on personal social relationships; family is still important; and communication remains informal and open. But in many areas family ties are weakening as economic opportunities and a modern lifestyle entice many people from their home communities, and as distance makes maintaining family relationships more challenging. The closeness of some rural communities is being challenged as new people and businesses move into the area.

In some areas the connection to the land is weakening. As farming and ranching become less viable, land may have greater value for other uses. Areas on the outskirts of cities may find that land is much more valuable for subdivisions than for agriculture, and so land is often sold off. Rural areas with good water or scenic beauty might find that land is worth more as resort property. And as exploitation of natural resources causes the oil, coal, or copper ore to play out, communities may face devastating economic consequences. Yet if new natural resources are found, their exploitation may scar the land and community.

Despite some attempts, rural economies still tend to have little diversity. Thus, a sudden shift in the economy; a decline in interest rates, goods, or prices; or the relocation of jobs can prove devastating to a rural area. Simply, there are fewer places for rural people to go to find alternatives for suitable work in the community. The outsourcing of jobs and industries has had a significant effect on rural workers. For example, the closing of textile plants in places like North Carolina has displaced many workers, and their jobs have not been replaced.

Rural people are still remarkably self-reliant, despite the poverty, poor education, and hard working conditions that many of them have faced. Their independence and can-do attitude remains strong and can be a major strength for social workers who work with them. Moreover, many traditional rural values have remained strong over the past century, and it is well that they did. The rural values of self-reliance, helping others, and community have allowed many rural areas to remain strong and to survive major social and economic changes. This is an important notion for any rural social worker to keep in mind, as these are assets to be incorporated into the professional helping process. True cultural competency in working with rural people involves understanding these values and the traditions of a rural area.

CONCLUSION

Social workers learn early in their careers that it is crucial to develop cultural sensitivity in order to successfully work with clients. The general perception is that rural people do not constitute a client group for which cultural competence is needed. Nevertheless, rural communities comprise people with a common language, values, customs, music, art, and skills that are in many respects distinct from those of people who do not consider themselves rural. This array of common characteristics is indeed what we would call culture, and social workers in rural practice should develop both knowledge of the culture and facility in interacting with rural people.

As with any cultural group, there are unique differences between individuals and communities. But these differences do not negate the many common traits found in rural life. These traits include attachment to the land, the importance of family, the importance of church and schools, informal helping networks, complex and close personal relationships, open communication, reliance on tradition, and self-reliance. Food, music, and recreation are also important areas of social activity and integration. Rural culture is rich and has helped both communities and people adapt and survive in sometimes challenging environments. Too frequently our society dismisses the values of rural culture and rural people.

Cultural competency is important for any social worker, including those working with rural people and in rural communities. Rural people know one another and value their personal relationships. Social workers are usually viewed as outsiders, no matter how competent they may be. Outsiders are not trusted and are typically dealt with at a distance, and until social workers get some degree of acceptance, building strong helping relationships is difficult, if not impossible. A good way to earn acceptance and credibility is by learning the culture and demonstrating behavior based on that knowledge. Rural people are a tight-knit group, and they can spot an outsider quickly by observing behavior and speech. In a rural community, word travels fast through informal channels and outsiders are obvious. Learning the community and the local culture may take some study and the help of insiders.

Even though a social worker holds an official position, some rural people just do not want to work with someone they do not know. But the effort is worth it. Once accepted, the social worker will have better access to people and services, both formal and informal. Rural social work is all about learning, understanding, and acting within the framework of the rural community. Our clients deserve nothing less from us.

REFERENCES

Barker, R. L. (2014). *The social work dictionary* (6th ed.). Washington, DC: NASW Press.

Bowman, B. (1995). *He's wetting on my leg, but it's warm and wet and feels good.* Lufkin, TX: Best of East Texas Publishers.

Carawan, L. W., Bass, L. L., & Bunch, S. G. (1999). Using narratives in educating social workers for rural practice. In I. B. Carlton-LaNey, R. L. Edwards, & P. N. Reid (Eds.), *Preserving and strengthening small towns and rural communities* (pp. 355–366). Washington, DC: NASW Press.

Carlton-LaNey, I. B., & Burwell, N. Y. (2011). Historical treasures of rural communities: Special characteristics of rural places. In L. Ginsberg (Ed.), *Social work in rural communities* (5th ed., pp. 21–37). Alexandria, VA: Council on Social Work Education.

Carlton-LaNey, I. B., Edwards, R. L., & Reid, P. N. (1999a). The importance of families. In I. B. Carlton-LaNey, R. L. Edwards, & P. N. Reid (Eds.), *Preserving and strengthening small towns and rural communities* (p. 71). Washington, DC: NASW Press.

Carlton-LaNey, I. B., Edwards, R. L., & Reid, P. N. (1999b). Small towns and rural communities: From romantic notions to harsh realities. In I. B. Carlton-LaNey, R. L. Edwards, & P. N. Reid (Eds.), *Preserving and strengthening small towns and rural communities* (pp. 5–12). Washington, DC: NASW Press.

Cassleman, B. (1995). *Canadian words.* Toronto, ON: McArthur.

Cavender, A. (2003). *Folk medicines in southern Appalachia.* Chapel Hill, NC: University of North Carolina Press.

CNNMoney. (n.d.). *America's most dangerous jobs.* Retrieved from http://money.cnn.com/galleries/2011/pf/jobs/1108/gallery.dangerous_jobs/index.html.

Daley, M. R., & Avant, F. (1999). Attracting and retaining professionals for social work practice in rural areas: An example from East Texas. In I. B. Carlton-La Ney, R. L. Edwards, & P. N. Reid (Eds.), *Preserving and strengthening small towns and rural communities* (pp. 335–345). Washington, DC: NASW Press.

Daley, M. R., & Avant, F. (2004a). Advanced generalist for rural practice. In A. Roy & F. Vecchiola (Eds.), *Advanced generalist practice: Models, readings, and essays* (pp. 37–57). Peosta, IA: Bowers.

Daley, M., & Avant, F. (2004b). Reconceptualizing the framework for practice. In T. L. Scales & C. L. Streeter (Eds.), *Rural social work: Building and sustaining community assets* (pp. 34–42), Belmont, CA: Thomson/Brooks Cole.

Daley, M. R., & Pierce, B. (2011). Educating for rural competence: Curriculum concepts, models and course content. In L. Ginsberg (Ed.), *Social work in rural communities* (5th ed., pp. 125–140). Alexandria, VA: Council on Social Work Education.

Davenport, J., & Davenport, J. A. (1998). Rural communities in transition. In L. H. Ginsberg (Ed.), *Social work in rural communities* (3rd ed., pp. 37–51). Alexandria, VA: Council on Social Work Education.

Davenport, J. A., & Davenport, J. (1999). Squeals and deals: The impact of corporate hog farming on rural communities. In I. B. Carlton-

LaNey, R. L. Edwards, & P. N. Reid (Eds.), *Preserving and strengthening small towns and rural communities* (pp. 57–70). Washington, DC: NASW Press.

Davenport, J. A., & Davenport, J. (2005). Rural communities in transition. In L. H. Ginsberg (Ed.), *Social work in rural communities* (4th ed., pp. 17–33). Alexandria, VA: Council on Social Work Education.

Farley, O. W., Griffiths, K. A., Skidmore, R. A., & Thackeray, M. G. (1982). *Rural social work practice.* New York, NY: Free Press.

Ginsberg, L. H. (1976). An overview of social work education for rural areas. In L. H. Ginsberg (Ed.), *Social work in rural communities: A book of readings* (pp. 1–12). New York, NY: Council on Social Work Education.

Ginsberg, L. H. (1998). Introduction: An overview of rural social work. In L. H. Ginsberg (Ed.), *Social work in rural communities* (3rd ed., pp. 2–17). Alexandria, VA: Council on Social Work Education.

Ginsberg, L. H. (2005). The overall context of rural practice. In L. H. Ginsberg (Ed.), *Social work in rural communities* (4th ed., pp. 4–7). Alexandria, VA: Council on Social Work Education.

Ginsberg, L. (2011). Introduction to basics of rural social work. In L. Ginsberg (Ed.), *Social work in rural communities* (5th ed., pp. 5–20). Alexandria, VA: Council on Social Work Education.

Gumpert, J., & Saltman, J. E. (1998). Social group work practice in rural areas: The practitioners speak. *Social Work with Groups, 21*(3), 19–34.

Gumpert, J., Saltman, J. E., & Sauer-Jones, D. (2000). Toward identifying the unique characteristics of social work practice in rural areas: From the voices of practitioners. *Journal of Baccalaureate Social Work, 6*(1), 19–35.

Hartley, D. A., Savage, T. A., & Kaplan, L. E. (2005). Racial and ethnic minorities in rural areas: Use of indigenous influence in the practice of social work. In L. H. Ginsberg (Ed.), *Social work in rural communities* (4th ed., pp. 367–385). Alexandria, VA: Council on Social Work Education.

Hickman, S. A. (2004). Rural is real: Supporting professional practice through the rural social work caucus and the NASW professional policy statement for rural social work. In T. L. Scales & C. L. Streeter

(Eds.), *Rural social work: Building and sustaining community assets* (pp. 43–50). Belmont, CA: Thomson/Brooks Cole.

Hickman, S. A. (2014). Rural is real: History of the national rural social work caucus and the NASW professional policy statement on rural social work. In T. L. Scales, C. L. Streeter, & H. S. Cooper (Eds.), *Rural social work: Building and sustaining community capacity* (2nd ed., pp. 19–28). Hoboken, NJ: Wiley.

Johnson, H. W. (1980). Working in the rural community. In H. W. Johnson (Ed.), *Rural human services: A book of readings* (pp. 143–148). Itasca, IL: Peacock.

Johnson, M., & Dunbar, E. (2005). Culturally relevant social work practice in diverse rural communities. In L. H. Ginsberg (Ed.), *Social work in rural communities* (4th ed., pp. 349–365). Alexandria, VA: Council on Social Work Education.

King, L. (2013, July 24). Does fracking lead to earthquakes? *Christian Science Monitor*. Retrieved from http://www.csmonitor.com/Environment/Energy-Voices/2013/0724/Does-fracking-lead-to-earthquakes.

Locke, B. L. (2009). The national rural social work caucus: 32 years of achievement. *Contemporary Rural Social Work, 1*, 1–7. Retrieved from http://journal.und.edu/crsw/issue/view/22.

Locke, B. L., & Winship, J. (2005). Social work in rural America. In N. Lohmann & R. Lohmann (Eds.), *Rural social work practice* (pp. 3–6). New York, NY: Columbia University Press.

Martinez-Brawley, E. E. (1990). *Perspectives on the small community: Humanistic views for practitioners*. Washington, DC: NASW Press.

Martinez-Brawley, E. E. (2000). *Close to home: Human services in the small community.* Washington, DC: NASW Press.

Mitchem, S. Y. (2007). *African American folk healing*. New York, NY: New York University Press.

Mohr, H. (1987). *How to talk Minnesotan*. New York, NY: Penguin Books.

Morris, J. H., & Morris, L. C. (1999). Small town murals: Remembering rural roots. In I. B. Carlton-LaNey, R. L. Edwards, & P. N. Reid (Eds.), *Preserving and strengthening small towns and rural communities* (pp. 186–195). Washington, DC: NASW Press.

National Association of Social Workers. (2008). *Code of ethics of the national association of social workers.* Washington, DC: Author. Retrieved from http://www.socialworkers.org/pubs/code/code.asp.

National Association of Social Workers. (2009). Rural social work. In *Social work speaks: National Association of Social Workers policy statements* (8th ed., pp. 297–302). Washington, DC: Author.

National Association of Social Workers. (2012). Rural social work. *Social work speaks: National Association of Social Workers policy statements* (9th ed., pp. 296–300). Washington, DC: Author.

Osgood, M. H. (1980). Rural and urban attitudes toward welfare. In H. W. Johnson (Ed.), *Rural human services: A book of readings* (pp. 159–171). Itasca, IL: Peacock.

Patterson, S. L., Memmott, J. L., Brennan, E. M., & Germain, C. B. (1998). Patterns of natural helping in rural areas: Implications for social work research. In L. H. Ginsberg (Ed.), *Social work in rural communities* (3rd ed., pp. 22–36). Alexandria, VA: Council on Social Work Education.

Peeples, L. (2012, October 18). Fracking pollution sickens Pennsylvania families, environmental group says. *Huffington Post.* Retrieved from http://www.huffingtonpost.com/2012/10/18/fracking-pollution-pennsylvania_n_1982320.html.

Riebschleger, J. (2005). Facilitating rural community planning groups. In L. H. Ginsberg (Ed.), *Social work in rural communities* (4th ed., pp. 109–122). Alexandria, VA: Council on Social Work Education.

Riebschleger, J. (2007). Social workers suggestions for effective rural practice. *Families in Society*, *88*(2), 203–213.

Rural America. (1980). *I.Q.s flunk rural test.* In H. W. Johnson (Ed.), *Rural human services: A book of readings* (pp. 42–43). Itasca, IL: Peacock.

Schott, M. (1980). Casework: Rural. In H. W. Johnson (Ed.), *Rural human services: A book of readings* (pp. 153–158). Itasca, IL: Peacock.

Tice, C. J. (2005). Celebrating rural communities: A strengths assessment. In L. H. Ginsberg (Ed.), *Social work in rural communities* (4th ed., pp. 95–107). Alexandria, VA: Council on Social Work Education.

US Census Bureau. (n.d.). *Metropolitan and micropolitan statistical areas main.* Retrieved from http://www.census.gov/population/metro/.

Walmart. (n.d.). *History timeline.* Retrieved from http://corporate.walmart.com/our-story/heritage/history-timeline.

Waltman, G. H. (1986). Main street revisited: Social work practice in rural areas. *Social Casework, 67*, 466–474.

Watkins, T. R. (2004). Natural helping networks. In T. L. Scales & C. L. Streeter (Eds.), *Rural social work: Building and sustaining community assets* (pp. 65–75). Belmont, CA: Thomson/Brooks Cole.

Weber, B. A., Geigle, J., & Barkdull, C. (2014). Rural North Dakota's oil boom and its impact on social services. *Social Work, 59*(1), 62–72.

Weber, G. K. (1980). Preparing social workers for practice in rural social systems. In H. W. Johnson (Ed.), *Rural human services: A book of readings* (pp. 203–214). Itasca, IL: Peacock.

White, C., & Marks, K. (1999). A strengths-based approach to rural sustainable development. In I. B. Carlton-LaNey, R. L. Edwards, & P. N. Reid (Eds.), *Preserving and strengthening small towns and rural communities* (pp. 5–12). Washington, DC: NASW Press.

Immigration is changing the face of rural communities: a Headstart program in Alabama.

CHAPTER THREE

Diversity in Rural Communities

THERE IS A COMMON ASSUMPTION that the people who live in rural communities are not a diverse group. Indeed, the stereotypical picture of a rural community is composed almost entirely of white residents. This view may be a product of the popular media's portrayals of rural life. No doubt the television programs that have depicted Mayberry, the Waltons, the Dukes of Hazzard, and the more recent show the Hatfields and McCoys have left an indelible image of the simple, rustic behavior of communities that are overwhelmingly male dominated and white. When we think *rural*, it is almost as if we expected the fictional Andy Taylor of Mayberry or the farmer and his daughter from the Grant Wood painting *American Gothic* to step forward and greet us.

The fictional Lake Wobegon of the radio show *Prairie Home Companion* portrays life in small-town Minnesota, with its Norwegian bachelor farmers. Traditional country and bluegrass music is sung primarily by white performers. Rural comedians often play to the "redneck" image and are predominately white. The term *redneck* is an unflattering reference to poor and uneducated whites, primarily from the South, yet today Southern conservatives have adopted it as a point of pride. The common thread in many depictions of rural life is that it is an almost exclusively white society. Given these visible images of rural people, the stereotype is not surprising.

Stereotypes, though, can be very misleading. While it is true that small rural towns and villages tend to be more homogeneous than large cities, it is a mistake to think that rural communities are either all white or all alike in their composition. That is too simplistic, and it ignores the needs of significant groups of people who may at some point need a social worker's services. To be responsive to all community members, social workers need to be aware of diversity in rural communities and how that diversity affects needs, services, and social problems. While looking at all minority and oppressed groups in the rural environment is beyond the scope of this chapter, identifying some of the larger groups and the problems they face is important for rural social workers because it is good social work practice. This chapter examines issues relevant for social work with rural African Americans, Hispanics, and Native Americans; gay, lesbian, bisexual, and transgender persons; and the elderly.

Indeed, rural communities are multicultural and multidimensional, as we will see in this chapter. Rural practice benefits from use of a culturally grounded approach, like that recommended by Marsiglia and Kulis (2009). This is an approach that includes not only cultural characteristics but also the effects of past and current oppression. Rural people are not simply rural, elderly, African American, female, lesbian, or of upper (or lower) socioeconomic class—they might identify as all of those characteristics simultaneously. So while good practice is grounded in the culture, practice may also need to focus on the intersectionality of multiple dimensions of people with whom a social worker is working. Clearly aspects of rural culture are the primary focus of this work, but it is best to remember that rural communities are not homogeneous, and failing to recognize the differences that exist even in a single community could be a mistake. Whether working with elderly or young people, Hispanic or African American people, lesbian or bisexual people—being rural gives them all something in common, even if they differ in other areas.

RURAL DIVERSITY

According to the National Association of Social Workers (NASW, 2012b), racial and ethnic minorities account for 18.3 percent of the residents in the rural United States, or almost one in five. This is a good indication that rural social workers will have to work with a range of people, despite the relative homogeneity of rural communities compared to urban ones. African Americans represent the largest racial minority in the rural United States, and Hispanics are the fastest-growing population in rural areas. In fact, in some smaller communities groups considered minorities nationwide may actually be in the majority, yet this does not keep them from facing discrimination and oppression.

An example is the so-called black belts of the rural South. These were originally named for the color of the soil, but today they have become synonymous with regions that have a high percentage of African American residents. The Southwest and southern border regions of the United States have many rural communities, and in many of those communities, most residents are of Hispanic heritage. Across the United States—Alaska, Hawaii, the Southwest, the Midwest, the Northeast—there are rural regions with concentrated populations of Native Americans. On the Gulf Coast, one can find rural fishing communities populated by Southeast Asian immigrants and in the West rural areas populated by Asian immigrants. There are many examples, but the ones here should serve to illustrate the rich racial and ethnic diversity of smaller towns and help debunk at least one stereotype of rural communities.

Race and ethnicity are not the only components of the rich diversity of rural communities. Small towns have a wider variety of religions, ages, and sexual orientations than is generally supposed. Often, some of this diversity is not immediately apparent because the rural community does not always embrace difference. Indeed, many minority groups opt to remain somewhat out of sight, to avoid the possibility of unfavorable treatment by community members. The reluctance to be visible and mistaken perceptions of what rural people are like may both play a role in people's assumptions that these areas have little in the way of diversity.

For example, the predominant religion in many rural communities is Christianity, particularly Protestantism, although several different religious groups may be represented. If the community is small, one religion and sometimes one church may be predominant, and other religions or churches are viewed with a jaundiced eye and little tolerance for other religious views. Understandably, members of a minority religious group may tend to keep to themselves, to avoid the reactions of others. The isolation of nonmajority religious groups may result in isolation from the broader structure of community support. For example, Waltman (2011) addresses the culture of the rural Amish, their self-reliance, avoidance of traditional social services, and their relationship to the broader rural community. Yet it is not unusual for rural communities to have a considerable amount of religious diversity that is not readily apparent.

There is often rich religious diversity in small communities. Regions that were settled by the Spanish or French may have many residents who are Catholic. For example, the rural Gulf Coast, Louisiana, states bordering Mexico, and parts of the border with Canada have significant Catholic populations. There are also rural settlements of Mormons in the West and Southwest United States and of Amish in Canada as well as the US Midwest, Northeast, and other parts of the country. There are Buddhist temples in places like Alabama and Virginia, and rural Jewish settlements in many areas, especially western United States and Canada. Indeed, there is a richness in religious diversity in rural areas that most people would not expect from typical portrayals of rural communities.

Rural communities also vary from nationwide norms with respect to age and the need for services. Small towns tend to have sizable elderly populations (Johnson, 2005; Yoon & Lee, 2004). In fact, elderly people are more likely to live in a rural community than in a city, and 26 percent of the nation's elders live in smaller communities (Sherr & Bloomheart, 2005). Rural communities are also the place of residence for high percentages of adults and children living in poverty, and of greater health-care needs, especially for minorities (NASW, 2012b; Nicholas, 2005). Since both the poor and minorities tend to have special needs for health care, income support, and other social welfare services, this type of age diversity has a direct impact on rural social work practice.

In what may often seem an almost invisible population, gay, lesbian, bisexual, and transgender (GLBT) persons also live in the country. Less is known about their numbers in rural areas and about sexual orientation in rural communities in general because of strong norms that condemn such relationships. Many rural communities have values and religious beliefs that condemn, on moral grounds, anything other than heterosexual relationships. Yet all such attitudes do is effectively encourage residents to remain invisible and isolate them from the rest of the community. A community's attitudes toward GLBT persons can restrict the services and supports that are available to them.

Immigration trends in the late twentieth and early twenty-first century have resulted in major shifts in the makeup of many rural communities today. For example, Hispanic migration to the United States today reaches many miles from the southern US border across the country (Cordova, 2004; Ringel, 2005). Migrant labor patterns that used to be temporary and follow agricultural crops have become long term, as families settle in rural communities to fill low-wage jobs in factories or to work in agribusiness or food-processing plants. As a result, many rural communities have begun to change from the fairly homogeneous society of the past to more diverse communities of the twenty-first century. Long-term residents of small towns and rural areas often resent the intrusion of new people as outsiders, particularly when those people have different cultural traditions. This difference might make people very uneasy. And the prevailing view becomes, "Why don't they learn to do things our way if they want to live here?" Frequently, the community isolates these newcomers. Minority groups may be tolerated to some degree, if only barely, if they are seen as fulfilling an important community function. Often, community members say they wish "they would go back where they came from."

To the new arrivals, many of whom are struggling to adapt to new environments and a new culture, this resentment and isolation only increases the problems they face. Working for low wages, trying to find adequate housing, trying to get health care, and getting children into school without documents—all while living in fear of detention and deportation—are some of the problems they must confront. In some cases, policies are put into place that even prevent immigrants from receiving needed services. Immigrants also have to address the lack of familiar religious institutions such as Catholic churches, Jewish synagogues, and Buddhist temples, and things as basic as finding the foods they are used to eating. Rural social workers might assist these immigrant families, and by so doing, they can sometimes earn the scorn of the community for helping "those people," which might be viewed as promoting dependency and a longer stay. Work with minorities in a rural community may end up involving almost as much work at the macro level with members of the majority community and power structure to help overcome prejudices and misunderstandings about minority people, in order to create an understanding of the broader needs and to create acceptance for disadvantaged people.

Who are some of the largest minority and oppressed groups in rural communities? The remainder of this chapter examines this question and identifies some of the important issues they face. The implications that arise for rural social workers and practice are considered in the context of this discussion.

AFRICAN AMERICANS

African Americans are one of the largest racial minority groups in rural areas (Avant, 2004, 2014; NASW, 2012b). While African Americans account for 13 percent of the US population, only 8.3 percent of rural Americans are black (Economic Research Service, 2011). But these figures can be somewhat misleading, given regional differences in the composition of the population. According to Avant (2004, 2014), 55 percent of African Americans live in the South, 17 percent in the Northeast, 18 percent in the Midwest, and 10 percent in the West. Even in rural regions generally believed to have few African American residents, like Appalachia, there are significant numbers (Hayden, 1993). In some parts of the rural United States, particularly in the South, African Americans are the majority.

Consider the following rural Southern counties and the percentage of the African American population residing there:[1]

- Marion County, South Carolina—population 32,846: 55.8 percent
- Greene County, Alabama—population 8,921: 80.4 percent
- Gadsden County, Florida—population 46,151: 55.5 percent
- Sumter County, Georgia—population 32,511: 51.8 percent
- Jefferson County, Mississippi—population 7,605: 84.7 percent
- Bertie County, North Carolina—population 20,874: 62.2 percent

African Americans who live in rural areas have traditionally been disadvantaged consistently compared to their urban counterparts (Avant,

[1] All data for individual counties in the following list come from the US Census Bureau website "State & County Quick Facts," with information for 2011 (http://quickfacts.census.gov/qfd/index.html).

2004, 2014). A primary concern for rural minorities is the high incidence of poverty. As both Summers (1998) and the NASW (2012b) have pointed out, the burden of poverty is particularly hard on rural minorities. Rural African Americans have a 32.2 percent poverty rate, more than twice the national average. For example, the poverty rate for Jefferson County, Mississippi, is 39 percent; Greene County, Alabama, 30.8 percent; Gadsden County, Florida, 27.6 percent; Sumter County, Georgia, 25.9 percent; Marion County, South Carolina, 25.1 percent. The nationwide US poverty rate for 2011 stood at 15 percent (US Census Bureau, 2011c). The poverty rate is already high for rural communities, but it is even higher for rural African Americans, thus making the effects of poverty additive. In addition, the rural poor usually count among them high percentages of highly vulnerable populations, such as children and elderly people, who may need the assistance of social workers and any available services (NASW, 2012b).

Of particular concern are health-care issues facing these rural African Americans. In general, health is strongly correlated with income, and the poor tend to be less healthy than those with higher incomes (Harley, Savage, & Kaplan, 2005; Institute for Research on Poverty, n.d.). The poor also tend to be uninsured more often than the rest of the population. This is certainly true for African Americans, as the rate of uninsured is 20.8 percent versus 16.3 percent for the population of the United States (US Census Bureau, 2011c). Perhaps the implementation of the more comprehensive health-care program known as "Obamacare" may make a positive change in rural health insurance, but it is still too early to tell. As if the co-occurrence of poorer health and less insurance coverage were not enough, it is well known that rural communities have fewer health-care professionals and health-related resources (Harley et al., 2005; NASW, 2012b).

African Americans are at a higher risk for specific diseases that can lead to death and disability. These diseases include heart disease, cancer, stroke, hypertension, and diabetes (Centers for Disease Control and Prevention, n.d.). Obesity, which creates greater long-term risk of contracting a number of health conditions, is also a high-risk condition for some rural groups. For example, rural African Americans are at higher risk for obesity than urban African Americans (Wong, 2012). Higher risk for health conditions coupled with less health insurance coverage and fewer health-care resources increase the possibility of more serious health issues for all rural residents including African Americans. Yet some rural African Americans may not use formal health care because of cost or distrust of formal organizations. They may favor the use of folk remedies over the use of formal health-care resources (Harley et al., 2005; Marsiglia & Kulis, 2009; Mitchem, 2007). Lack of access to and distrust of formal health-care resources has led some African Americans to rely on folk healers, spiritual methods, hoodoos, and conjurers for healing (Marsiglia & Kulis, 2009; Mitchem, 2007). Doing so is not a uniquely African American practice and is common with other groups too, and in rural communities—in any case, it may result in some health conditions not receiving effective treatment.

Poorer health among rural African Americans and poorer health care in their home communities can result in premature death or disability. Death of a family member from disease may result in loss of needed income and greater dependency on public assistance programs. Disability from disease for rural residents may affect their ability to get treatment or to follow up with doctors, or may lead them to go without treatment because there are no treatment or support services within a reasonable distance of their home.

Poverty and health care are not the only social welfare issues facing African Americans who live in rural communities. There are issues with unemployment, substandard housing, proof of property ownership, mental health, child welfare, and transportation. For example, Hayden (1993) discussed unsavory practices of selling land in Appalachia that were used to exploit African Americans and keep them from achieving social status and power. Such practices tend to be more prevalent among the poor, and the poverty rate is particularly high among rural African Americans. Yet social welfare services for addressing these problems are neither as numerous nor as complete as those available in larger cities. When families need specialized services, they often have to travel a considerable distance to receive them. Some of these social problems are borne of long-standing discriminatory practices designed to maintain the status quo and keep rural African Americans from attaining social and economic mobility.

Many social issues like the nineteenth century Jim Crow laws and subsequent loss of land led rural African Americans to migrate to urban areas, often outside of the South, to pursue better opportunities (Axin & Levin, 1997). Poverty, lack of educational opportunity, employment discrimination, poor housing and health care, and segregation offered little in the way of hope that things would ever improve. But moving to other regions, or greener pastures, did not always work out well. Thus, the promise of a better life was not always fulfilled—in some respects, life in the cities and in a new environment did not prove significantly better.

What this has meant for rural communities, especially in the South, is that in the past twenty to thirty years African Americans have been returning to and often settling in rural communities (Avant, 2004, 2014; Blundo, McDaniel, & Wilson, 1999). Several factors appear to motivate this reverse migration, including a desire to reestablish roots and improve economic conditions (Avant, 2004, 2014). Some appear to be returning to be near family, some are seeking the comfort and safety of rural life, and others are going back to the country to retire (Waites & Carlton LaNey, 1999). The expanding economy of the US South has also made the region attractive for relocation. People moving there are often returning to a life or to people they knew and were comfortable with. The slower pace and personal relationships of the country are appealing enough to induce people to move back. Being near old friends, family, and church is attractive because it offers a source of support.

The influx of in-migration to rural communities has created some social strains, as often these African Americans moving to the country have lived in cities for some time, with a broader range of services available to them. The absence of needed services has led to pressure to establish them, which is not always what a community expects to hear. As new arrivals ask for services they expect or need, rural community members may not want to address that need and begin to resent the newcomers.

* * *

It is erroneous to assume that African Americans are a homogeneous group. Indeed, there are differences in generational and socioeconomic factors, gender, rural or urban origin, and region of the country in which they live. Whatever the differences, rural African Americans face many kinds of social problems. There may be shortages of adequate services to meet their needs, many of which may be of long standing. Social workers who respond to a request for assistance can become hindered in assisting African American clients, especially if they rely exclusively on the formal resources that are available, especially in communities that are service poor. African Americans, though, have a tradition of informal helping (Marsiglia & Kulis, 2009). Racial discrimination is still an issue in some rural communities, and although it has been illegal for more than half a century, discrimination may still mean, unfortunately, that some agencies are less than helpful in providing services to African Americans.

African Americans, especially in the rural environment, tend to be incredibly resilient and often have several informal resources that they can mobilize to help them resolve crises. In many ways, rural African Americans have many strengths and assets that can help them overcome any difficulties they may be experiencing. For example, family, friends, spirituality, and the church community often offer good sources of support and assistance (Marsiglia & Kulis, 2009). Of course, this is true for many rural people, but these resources are often even more important for some African American individuals and families, as they are time-tested supports developed to deal with racism. But often, supportive services are unlikely to be found in a formal resource directory; social workers will have to learn about them and engage them. Indeed, many rural people, African Americans included, are somewhat wary of formal resources because of the stigma attached to their use. African American clients may simply prefer to work with the informal system of assistance that they know.

One of the biggest hurdles to clear in working with rural African Americans may be in establishing a strong working relationship. The worker-client relationship is essentially a mutual partnership (Compton, Galaway, & Cournoyer, 2005). To engage clients in this kind of partnership, workers have to establish authenticity, a sense of trust, and competency. African Americans, especially in a rural community, often deal in personal relationships, and a social worker may not be someone whom they know. Further, some might view social workers as representing a formal system and authority, which may engender caution given experiences with oppression and discrimination. For rural social workers, building relationships based on authenticity, trust, and competency begins with cultural competency. Until clients or the community believes that a social worker understands them and is there to help, progress, if any, will be slow.

All good social work requires cultural competency on the part of the social worker, and this includes work with rural African Americans. In effect, rural social workers who want to empower rural African Americans must be to some degree bicultural or in some cases "tricultural," simultaneously demonstrating competency in working with African Americans, across one's own culture, and with the rural culture. This kind of cultural competency entails not only a basic understanding of cultural characteristics but also facility in acting to respect those characteristics and traditions. In effect, social workers must not only "talk the talk, but walk the walk."

Using an Afrocentric perspective for social work with rural African Americans is a conceptual approach that has been suggested to be effective. The Afrocentric perspective helps develop cultural sensitivity by creating shared realities between worker and clients (Avant, 2004, 2014; Marsiglia & Kulis, 2009). The Afrocentric perspective is built on African American culture and values and provides a frame of reference for understanding those things. The perspective is built on African American history, culture, and worldviews (Avant, 2004, 2014). Incorporating this kind of approach into practice is helpful for workers to understand the outlook and approach to problem solving used by the people whom they are attempting to empower.

When one examines the traditional values and traditions of African Americans, it is striking how many of those values and traditions are similar to those of rural people in general. Among aspects of African American culture that have been discussed are the use of informal resources, importance of family, spirituality and importance of the church, importance of community, value of history and traditions, importance of reliance on personal relationships, and connection to the land (Avant, 2004; Carlton-LaNey & Burwell, 2011; Harley et al., 2005; Marsiglia & Kulis, 2009; McMahon, 1996). Among African Americans there also tends to be a more collective view of the interdependence of people and the close relationship of the individual and society—this is something that rural people also share.

Many African American families, at some point in their history, have rural roots. Many of the values developed in rural life were undoubtedly passed down to the present generation. Indeed, rural life probably produced common experiences like hard work, low pay, discrimination and oppression, reliance on both the family and church—all of these things rural African Americans share with rural communities in general.

For social workers, while learning traditional values and traditions of rural African Americans is an important step in developing cultural competency, it is also important for the development of strategies to empower clients. Traditional values and traditions are a source of strength for African Americans, particularly in rural areas. They have helped generations of people cope, survive, and flourish in environments that were often harsh and oppressive.

Despite the common ground that may exist between African Americans and other community residents, in many respects in rural areas subgroups in a community essentially live separately and have only limited interaction. This suggests that the challenge of a dual cultural competency (i.e., African American and rural) in working with rural African Americans may not be quite so formidable. This is not to say that rural African Americans are the same as other rural people or don't have a particular culture, but in many respects, all rural people have common bonds and characteristics that may facilitate the process of social workers developing a broader competency across groups of people and communities.

HISPANICS

According to the US Census, in 2010 there were 50.5 million Hispanics in the country, representing 16 percent of the population. The Hispanic population in the United States has increased dramatically over the past few years, a 43 percent increase since 2000 (US Census Bureau, 2011b). The highest concentration of Hispanics is in the West and South, with the greatest density near the US-Mexico border. Approximately two-thirds of the Hispanic population lives in just four states: California, Texas, Florida, and New York (US Census Bureau, 2007).

The percentage of the Hispanic population varies considerably according to the part of the country and the specific community. For example, Hispanic residents in both California and Texas account for more than 37 percent of the states' total population, and Texas has fifty-one counties in which Hispanics constitute the majority (US Census Bureau, 2011b). Maine, in contrast, has only slightly more than 1 percent of residents who are Hispanic. Moreover, Hispanics represent a diverse cultural group in the United States, with 70.9 percent of Central American origin (including Mexican), 15.5 percent of Caribbean origin, and 5.5 percent of South American origin (US Census Bureau, 2011b). Of course, it is important to remember that many Hispanics never even crossed a border—they are native born in the United States. In fact, in parts of the West and Southwest, many people are descendants of Mexicans or Spanish settlers in lands that were subsequently annexed to the United States. In a very real sense, the border crossed them, not vice versa.

Rural areas saw a 22 percent increase in Hispanic population growth between 2000 and 2006, with an estimated 3.2 million Hispanics living in rural areas. Hispanic growth in rural communities is not quite as dramatic as in cities, but it is significant nonetheless. Beginning in the 1990s, immigration patterns for Hispanics in the United States shifted to rural areas outside of the traditional destinations of California, Florida, and Texas (Villalobos, 2014). States like Illinois, Georgia, Pennsylvania, and Alabama saw a significant influx of new immigrants. The increase in Hispanics has more than compensated for the decline in other groups of rural residents (Mather & Pollard, n.d.). In fact, Hispanics have often assumed jobs that were vacated as other rural residents moved to the city to seek more attractive economic opportunities.

Despite some people's perceptions that Hispanics are a heterogeneous group, the term includes persons of Mexican, Cuban, Puerto Rican, Central American, and South American descent (Villalobos, 2014). While Spanish is a common language most Hispanics share, not all speak or understand Spanish well, as many immigrants are indigenous people who speak native languages. Even in the Spanish language there are a number of dialects and different cultural practices that reflect the vast geographic areas from which people immigrate. Social workers who work with Hispanic immigrants benefit from learning the characteristics of the culture and the effects of acculturating to the United States on each individual and family (Villalobos, 2014).

Looking at a few sample counties indicates that in some rural counties persons of Hispanic or Latino origin are a majority of the population:[2]

- Kleberg County, Texas—population 32,196: 70.3 percent
- Presidio County, Texas—population 7,761: 83.7 percent
- Santa Cruz County, Arizona—population 47,676: 82.7 percent
- Costilla County, Colorado—population 3,662: 64.2 percent
- Hidalgo County, New Mexico—population 4,862: 56 percent

Rural Hispanics face many of the same kinds of issues that confront other minorities and oppressed groups. Among these problems is poverty. The poverty rate for rural Hispanics is about one in four (US Department of Agriculture, 2004; Villalobos, 2014). The national poverty rate for Hispanics is similar, at 26.6 percent (US Department of Health and Human Services, 2011), although this is almost double the national average. The five counties listed earlier show high poverty rates, with Santa Cruz County at 26.2 percent; Kleberg County, 24.8 percent; Hidalgo County, 23.7 percent; Presidio County, 22.9 percent; and Costilla County, 22.2 percent.

Like any other group of people who disproportionately face poverty, Hispanics face issues in getting adequate housing, maintaining an adequate diet, accessing health care and mental health care, living in unstable employment markets, and accessing transportation. The influx of migration stretches the ability of many rural communities to provide adequate housing and can result in overcrowded local schools (Dalla & Christensen, 2005). Hispanics also face disparities in health and mental health care (Villalobos, 2014). When communities look to address these kinds of challenges, there can be a backlash based on prejudice and discrimination. As Hispanics who are new residents need services, the demand on community resources increases, especially in rural communities, where social welfare resources may not be plentiful and local residents are reluctant to add more. Access to some of the community's informal resources

[2] All data for individual counties in the following list come from the US Census Bureau website "State & County Quick Facts," with information for 2011 (http://quickfacts.census.gov/qfd/index.html).

may also be restricted if community members view Hispanics as outsiders. For example, community homeless shelters may be more reluctant to serve people who they view as transient. The attitude may be that they were not invited to live in the community and are welcome to leave if they cannot take care of themselves without outside help. This is the harsh reality of how many rural people and communities view newcomers and/or outsiders, and it may appear to some as overt racism.

Hispanics face some barriers to acceptance and can face difficulties when trying to meet their own social welfare needs. The most obvious barrier is language. In most parts of the country English is the language of commerce, and there may be few bilingual people to help those for whom English is not a first language. Language skills can affect one's ability to get certain employment and thus affect income. But it may also affect a person's ability to purchase a car or even get adequate medical care. In some instances, children or low-wage workers who understand English are used as translators. If a client's family has a limited command of English, then communication with service providers such as health-care staff may be difficult. And where immigrants or migrants are new arrivals, there may be no one who speaks the language. Obviously, not being able to tell a physician what is wrong, for example, is a problem. I have seen some patchwork attempts at translation by janitors or children, but these are not prudent approaches for social work in general, because lay translators may not know things like medical terminology, and translation by nonprofessionals also creates issues of confidentiality.

Hispanics also face prejudice and discrimination based on societal views toward immigration. Small towns are typically not the melting pot that cities are, and they also have less tolerance of difference and a distrust of outsiders. There may be a prevailing view that most Hispanics are not legal residents of the United States, and there may be resentment toward their language, religion, and culture. There is often resentment that these things, which Hispanic migrants bring with them, will create change for the worse in the traditional culture of the community. It is interesting to note that Mexican accounts from the 1830s reflect similar concerns about Anglo-Americans who were crossing the border into Texas when it was still part of the state of Coahuila (Davis, 1998). There may also be resentment based on a belief that Hispanics are taking jobs away from other members of the community. However, Hispanics are commonly taking jobs that have remained vacant because others would not take them at the prevailing wage.

Many Hispanics are working in agriculture or agribusiness. These jobs typically offer low pay and few benefits, thus leading to economic instability. Dalla and Christensen (2005) reported that Hispanics working in Midwestern meatpacking plants reported financial concerns that included inability to save money for emergencies, inability to move to better jobs, and the safety conditions in which their families were living. They also had employment concerns related to increased production demands, and an increased possibility of injury. Residents of this community also expressed concerns about language barriers, teen parenting, alcohol use, and community prejudice (Dalla & Christensen 2005).

Of course, ideas about immigrants are stereotypes. No one can tell whether a person is in the country legally, illegally, or is a natural born citizen just by appearances. Still, hostility and discrimination are real and have harmful effects. This kind of prejudice has led states like Georgia and Alabama to pass harsh laws targeting illegal immigrants. The laws essentially criminalize being in those states without having appropriate legal documentation. They also deny public benefits to those who are undocumented, bar college attendance, and require the identification of schoolchildren who are illegal immigrants. Essentially, these types of laws bar those who are undocumented from many kinds of social welfare services. States that have passed such laws have found that there are sometimes unintended consequences, like sudden drops in school enrollment and labor shortages for harvesting crops (Constantini, 2011; Rawls, 2011).

These laws are primarily targeting Hispanics as the largest immigrant group, particularly in the South and West. These anti-immigration laws create a climate of fear in which people worry about being identified and/or arrested and facing deportation. This fear makes them vulnerable for exploitation in the workplace, and it creates difficulty in finding housing, problems with financial transactions, lack of access to services, and difficulty in many other aspects of life. As a result, some work for low wages and minimal benefits in what are often dangerous jobs and find difficulty in getting adequate housing. For example, agricultural work often exposes employees to hazardous chemicals and pesticides and employment in the meat-processing industry can produce disability from repetitive motion over time. And if they fall into need, they are excluded from most social welfare benefits. They may not be excluded from emergency medical care, although they may have some difficulty in accessing it, or some fear in using it. Their children may also be able to attend school, but when they do, they are typically identified as outsiders.

* * *

Unfortunately, too little has been written about social work with rural Hispanics to date. Some of this is understandable given that most of Hispanic immigrants tend to settle in urban communities, and many undocumented immigrants in rural areas try to maintain a low profile. There may also be a small number of Hispanic social workers who work in these rural areas, especially in communities that have seen a lot of recent immigration. As the rural Hispanic population continues to grow, social workers are likely to work more frequently with Hispanic individuals, families, and communities. Clearly, this area of rural practice needs more attention.

Many Hispanics who live in rural communities also have rural roots. Either their families have lived in the country for some time or immigrants may have come from rural regions themselves. Cordova (2004) describes the settlement of Hispanic immigrants in a rural Texas *colonia*, or neighborhood. In general, a *colonia* refers to a community located within 150 miles of the border, but one such settlement described by Cordova (2004) is some 500 miles from the border (see also Texas Secretary of State, 2014). Given recent immigration patterns and patterns of settlement undoubtedly the numbers of *colonias* outside of the 150-mile radius are growing.

Of concern to social workers is the typical infrastructure of these communities. They usually have substandard housing, and they often lack running water and adequate sewage, street lighting, paved roads, and electricity (Cordova, 2004; Texas Secretary of State, 2014). These communities may also have a weak network of social relationships. The attraction of *colonias* is that they usually offer relatively cheap housing and people can live near others whose culture is more like their own. But the lack of infrastructure may mean that housing and occupancy codes are not enforced, public health issues may arise, and it is difficult to get children to school and adults to work. In effect, the housing may be overcrowded and the water and sanitation poor. These are conditions that are seen to some degree in inner cities and that re-create in rural communities the modern equivalents of the tenements of the early twentieth century. These neighborhoods may also have little in the way of services like police and fire protection.

The residents of a *colonia* settle in the area for employment, and many pay taxes directly or indirectly. Yet they get very little back in the way of services or infrastructure. For example, many residents of Cordova's (2004) rural community called La Selva lived near a poultry hatchery or chicken-processing plant operated by a large agribusiness company. Many of them were employed in the meat-processing facility (Rodriguez, Cooper, & Morales, 2004). Yet many of them lived in the *colonia*, where roads are unpaved. The local city and county governments refused to take responsibility for improving conditions in the *colonia* (Cordova, 2004). This is often the case in rural communities, as they are apathetic to the needs of such neighborhoods because there are not high population concentrations or voters there. In a very real sense, these types of situations are fertile fields for macro practice, as community development efforts to improve infrastructure can make a real difference in the lives of many rural residents. Rural social workers can employ their organizing skills to help mobilize local resources for improving these neighborhoods.

In providing direct practice services for Hispanics, social workers should appreciate that, like most rural people, Hispanics tend to be traditional in their worldview. Traditional Hispanic families tend to be close to their families and make decisions in a collective manner (Villalobos, 2014). The family unit can provide support, which is especially important in rural communities where Hispanics are isolated from the rest of the community. Traditionally, men tend to be decision makers and women have primary roles in taking care of the household and raising children, even when they work. There is an emphasis on respect (especially for elders), formality, congeniality (*simpatía*), and personalism (*personalismo*) (Villalobos, 2014). These values often conflict with the dominant US culture, and they may even conflict across generations in families.

There is also a tendency to use informal helping networks instead of formal agencies for help in the Hispanic community. Many of the services traditionally provided by public social welfare services are effectively unavailable to many immigrant Hispanics, who are either legally barred from eligibility or afraid of being identified as undocumented. Thus, churches and church-based services, like Catholic Social Services, are very important sources of assistance.

Traditionally, Hispanics often rely on informal and folk healing methods, and they are more likely to have seen a priest, pharmacist, or folk healer than a health-care professional (Poole & Espadas, 2014). Many Hispanic families visit a *curandero* or *curandera*—a healer to help heal spiritual as well as physical ailments. The healing methods of a *curandero* might use herbs, prayers, candles, and other elements to help effect a cure. These methods may also be used to help improve mental health and other socio-psychological conditions, or they may be used in conjunction with traditional medical and mental health services to help improve an individual's condition. But it is important for rural social workers to understand that traditional rural families may distrust traditional medicine and mental health services and that, at some level, folk healing may need to be employed in the helping process.

Some knowledge of Spanish may be helpful in working with Hispanic families that have a limited command of English. But unless a social worker is truly bilingual and fluent, it is not likely that the complicated interactions of professional helping can be transacted successfully. There may also be some communication issues in addressing the multiple dialects of Spanish. Clients may not use the same dialect, idioms, or vocabulary that someone who learned Spanish in college is familiar with. Translators can be used, but it can create confidentiality issues if a translator is not a professional bound by a code of conduct. Some translators, like children, even though bilingual, may not know the vocabulary and technical terms and may not be able to provide accurate translations.

Many of the principles of rural practice apply to doing social work with Hispanics in small towns. As with other rural residents, Hispanics often value traditions, family, and church, and use informal resources to assist them in times of need. The key challenge for social workers is establishing trust in the professional working relationship. Gaining trust takes cultural competence, but it may also be complicated by language barriers and a potential client's concerns about the social worker's position as an "official." Social workers often have to overcome distrust of formal agencies, which many see as an extension of an oppressive government that seeks to arrest and deport them. To the extent that social workers are viewed as representing this power structure, there may be some reluctance to open up and collaborate with them. In many instances, rural workers need to collaborate with informal resources and the church to empower rural Hispanic clients. Moreover, social workers may have to help negotiate state and federal policies that place barriers in the way of good employment and access to services. All of this can be challenging, but Hispanic families who live in rural communities are resilient like other rural people. They have many types of strengths that must be recognized and developed as part of the helping process.

NATIVE AMERICANS

Native Americans represent 1.7 percent of the US population, or about 2.9 million people, and the number of Native Americans in the United States is growing. Since 2000 the Native American population has increased by 18 percent, about twice that of the national average (US Census Bureau, 2012). The largest numbers of Native Americans are in the West, where 41 percent of the Native American population lives. There are also significant numbers of Native Americans in the South, the Upper Midwest, Arizona, and New Mexico (US Census Bureau, 2011a). States with the largest numbers of Native Americans include California and Oklahoma, and there are especially high concentrations of Native Americans in the latter. Most Native Americans, like most Americans, live in cities, with New York and Los Angeles having the greatest numbers of them.

Yet there are still many Native Americans who live in rural communities. Thirty-nine percent of American Indians and Alaska Natives live in rural areas (Conway, BigFoot, & Sandler, 2011). In several rural Western counties, Native Americans constitute the majority population. Examples of these counties include the following:[3]

[3] All data for individual counties in the following list come from the US Census Bureau website "State & County Quick Facts," with information for 2011 (http://quickfacts.census.gov/qfd/index.html).

- Apache County, Arizona—population 72,401: 71.6 percent
- McKinley County, New Mexico—population 73,664: 74.6 percent
- Sioux County, North Dakota—population 4,280: 81.7 percent
- Buffalo County, South Dakota—population 1,988: 80.5 percent
- Bethel Census Area, Alaska—population 17,416: 81.7 percent

Communities with six or fewer people per square mile are generally considered very rural, or "frontier." The Bethel Census Area, for example, has 0.4 persons per square mile; Sioux County, 3.8; Apache County, 6.4; Buffalo County, 10.7; and McKinley County, 17.0. Clearly, two of these examples are frontier and one is very close to being so, which indicates that these communities have large areas with few people—and often few resources. Many other counties also have low population densities but are considered rural, not frontier.

The poverty rate for Native Americans in 2010 was 28.4 percent, almost double the national average. Of the sample of Native American–majority counties listed here, poverty rates are mixed. In all but one of the five counties listed, the poverty rate is greater than the national average, and in two it is above the average for Native Americans. Sioux County had a 42.3 percent poverty rate; Apache County, 34.7 percent; Bethel Census Area, 19.8 percent; McKinley County, 19.0 percent; and Buffalo County, 13.8 percent.

Twenty-nine percent of Native Americans lack health insurance coverage (US Census Bureau, 2011a). This obviously creates a problem of accessing and using health care for many families. This may be an even bigger problem in rural areas, where there are limited health-care resources. There are also a number of mental health issues for Native Americans living in rural areas, including high rates of depression, suicide, and substance abuse (Conway et al., 2011). Winship (2014) also has reported concerns with homelessness and substandard housing on Native American reservations, where people face overcrowding, difficulty in financing housing, and people living in substandard conditions such as dry riverbeds and sheds.

Native Americans, as defined by the US Census Bureau, are American Indians and Alaska Natives. They are a diverse group, comprising many tribes and representing many diverse cultures that can be very different from each other. Even within tribes there can be strong political differences in terms of positions on things like assimilation, sovereignty, education, health care, and many others. Language can also be an issue for Native Americans—28 percent speak a language other than English at home, and for some groups like the Navajo, that percentage is even higher. Systematic discrimination and genocide against Native Americans in the United States has been well documented. The Native American experience of genocide that resulted from colonialism has had lasting consequences for contemporary Native Americans (Marsiglia & Kulis, 2009). Of course, stereotypes and prejudices against Native Americans persist in the twenty-first century. These prejudices often lead to discrimination, which has negative effects on Native peoples.

Many Native Americans live on or near reservations or tribal lands. Approximately one million Native Americans live on tribal lands (US Census Bureau, 2012), most of which are rural. There is also frequent movement back and forth between reservations and cities (Marsiglia & Kulis, 2009). The largest of the tribal lands in terms of population are the Navajo Reservation (New Mexico, Arizona, and Utah), with 173,667 people; Knik Native Village (Alaska), 65,768; Osage Reservation (Oklahoma), 47,472; Kenaitze Native Village (Alaska), 32,902; and Flathead Reservation (Montana), 28,359 residents (US Census Bureau, 2012). The largest tribes are the Navajo, Cherokee, Chippewa, and Sioux. Many tribes maintain sovereignty over tribal matters and are self-governing. As a result, these tribes maintain a variety of their own services to assist members.

* * *

Unfortunately, too little has been written about work with Native Americans in rural communities. Clearly, cultural grounded practice is essential for working with Native Americans in rural communities. A key to working with Native Americans is developing an understanding that all Native peoples are not alike, and there is considerable diversity among them. It is also important to engage Native Americans in an intervention process that embraces their perspective and builds on strengths.

Weaver (1999) indicates that the elements of culturally grounded practice include knowledge about the diversity, history, culture, and current realities of the people with whom one is working. Marsiglia and Kulis (2009) add that knowledge of Native American experience with colonialism and genocide may help explain some of the problems this group of people faces today. Spirituality may also be an important element in understanding how Native Americans live their daily lives, especially with their concept of subjective well-being (Yoon & Lee, 2004). Spirituality may also play an important role in helping empower them. Spirituality and folk healing play into Native concepts of health and health care as well. For Native Americans medicine men or shamans serve as physicians, psychiatrists, and spiritual leaders (Marsiglia & Kulis, 2009). Rituals such as sweat lodges, sand paintings, and fetishes, as well as use of herbs like wild ginger and boneset, may be used to effect cures. Social workers may need to embrace these traditions and incorporate them as part of a strengths-based plan in working with Native Americans. Native Americans often have a distrust of outsiders that is usually founded on personal and historical experiences. In Native American communities, there is a strong sense of family and community, and traditions are important. To be more sensitive to the culture of Native Americans, it is important to work cooperatively with members of a person's family and tribe.

Native Americans who live in rural communities are members of their own culture and are *also* rural people. Thus, culturally grounded practice for the social worker involves evaluating the complexities of the person-in-environment approach in working with Native Americans. Failure to appreciate the complexity of a specific person's or family's culture can lead to serious errors in developing assessments and in executing interventions to help them. For example, cross-cultural misunderstanding by child welfare workers of Native American behavior has been a cause for the removal of children from families. Social workers who are not Native Americans could easily, and mistakenly, interpret traditional practices as harmful and take action to remove a child from his or her family. The federal Indian Child Welfare Act of 1978 was passed to lower the rate of removal of Native American children from their families and communities. One of the ways the act does this is by attempting to involve the tribe and family in child welfare services and placement decisions (Administration for Children & Families, n.d.).

SEXUAL ORIENTATION: GAY, LESBIAN, BISEXUAL, AND TRANSGENDER

Rural communities, in general, are not noted for their tolerance of difference from what is considered the mainstream. As a result, community members whose sexual orientation is other than heterosexual in small communities are at risk for experiencing both discrimination and oppression. They typically face heterosexism, homophobia, and stigma if community members discover their sexual orientation (Comerford, Henson-Stroud, Sionainn, & Wheeler, 2004). As a result, there are few services in small communities that are sensitive to the needs and issues of rural gays and lesbians. Rural social workers are not immune from this type of bias and have to be careful in dealing with their own views to avoid compounding this oppression in their work with gays and lesbians (Kulkin, Williams, & Woodruff, 2005).

Rural gay, lesbian, bisexual, and transgendered persons face heterosexism and homophobia, and have a limited ability to express themselves, which forces them to remain invisible, compartmentalize their lives, or become isolated (Russell, 2014). They need to remain quiet about their identity because they may be viewed as a threat to social or religious groups, and they face exclusion (Russell, 2014). Given the fishbowl atmosphere of small towns, where little escapes notice, this kind of environment presents a major challenge for the person who is gay, lesbian, bisexual, or transgendered (GLBT). In addition, because GLBT persons often maintain a low profile, there is not a great deal of literature to guide rural social work with this population.

Rural norms, attitudes, and behaviors toward GLBT persons stem from the conservative perspective with which many rural people approach life, and their lifestyle is devalued or the subject of intolerance (Russell, 2014). In this sense, GLBT persons are not seen as people who engage in "normal" types of relationships. Prevailing religious beliefs can help reinforce the idea that GLBT persons are not to be accepted.

This kind of environment can prove very challenging for the GLBT person who lives in a rural community (Neely, 2005), as they face the very real possibility of social ostracism, alienation from family, loss of employment, and potential physical violence if this essential part of their identity is discovered. As a result, GLBT persons in rural areas often keep their sexual orientation a closely guarded secret and are less likely to identify and associate with other GLBT persons in the community for fear of their sexual orientation being revealed. Social disapproval and outright hostility have led many GLBT persons to relocate to cities, where they can often be more anonymous, live more openly, connect with a GLBT community, and face less discrimination (Kulkin et al., 2005; Russell, 2014). Yet in the twenty-first century this trend appears to be reversing somewhat, as more GLBT persons are found in smaller communities, possibly because they are better able to interact with other members of the GLBT community through electronic media (Neely, 2005). Perhaps the advent of communications like the Internet, increased societal visibility, and political changes have helped make rural life somewhat easier.

So, given the social environment and culture of the rural community, which types of problems and issues might social workers expect GLBT persons to face?

Identity Formation

The social isolation that GLBT persons frequently face in a rural setting may affect identity formation and the coming-out process (Comerford et al., 2004; Kulkin et al., 2005; Russell, 2014). Simply stated, GLBT persons may not have access to peers, role models, or other types of community (Neely, 2005). They may also be isolated from their families (Comerford et al., 2004; Russell, 2014).

Social Isolation

The isolation borne of conditions that oblige GLBT persons to keep an important part of their identity secret can lead to feelings of social isolation and guilt. A great deal of energy is required for an individual to manage the concept of being "different" and to manage concerns about how others in a community may react. This kind of isolation also affects the availability of a social support structure for GLBT persons, at least for issues related to identity and relationships. Simply discussing these kinds of issues with one's friends and family, who provide social support, may run the risk of alienating them, risking wider disclosure, and generating negative consequences for all involved (Russell, 2014). In many cases this could be too threatening, and in others, a full range of social support may not be available.

Civil Rights

GLBT persons face workplace discrimination and may be harassed on the job (Neely, 2005). They may also be denied the ability to marry, raise a family, share financial and health-care benefits, and they may even experience outright violence (Russell, 2014). Indeed, in rural areas, the distrust and prejudice against anyone who is not heterosexual may be so strong that GLBT persons have difficulty finding and keeping employment, experience discrimination, and are socially ostracized. In any event, many social situations and conditions can become so unpleasant that it might be difficult for them to remain in a rural area. Verbal harassment for being "different" is not uncommon, and they may find a poor response to any requests for redress to violations of their rights (Russell, 2014).

Family

In small communities with little acceptance of GLBT persons, families may also feel pressure to not accept a GLBT family member. In other words, the community's discomfort and hostility toward a GLBT person could reflect on that person's family, and there may be social consequences for the family. The family may even be pressured to have the GLBT person change his or her behavior to a more "normal" behavior. This kind of social pressure can affect the GLBT person's relationship with his or her family (Comerford et al., 2004). These issues are not unique to rural life, but they do become magnified there, because a greater proportion of people know other people's business in small towns. It is also difficult for a GLBT person to start or maintain a relationship with a partner. Engaging in relationships invariably involves some degree of "coming out" about one's sexual orientation, and this is likely to be observed or noticed one way or another in a small community. Social consequences, or at least fear of social consequences, may ensue. In a rural area the consequences a GLBT person may face could be more serious because there are fewer options for churches, social relationships, redress of grievances, school, and employment.

Religion

Churches and spirituality are significant aspects of rural life. Yet many religious groups and churches, including more fundamentalist forms of Christianity, do not accept GLBT persons (Russell, 2014). Disclosure or discovery of a GLBT person may expose him or her to exclusion from a religious community, and even persecution, which can be a substantial problem for a GLBT person in a small community, where places of worship may be limited. This is a serious price to pay, and rural GLBT persons are usually well aware of it. Exclusion from a spiritual community can have a serious impact on the life of a person, and GLBT persons try to remain invisible in this aspect of their lives to avoid exclusion and religious condemnation.

It is critical for social workers in rural practice to be aware of the basic life issues that GLBT persons in small communities confront. As a very practical matter, they confront the harsh reality that if someone finds out about their sexuality, it may threaten their life, livelihood, or family. As a result, GLBT persons are likely very careful about where, how, and to whom they disclose any information about their sexuality. This means that social workers need to build trust, and maintaining confidentiality is especially important. Rural GLBT persons are an oppressed group, and they may face even more or harsher oppression than their counterparts in larger communities. Thus, it is extremely important for social workers to be affirming for the GLBT client. To do this, it may be necessary for social workers to address some of their own personal biases and feelings about GLBT persons (Kulkin et al., 2005). Acknowledging the challenges that clients face—isolation, identities, families, social interaction, discrimination, employment, and spirituality—and addressing these issues in a sensitive way are critical to empowering GLBT persons. Indeed, social workers may be the only people who understand and who can assist the GLBT person to negotiate what is potentially a very hostile environment.

SENIOR CITIZENS

According to the US Census (2011c), people older than age sixty-five currently make up 13.3 percent of the US population. In the rural United States, the proportion is slightly higher, with 15 percent, or 7.5 million seniors (Rural Assistance Center, 2012). The number of seniors is expected to double by the year 2030, creating an even greater need to focus on this group and provide more services for them.

Rural seniors face a number of issues of concern to social workers. Some of the more common problems the rural elderly face include the following:

- Movement of family from rural communities: Seniors may have few remaining family resources locally, as family members move to economically "greener pastures." Seniors may be the last family members to move, and if they follow family to a new environment, they often experience adjustment problems.
- Remoteness: In a rural area it may be many miles to a city where services are located. Transportation is a significant issue for many rural Americans, and it may prove more difficult for the elderly, who might have older cars and trucks or whose driving skills have declined. The communications network in rural areas is not particularly strong if seniors need to get help, and in emergencies response times may be slow.
- Health: Some of the more common health-related issues that affect the rural elderly include poor nutrition, obesity, diabetes, Alzheimer's disease, and depression. These are chronic conditions that require regular, long-term treatment, and so access to appropriate health care is a potential concern.
- Living conditions: These may include substandard or poorly maintained housing, poor-quality drinking water, inadequate sewage, poor roads, and bad weather conditions at some times of the year. Such conditions can lead to illness, exposure, or complete isolation for periods of time. For example, if a blizzard hits, rural roads are often the last to be plowed (Rural Assistance Center, 2012).

With age, family income typically declines, and frequently there is a need for more health care. While the elderly may be covered by Medicare and/or Medicaid, often rural health and mental services are not entirely adequate to meet their needs. Health-care and mental health-care resources in small communities are not as numerous or as specialized as seniors may need, and seniors may have trouble accessing transportation to and from medical appointments. Where rural transportation networks are weak, informal support for the elderly is more important, which usually means that family members or a church provides transportation. But in some instances family may have moved away, or in the case of the very old, family members may have passed away before them. In any event, in the twenty-first-century rural community, family and friends may not be as available to provide needed support and transportation. In any event, some, if not all, of these factors contribute to the rural elderly using needed health-care resources less than their urban neighbors do (Coward & Dwyer, 1998). The result could be poorer health and greater occurrence of chronic conditions.

A particularly vulnerable group is elderly women in rural areas (Carlton-LaNey, 1998; Sherr & Bloomheart, 2005). In small towns most seniors have grown up with traditional values and roles. These traditional roles for rural women have been taking care of the home and raising children, and some helped with farm work. Elderly women typically have no children at home, and many did not have a career outside the home. Even if they did work, most rural women were in low-wage employment. The income of rural seniors is generally better if they are married, and if a spouse passes away, this can mean a significant loss of income, from which it is difficult to recover. Among rural elderly women, minorities appear to be especially at risk for lower incomes, poverty, and health conditions than the rest of the rural population (Carlton-LaNey, 1998; Comerford et al., 2004).

* * *

Social workers who provide services for the rural elderly should recognize that they are a diverse group (Coward & Dwyer, 1998). There may be considerable differences in age, education, and cultural background. For example, elderly persons range in age from sixty-five to older than one hundred, and there can be generational differences between them. There also tend to be different needs in terms of health and mental health as the population ages. Rather than viewing the elderly as a homogeneous group based on age, it is often helpful to look at them individually on the basis of age. One method of doing this is to group seniors into three categories: the young-old (age fifty-five through seventy-four), the old-old (age seventy-five to eighty-four), and the very old (age eighty-five and older) (Sherr & Bloomheart, 2005). Obviously, the needs even within these groups change depending on a number of factors, including physical and mental condition, educational level, socioeconomic status, and individual resources. For example, even though people may be of the same age, different levels of education, income, and work experience can mean that they have very little in common except their age.

Individual differences between the elderly can make big differences in a social worker's assessments and interventions with them. One example is the educational level of a client, which can affect how social workers engage them in the empowerment process. Failure to identify and recognize this can lead to poor or even harmful results. My own experience in assisting an elderly relative helps illustrate this point. The individual was in her mid-nineties and cognitively functioning well. She was a college graduate, had worked for a long time as a professional, and was still employed in accounting when she contracted an illness that required rehabilitation in a nursing home. The care staff at the nursing facility assumed because of her age that she had dementia because she was not appropriately responsive to them, and they were giving her treatment based on that observation. In fact, what they were observing was a result of her poor hearing, which was accentuated when they removed her hearing aids for safekeeping. She was also upset over her loss of independence and the fact that she had very little in common with other residents at the facility. When these issues were identified for rehabilitative staff and her care changed, she was more responsive. Her desire to regain her independence was a strong motivating factor for her in following the treatment plans, and she was able to return home after a brief period.

Rural seniors have generally lived in the community for a long time, and this tends to make them have a very traditional outlook. It may also mean that they are reluctant to reach out and request services, or to use them when offered. They may think that others will see them as dependent or as on "the welfare." Neither of these traits is particularly valued in a rural community, where self-reliance is often expected.

Being a member of a rural community has some benefits that serve as strengths for rural seniors. Because they have lived in the community for a long time, the rural elderly are usually known and accepted as community members. This can give them access to informal resources, such as family members, friends, the church, and other local organizations that can provide valuable support. A person's particular situation will determine which of these informal resources may be helpful. Use of informal resources is a sensitive way to empower seniors because they might feel more comfortable with this type of help, on the basis of their past experience. If informal resources alone cannot fully address a need, then some formal resources may be needed. A good assessment and discussion with the client can help clarify a mutually agreeable approach. In working with the elderly, it is important to get their input as to potential solutions and the services with which they are most comfortable, in order to facilitate their sense of independence and dignity.

CONCLUSION

This chapter has discussed diversity in the rural environment. Understanding the richness of rural diversity is critical to the process of social work practice because it is exceedingly difficult to resolve social problems and empower clients if workers do not understand them and their worldview. Rural social workers should develop not only a basic knowledge of the people and clients with whom they are working but also a degree of cultural competency, so that they can be effective.

This chapter has examined only some of the larger diverse groups that make up rural communities. Among the rural populations discussed are African Americans, Hispanics, American Indians, GLBT persons, and seniors. There are, of course, many other diverse groups that can be considered, including Asian Americans, women, religious groups, and other ethnic groups. And there might be subgroups within each of these, as well. But a full discussion of each group that represents rural diversity is beyond the scope of this chapter and this book. There are many other fine works that address the characteristics of diverse populations that can be used to expand on what has been covered here.

The purpose of this chapter is to sensitize readers to the importance of diversity and cultural competency in rural practice. Indeed, all rural social work incorporates cultural competency as a central element. First and foremost, rural people who are part of a diverse cultural group are a minority, all too often misunderstood; they also are oppressed and face barriers because of discrimination. But within rural society there are other groups of people who face the same issues. They are all rural people, but because of their race, ethnicity, sexual orientation, age, religion, or some other factor, they face additional issues. As rural people grow to need the help of a social worker, it is essential that social workers understand them to provide that help effectively.

All people with whom social workers work are complex and multifaceted. A person may be rural, African American, and elderly, and each attribute contributes something to the person's worldview, response to social needs, reaction to a social worker, and ideas about how best to resolve the life issues he or she is facing. In a rural community the whole may be more than the sum of the parts: each cultural factor contributes individually but all the factors interact to contribute to the individuality of the person.

It is incumbent on social workers to understand as much as they can about the people with whom they are working. There should be a serious attempt to understand the individual within the context of his or her own complex set of cultural factors. In some cases social workers may be the only people who even try to understand a person's background and a person as an individual. As professionals we owe our clients no less.

REFERENCES

Administration for Children & Families. (n.d.). *Indian Child Welfare Act.* Retrieved from https://www.childwelfare.gov/systemwide/courts/icwa.cfm.

Avant, F. L. (2004). African Americans in rural areas: Building on assets from an Afrocentric perspective. In T. L. Scales & C. L. Streeter (Eds.), *Rural social work: Building and sustaining community assets* (pp. 77–86). Belmont, CA: Thomson.

Avant, F. L. (2014). African Americans living in a rural community: Building on assets from an Afrocentric perspective. In T. L. Scales, C. L. Streeter, & H. S. Cooper (Eds.), *Rural social work: Building and sustaining community capacity* (2nd ed., pp. 99–112). Hoboken, NJ: Wiley.

Axin, J., & Levin, H. (1997). *Social welfare: A history of the American response to need* (4th ed.). New York, NY Longman.

Blundo, R., McDaniel, C., & Wilson, F. (1999). Change and survival in a small, multiracial Southern town. In I. B. Carlton-LaNey, R. L. Edwards, & P. N. Reid (Eds.), *Preserving and strengthening small towns and rural communities* (pp. 213–224). Washington, DC: National Association of Social Workers.

Carlton-LaNey, I. (1998). Elderly black farm women. In L. H. Ginsberg (Ed.), *Social work in rural communities* (3rd ed., pp. 150–163). Alexandria, VA: Council on Social Work Education.

Carlton-LaNey, I., & Burwell, N. Y. (2011). Historical treasures of rural communities: Special characteristics of rural places. In L. H. Ginsberg (Ed.), *Social work in rural communities* (5th ed., pp. 21–37). Alexandria, VA: Council on Social Work Education.

Centers for Disease Control and Prevention. (n.d.). *Minority health: Black or African American populations*. Retrieved from http://www.cdc.gov/minorityhealth/populations/REMP/black.html.

Comerford, S. A., Henson-Stroud, M. M., Sionainn, C., & Wheeler, E. (2004). Crone songs: Voices of lesbian elders aging in a rural environment. *Affilia*, *19*(4), 418–436.

Compton, B. R., Galaway, B., & Cournoyer, B. R. (2005). *Social work process*. Belmont, CA: Thompson Brooks/Cole.

Constantini, C. (2011). Alabama immigration enforcement law has a 'chilling effect' in classrooms, critics say. *Huffington Post*. Retrieved from http://www.huffingtonpost.com/2011/10/06/new-immigration-law-chilling-effect_n_998628.html.

Conway, P., BigFoot, D. S., & Sandler, E. P. (2011). Resiliency and behavioral health challenges among American Indians and Alaska natives in rural communities. In L. H. Ginsberg (Ed.), *Social work in rural communities* (5th ed., pp. 249–269). Alexandria, VA: Council on Social Work Education.

Cordova, W. (2004). Life in a *colonia*: Identifying community assets. In T. L. Scales & C. L. Streeter (Eds.), *Rural social work: Building and sustaining community assets* (pp. 164–182). Belmont, CA: Thomson.

Coward, R. T., & Dwyer, J. W. (1998). The health and well-being of rural elders. In L. H. Ginsberg (Ed.), *Social work in rural communities* (3rd ed., pp. 213–232). Alexandria, VA: Council on Social Work Education.

Dalla, R. L., & Christensen, A. (2005). Latino immigrants describe residence in rural Midwestern meatpacking communities: A longitudinal assessment of social and economic change. *Hispanic Journal of Behavioral Sciences*, *27*(1), 23–42.

Davis, W. C. (1998). *Three roads to the Alamo*. New York, NY: HarperCollins.

Economic Research Service, US Department of Agriculture. (2011). *Rural America at a glance, 2011 edition.* Retrieved from http://www.ers.usda.gov/media/123318/eib85.pdf.

Harley, D. H., Savage, T. A., & Kaplan, L. (2005). Racial and ethnic minorities in rural areas: Use of indigenous influence in the practice of social work. In L. H. Ginsberg (Ed.), *Social work in rural communities* (4th ed., pp. 367–400). Alexandria, VA: Council on Social Work Education.

Hayden, W. (1993). African-American Appalachians: Barriers to equality. In L. H. Ginsberg (Ed.), *Social work in rural communities* (2nd ed., pp. 130–149). Alexandria, VA: Council on Social Work Education.

Institute for Research on Poverty. (n.d.). *Health & poverty*. Retrieved from http://irp.wisc.edu/research/health.htm.

Johnson, C. (2005). Demographic characteristics of the rural elderly. In N. Lohmann & R. A. Lohmann (Eds.), *Rural social work practice* (pp. 271–290). New York, NY: Columbia University Press.

Kulkin, H. S., Williams, J., & Woodruff, L. (2005). Social workers in rural areas: An assessment of homophobic attitudes. In L. H. Ginsberg (Ed.), *Social work in rural communities* (4th ed., pp. 427–441). Alexandria, VA: Council on Social Work Education.

Marsiglia, F. F., & Kulis, S. (2009). *Diversity, oppression, and change.* Chicago, IL: Lyceum Books.

Mather, M., & Pollard, K. (n.d.). *Hispanic gains minimize population loss in rural and small-town America.* Washington, DC: Population

Reference Bureau. Retrieved from http://www.prb.org/Articles/2007/HispanicGains.aspx.

McMahon, M. O. (1996). *The general method of social work practice* (pp. 221–222). Needham Heights, MA: Allyn and Bacon.

Mitchem, S. Y. (2007). *African American folk healing*. New York, NY: New York University Press.

National Association of Social Workers. (2012a). Code of ethics of the National Association of Social Workers. In *Social work speaks: National Association of Social Workers policy statements* (pp. 375–391). Washington, DC: Author.

National Association of Social Workers. (2012b). Rural social work. In *Social work speaks: National Association of Social Workers policy statements* (9th ed., pp. 296–300). Washington, DC: NASW Press.

Neely, C. (2005). Gay men and lesbians in rural areas: Acknowledging, valuing, and empowering this stigmatized invisible people. In N. Lohmann & R. A. Lohmann (Eds.), *Rural social work practice* (pp. 232–254). New York, NY: Columbia University Press.

Nicholas, D. (2005). The health of rural minorities. In N. Lohmann & R. A. Lohmann (Eds.), *Rural social work practice* (pp. 211–231). New York, NY: Columbia University Press.

Poole, D. L., & Espadas, A. (2014). Help seeking pathways to care: Culturally competent practice with rural Hispanics with high migratory traditions to the United States. In T. L. Scales, C. L. Streeter, & H. S. Cooper (Eds.), *Rural social work: Building and sustaining community capacity* (2nd ed., pp. 163–174). Hoboken, NJ: Wiley.

Rawls, P. (2011, October 5). Alabama workers leave state as immigration law takes effect. *Huffington Post*. Retrieved from http://www.huffingtonpost.com/2011/10/06/alabama-workers-immigration-law_n_997793.html

Ringel, S. (2005). Mexican American adolescents in rural areas: Education, culture and mental health. In L. H. Ginsberg (Ed.), *Social work in rural communities* (4th ed., pp. 387–400). Alexandria, VA: Council on Social Work Education.

Rodriguez, R., Cooper, H. S., & Morales, L. (2004). Working with Mexican immigrants in rural East Texas. In T. L. Scales & C. L. Streeter (Eds.), *Rural social work: Building and sustaining community assets* (pp. 118–131). Belmont, CA: Thomson.

Rural Assistance Center. (2012). *Aging*. Retrieved from http://www.raconline.org/topics/aging/.

Russell, A. C. (2014). Building community among rural gay, lesbian, bisexual, and transgendered persons: Connecting community through families of choice. In T. L. Scales, C. L. Streeter, & H. S. Cooper (Eds.), *Rural social work: Building and sustaining community capacity* (2nd ed., pp. 99–112). Hoboken, NJ: Wiley.

Sherr, M. E., & Bloomheart, F. (2005). Rural elderly women: A triple jeopardy population. In L. H. Ginsberg (Ed.), *Social work in rural communities* (4th ed., pp. 465–486). Alexandria, VA: Council on Social Work Education.

Summers, G. F. (1998). Minorities in rural society. In L. H. Ginsberg (Ed.), *Social work in rural communities* (3rd ed., pp. 165–176). Alexandria, VA: Council on Social Work Education.

Texas Secretary of State. (2014). *What is a colonia?* Retrieved from http://www.sos.state.tx.us/border/colonias/what_colonia.shtml.

US Census Bureau. (2007). *The American community—Hispanics: 2004*. Retrieved from http://www.census.gov/prod/2007pubs/acs-03.pdf.

US Census Bureau. (2011a). *American Indian and Native Heritage Month 2011*. Retrieved from http://www.census.gov/newsroom/releases/archives/facts_for_features_special_editions/cb11-ff22.html.

US Census Bureau. (2011b). *The Hispanic population 2010*. Retrieved from http://www.census.gov/prod/cen2010/briefs/c2010br-04.pdf.

US Census Bureau. (2011c). *Income, poverty and health insurance coverage in the United States: 2010*. Retrieved from http://www.census.gov/newsroom/releases/archives/income_wealth/cb11-157.html#tablec.

US Census Bureau. (2012). *American Indian and Native American population: 2012*. Retrieved from http://www.census.gov/prod/cen2010/briefs/c2010br-10.pdf.

US Department of Agriculture. (2004). *Rural poverty at a glance*. Retrieved from http://usa.usembassy.de/etexts/soc/ruralpoverty.pdf.

US Department of Health and Human Services. (2011). *Information on poverty and income statistics: A summary of 2011 Current Population Survey data*. Retrieved from http://aspe.hhs.gov/poverty/11/ib.shtml.

Villalobos, G. (2014). Latino populations in rural America. In T. L. Scales, C. L. Streeter, & H. S. Cooper (Eds.), *Rural social work:*

Building and sustaining community capacity (2nd ed., pp. 87–98). Hoboken, NJ: Wiley.

Waites, C., & Carlton-LaNey, I. B. (1999). Returning to rural roots: African American return migrants' use of senior centers. In I. B. Carlton-LaNey, R. L. Edwards, & P. N. Reid (Eds.), *Preserving and strengthening small towns and rural communities* (pp. 236–247). Washington, DC: NASW Press.

Waltman, G. H. (2011). Amish society: Clinical approaches and community services. In L. H. Ginsberg (Ed.), *Social work in rural communities* (5th ed., pp. 271–296). Alexandria, VA: Council on Social Work Education.

Weaver, H. N. (1999). Indigenous people and the social work profession: Defining culturally competent services. *Social Work*, *44*(3), 217–225.

Winship, J. (2014). Living in limbo: Homeless families in rural America. In T. L. Scales, C. L. Streeter, & H. S. Cooper (Eds.), *Rural social work: Building and sustaining community capacity* (2nd ed., pp. 237–249). Hoboken, NJ: Wiley.

Wong, J. (2012, September 14). Rural America fatter than urban America. *ABC News*. Retrieved from http://abcnews.go.com/Health/rural-america-fatter-urban-america/story?id=17231029#.UNCuGaywfQg.

Yoon, D. P., & Lee, E. O. (2004). Religiousness/spirituality and subjective well-being among rural elderly whites, African Americans, and Native Americans. *Journal of Human Behavior in the Social Environment*, *10*(1), 191–211.

Energy development is good economic policy for rural areas, yet it often has unforeseen consequences.

CHAPTER FOUR

Rural Social Welfare Policy

NETTING (2014) DISCUSSES a general definition of policy as a course of action. Social welfare policy can then be viewed as a set of guidelines or actions related to meeting the social welfare needs of people. Policy is important, but sometimes it might not seem the most engaging of subjects for social workers. The fact is that a majority of most social workers' time is spent in direct practice with individuals and families, and workers are typically most interested in matters that most directly affect their clients. For some social workers policy seems too far removed from their day-to-day responsibilities to be relevant to the services they provide and to what they do on a day-to-day basis. This is typically the case in rural practice, where decisions about programs, services, funding, and procedures appear to be the work of remote groups who either do not consider the impact of policy on rural communities or do not fully understand how best to meet the needs of rural people.

For some in social work, social policy is viewed as little more than irritating rules or an abstract set of ideas with only a very general connection to the kind of work they do. Yet social work does not occur in a vacuum, and there is more to service delivery than just the worker-client relationship. Social policy is an important factor that pervades the work that is done to empower clients, it helps shape the social environment, and it influences much of what social works do and how. Also, social welfare policy is an area that generally pays too little attention to the needs of rural people.

Social welfare policy is relevant for all social workers, but it is certainly very relevant for rural social work because of the importance of the surrounding environment to both worker and client in this field of practice. While the preferred mode of social interaction among rural people is informality, social workers tend to find themselves in many situations in which too much informality may be problematic. Many social workers are employed by agencies—rural or not, agencies have standardized rules or policies for what social workers can do. Policies help determine who social workers can see, the ways they can provide help, how long they can provide services, which records they must keep, general expectations for workers' behavior, and many other things that have a profound influence on how rural professionals provide social work services. The social work profession itself lays down some general rules of how social workers should interact with clients, colleagues, their agency, and society. Although these behavioral expectations are contained in a professional code of ethics, the expectations comprise a general set of rules for appropriate behavior that takes on many aspects of a professional policy of sorts. Within limits, rural social workers may be able to exercise some discretion in how they apply policies to be more responsive to the needs of rural clients and communities. But it certainly helps to understand the intent of such policies to know the limits of that discretion.

Indeed, social welfare policy does affect clients in many ways. Agency policies determine hours of operation, the application process for services, the kinds of problems addressed by the agency, where services are available, how to contact the agency, and many other aspects of services that are important to people being able to access assistance. Broader social policy helps determine who may be eligible for services, the type of help available, how much service is offered, worker qualifications, staffing patterns, and other factors that shape the services themselves. For clients this may mean the difference between some or no service being available. This chapter examines social welfare policy in the rural environment and explores its effects on rural communities and how policies may or may not serve people in rural areas and small towns as well as they intend.

A couple of examples may help illustrate the importance of rural social welfare policy to the helping process. Consider the following hypothetical scenario: Mary Jo has recently become concerned about her grandmother Martha, who just turned eighty-nine. Martha's husband of sixty-five years passed away eighteen months earlier, and since that time Martha has seemed different. Her house, which used to be very clean, is messy and not straightened up or cleaned. Martha used to be an excellent cook and enjoyed cooking for the family, but she rarely cooks now, skipping meals and eating frozen dinners. She has also lost interest in most of her activities, as she rarely quilts, cans fruit, or works in the garden. She rarely talks to or visits with her friends or neighbors anymore.

Mary Jo is worried that her grandmother is experiencing depression, and she thinks she might need help. The family doctor, a general practitioner, was consulted, and he recommended that Martha be evaluated at the regional mental health clinic. He stated that her Medicare might pay for treatment services if needed. The problem is that Mary Jo and Martha live in Pikeville, a one-stoplight town fifty miles from the county seat where the mental health clinic is located. The trip there takes about an hour and a half each way, on a narrow road that winds through the mountains. There are times in the winter when the road becomes impassable and commuting to the county seat is not practical.

The Green River Valley mental health agency requires that each person who requests nonemergency services appear at the main office in person and fill out an application. Once the application is completed, the person will be put on a wait list for screening to determine whether services will be provided. It is likely that Martha will be put on a waiting list for services, but the wait could be several months because the clinic has limited staff. But the services Martha needs are not provided any closer to Pikeville than at the main office, so treatment would require frequent trips back and forth. The problem is that Mary Jo's truck already has ninety-eight thousand miles on it, she will have to take off work without pay for each visit, and she risks being fired for missing too much work.

Social policy in this case affects whom the agency will see and how soon Martha might be screened and served, and it places major barriers in the way of clients and family who are trying to resolve problems in a responsible way. Given the wait and difficulty in accessing services, Martha may not get help until she gets much worse. Undoubtedly these services were designed to help people like Martha, and not to intentionally put her at a disadvantage. But given the low population density of the region and the funding limitations, the model of service that was designed in the state capital may not work well for those who live in Pikeville.

Or consider this second hypothetical example. Jenkins Ferry, a town of ten thousand, is the county seat of Semmes County, located in the pine woods, red clay, and rolling hills of the Deep South. Logging and sawmills are the chief industries, along with raising chickens for sale to large poultry producers. The county has a population of 37,445, and the average income is low, with a 31.8 percent poverty rate. Although the county unemployment rate is just slightly above the national average, many people work part-time at low-wage jobs and are underemployed.

Jenkins Ferry is a fiercely independent community with the strong belief that people should support themselves and their families and not ask anyone for a "handout." A motto seen in some places in town is "Poor but proud." Many county residents would benefit from food stamps and/or public assistance. But the only place to apply for financial assistance in the county is in Jenkins Ferry. The financial assistance office is located on Main Street, so applicants have to park on the street and pay the meter. The waiting area for the office faces Main Street, and applicants must sit in front of a large window that allows everyone who passes by to see them. This discourages many applicants, and in the county food stamps are especially underutilized. The staff informally says that the design of the office is intentional, because it helps discourage those who don't need help from "feeding at the public trough" and gives help only to those who really need it.

In this case the agency's policy is intentional, designed to discourage use. Anyone who applied for aid stands a good chance of being recognized. Given the community gossip network and prevailing values, an applicant for assistance may expect to be the subject of unfavorable discussions that might spread widely. So people do not submit applications to a program for which they are otherwise eligible, and instead struggle to feed their families.

SOCIAL WELFARE POLICY

A clear and common use of the term *social welfare policy* is, at times, difficult to pin down, because the term is employed in diverse ways in both general and professional contexts to describe collective approaches to achieving a common good. *Policy* is most commonly used to describe pieces of legislation, administrative regulations for implementing programs, or specific operating procedures or rules of agencies. In other words, policy represents conventions or patterns used in taking action. This kind of broad and varied usage of the term *policy* can sometimes make it unclear as to just what it is that people are discussing.

A useful definition of *social welfare policy* is suggested by Popple and Leighninger (2008, pp. 25): the "principles, guidelines, or procedures that serve the purpose of maximizing uniformity in decision making regarding the problem of dependency in our society" (p. 25). This is a more specific way of saying that policy is an objective and standardized approach to a course of action designed to help those in need. This standardization of principles, guidelines, and procedures through social policy provides a degree of rationality, consistency, and uniformity to how social welfare programs serve those in need. Yet the very regularity that policy provides also means that the same kinds or levels of service may be provided to people whose basic conditions are similar but whose circumstances may differ markedly in some respects. For example, the provision of child welfare services may extend into all counties and communities. But to operate efficiently, services are usually concentrated into larger towns and regional centers. A worker may do outreach and provide services to a rural area, but sometimes foster homes, psychological testing, court visits, homemaker services, and counseling services could be provided at distant locations. Standard policies on caseload size, response times, periodic visitation, and family involvement may prove more difficult in small communities because of the distance and time involved in travel. Since policy makers are increasingly urban in outlook, the contextual factors of rural communities that make it desirable for residents to live there may actually create a disadvantage, as the array of local services may not be as wide and accessing services that do exist could be more challenging.

The number of people who need help in our society is large, and the resources for providing that help are limited, so policies are designed to deliver services with the resources available. For some kinds of social needs and social welfare issues, the cost of providing assistance can become an overriding concern. For example, the poor currently represent 15 percent of the population, or forty-seven million people. Even if a policy were created to offer each poor person only $100 per year, the cost of that would be $4.7 billion. Of course, as a society we generally provide more than $100, even less generous programs. Programs to help the poor are expensive because of the sheer numbers of people who need help. From a practical standpoint most of society's social welfare problems involve hundreds of thousands, if not millions, of people who could benefit from assistance, and the potential cost of helping is quite large. Social policy makers are very mindful of program costs in carefully managing the taxpayer dollars or private contributions that are necessary to provide services to those in need, and they manage social welfare resources efficiently. But providing services efficiently tends to be difficult when the recipients of services tend to be widely dispersed, as in rural communities.

Thus, when designing social policy, policy makers have to make some choices. Often, to use resources "wisely," policy makers target only those who are deemed most needy or deserving. Many social welfare policies attempt to promote client self-sufficiency and reduce costs, and self-sufficiency is often viewed as a desirable end. This is compatible with prevailing values in most rural communities, where belief in self-sufficiency is particularly strong.

While policy makers often reside in urban settings, rural communities are not exempt from their share of social problems and people who need assistance. For example, the percentages of people living in poverty are typically high in many rural communities, and there are unmet health-care needs (National Association of Social Workers, NASW, 2012). As a result, policies to address financial need assume greater significance for people in rural communities. Food stamps are an excellent illustration of this. According to a Carsey Institute (2005) report, the rural poor are more reliant on food assistance than are their urban counterparts. Thirty-one percent of food stamp recipients are rural residents, who represent only twenty-two percent of the population. Many rural recipients of food stamps are employed, but low wages do not provide them with enough to make ends meet, so food stamps fill in the gaps. Yet this is just one type of rural issue; there are also people in rural areas with health-care needs who have no insurance, shortages of mental and behavioral health care, people who are exploited or abused, underserved veterans, and those who have substandard housing or are homeless, just to name a few (Belanger, 2008; NASW, 2012; Winship, 2014).

A core concept embedded in our social welfare policy is the idea that society expects people to meet their own basic needs in areas such as economic support, education, social interaction, and health-care needs (Barker, 2003). There are always people who, for some reason or another, cannot meet all of these needs. Perhaps they are too young or too old to work, they might be disabled, those entrusted with their care might not be fulfilling their duties adequately, or they might be unemployed and unable to find a job. In our society, we could just say "too bad" or "tough luck" and move on—sometimes we do. But we tend to be compassionate people, and we don't always do that. For a variety of reasons, including compassion, a collective sense of the common good, the intrinsic value of doing good works, and helping maintain the social order, we believe that we have some responsibility to help those in need. But because of issues of access and availability, rural people often fall into the "tough luck" category, or at least they may find social welfare services more difficult to access. As much as they can, rural people do their best to make informal resources work in lieu of traditional services that may be available elsewhere.

In a very broad sense, society expects that everyone has the basic responsibility of meeting his or her own basic needs. Usually that is done through the free-market economy, in which a person exchanges labor for a wage and then uses those wages to purchase what he or she needs. But even though society places a high value on the free market, work, and self-sufficiency, we do not place the entire burden for self-support or meeting human needs on every individual. For example, there are children who are not allowed to work, disabled people who may not be able to work, and elderly people who have withdrawn from the labor force. But we do not always immediately intervene to provide social welfare services for these groups unless they have demonstrated a compelling need that cannot be met otherwise.

The economic recession in the twenty-first century has at times overwhelmed the public system designed to cushion the loss of employment. For example, many people received unemployment compensation benefits as a result of long-term unemployment. This occurred at a time when unemployment rates were high, and it was not always possible to get reemployed, especially at wages close to what one might have been earning before. For many, especially low-income workers and the poor, the free market has never worked well, making their income periodic, marginal, and unpredictable. Some of them may not even be eligible for the temporary relief of unemployment benefits because the jobs in which they worked were not covered by unemployment insurance. Rural economies may also provide fewer opportunities for reemployment at a self-supporting wage once a person is unemployed.

When the free market is not enough to meet the basic needs of people, society also promotes the use of informal and private resources to meet those needs. In work with clients, private and informal sources, such as family and friends, are important avenues of assistance and the ones with which clients may be most comfortable. For example, with those who are too young for us to expect self-care and support, we expect their family to provide for them. A grandparent, aunt, or uncle may take in a child whose parents die suddenly or who has drug-dependent parents. Many people are also able to turn to their church or a local charity, like a food bank or clothing closet, for help in meeting some of their needs. Local churches may maintain food pantries and clothing closets for short-term assistance. Churches are also often involved in assistance in the aftermath of disasters that cause loss of property and employment. The church can spearhead organizing help and collecting resources to meet extraordinary needs.

When society makes a decision that some group of people is in need and deserving of help, it often develops social welfare policy, and programs to deliver services to address the situation. These needs can be for basic physical resources that are essential for life (e.g., food, shelter, and clothing), family support, basic protection, or health care. In an attempt to address basic needs, social policies consist of a well-intentioned plan of activities and programs to help, and they may be designed to provide only partial assistance, in order to encourage self-support. Social policy is often designed to cast a wide net to reach a substantial portion of those who have specific kinds of common needs. Because they are broadly conceived, the effects of social policy often vary for different subgroups among people who receive help, depending on the specifics of the situation. Rural people are often a subgroup that experiences differential effects of social policy because of the characteristics of their home communities, which tend to spread services thinner, provide less specialization, and create more difficulty in access.

SOCIAL POLICY AND RURAL PEOPLE

Decision makers who develop social policy often neglect to consider the effects on rural communities. This neglect might not be intentional, as the intent of the policy is to create benefit for the greatest number of people—and indeed, most people live in urban areas. Or, policy makers may base decisions on misconceptions about what life in the country is like, which is typically not malicious, since media stereotypes play a role in people's views about small towns. In the political arena the voice of rural people has been diminished, as over the years the political influence of rural areas has decreased as the population has shifted to the cities (Locke & Winship, 2005; Lohmann & Lohmann, 2005). As a result, social policies that affect rural people are increasingly made by representatives who live in metropolitan areas and may have an urban outlook. Some rural areas can be far away from the representative's base, and the people's problems remote. This can result in rural people not being as well served by social welfare policy and services as some other groups. Popular myths of idyllic country life to the contrary, rural communities and the people who live in them do experience a need for social welfare services, sometimes an even greater need and with more frequency than in the cities.

Not surprisingly, in rural communities there is a healthy distrust of policies made in distant locales. The value that rural people place on personal relationships leads them to question decisions and actions taken in distant places like Washington, DC, or a state capital. Moreover, there is awareness that many people who shape social policy are city folk, who live in a "different world" and do not understand rural life. Rural idioms depicting urban dwellers and their outlook on life are colorful and speak to the lack of mutual understanding between city and country. To rural people, their urban neighbors are "raised on concrete" (don't understand the country), have things "all cattywampus" (askew or awry), make about as much sense as "talking Dutch to a duck" (are incomprehensible), are as "confused as a boy who dropped his gum in a chicken yard" (don't know what to pick up), do not know to "never approach a bull from the front, a horse from the rear, or a fool from any direction" (do not "get" country life).

In other words, many of the policy makers simply do not understand rural people, and thus they make policies and design programs that are not well suited to the realities of life for rural people. Because of differences between rural and metropolitan communities, a one-size-fits-all approach to social policy may not only not work well; it could effectively further disadvantage the people and communities that a policy is trying to help.

For example, several years ago there was a proposal in the US Southwest to streamline the federal Temporary Assistance for Needy Families program, which provides cash assistance to poor families. The idea was to cut costs and make the program more efficient by using an automated application process. Applicants were to apply online or by phone, which would help eliminate several field offices. The problem was that many rural poor did not have computers with Internet access. Traveling to a local library to get online was not always feasible and did not provide much privacy. Phone applications were a problem as well, because many poor families did not have touch-tone phones and the automated system disconnected people who dialed from a rotary phone. The plan was eventually scrapped.

Public policy makers, particularly politicians, are another subject of distrust and scorn in rural communities. Some basic rural idioms about politicians help make the point: "Politicians and preachers are the same—both bless the public, damn 'em, and take their money" (don't trust them—what they say and do does not match); "Politicians love money like a hog loves slop" (don't trust the motives of a politician because they only care about the money); "Politicians are like cockroaches—it's not what they carry off, but what they fall into and mess up" (they only mess things up); "Politicians flock to funerals like flies to the syrup pitcher" (they are all show); and "The only thing he ran successfully for was the county line" (they are incompetent) (Bowman, 1995, pp. 120–121).

Despite the droll humor in some of these sayings, there is a biting undercurrent that portrays politicians in general as greedy, insincere, inept, and incompetent. Not surprisingly, with this point of view, rural people are not likely to trust what policy makers and politicians do. And since the result of their work is often public social welfare policy, they do not trust that either. There may be some exceptions, though, for example, a local person who is well known, respected, and liked.

Rural communities are traditionally conservative politically and often oppose the creation or extension of social welfare services, either in general or into their communities. Self-reliant and independent rural people commonly view social welfare programs as being imposed by outsiders, siphoning off and wasting scarce resources, promoting dependency, and discouraging work. Public agencies are seen as impersonal and as operating under typically rigid, formal rules. Rural people who are used to personal interactions and relationships find the impersonality of an agency downright unfriendly. As a result, they tend not to embrace social welfare programs and services, although sometimes they are considered a necessary evil. The exception to this is the locally derived helping effort, through churches, community groups, and private organizations. Country people have compassion for their neighbors and understand that there are people in their community who need assistance. But the existence of formal services, especially publicly funded ones, goes against traditional rural values of self-reliance, support from family, and the church. Out of necessity, there is an uneasy tolerance of many formal social welfare programs and services.

In any event, rural people tend to be reluctant to use formal social welfare resources even when available, except as a last resort, because there can be community stigma attached to them. The strong values of self-reliance and independence come into play here; when people need help from a formal program, they often feel like they have failed or feel guilty. This is usually reinforced by the community, which may view taking help from outsiders as freeloading or being a failure. In a community where everyone knows everyone, it is not a good thing to be viewed in that way. Social connections and interactions are undoubtedly affected for someone who is viewed as not living up to the community's values and expectations. And no matter how discreet a person or agency is, in a small town, everyone knows.

Rural people who need social welfare tend to favor private and locally based services instead of publicly funded services. Locally based private services tend to be offered by people who are known in the community and trusted. This kind of assistance is often associated with the traditionally respected helping institutions of communities, like local churches, local civic organizations, grassroots help, and charities. Seeking help from these sources keeps supporting needs within the community and is much less likely to be met with social disapproval, because community members feel that they know who "really" requires help and who is taking unfair advantage of help. The informal, private system tends to work best for those who are connected to and accepted in the community. It may be less generous to those without those connections.

Unfortunately, people without those community connections are the very ones who need help the most, as they may be members of minority groups, recent immigrants, or a family with a bad reputation in the community. Private efforts also have limited resources, so that they might not reach all who need them. But this is fine with many rural people, who believe that if people cannot take care of their own needs or benefit from limited assistance, they need to move on. Some might even say that the community would be better without them.

I learned of these kinds of differences between rural and urban communities many years ago while collecting information as part of a national study of homelessness. Larger cities, especially those with harsh winters, would attempt to locate and assist the homeless with food and shelter during the worst times of the year. While these cities did not provide for everyone, and sometimes the temporary shelter was the jail, there was an effort to provide help when most needed. In contrast, smaller towns made little provision for the homeless, under the assumption that if the community was inhospitable, the homeless people would leave. Some communities were even more active in sending the homeless on their way. In one beach community in the South, police officers would check in on winter campers to see that they had appropriate means of support. If the campers were vacationing, they were wished a nice day; if they appeared to be homeless, they were threatened with arrest. In another small Southern community the police actively watched for homeless people entering the town. When it was time for the bus to arrive at the station, so did the police. Anyone who did not have someone waiting was questioned, and people who appeared homeless were given a ride to the county line with a strong suggestion that it would not be advisable to return. These policies, despite their questionable legality, were supported locally in terms of promoting self-support and reducing reliance on local social welfare resources.

One area of social welfare assistance in which rural communities appear to mobilize for action is providing assistance to those who experience a disaster. Disasters like hurricanes, tornadoes, fires, droughts, and oil spills can broadly affect a whole community or region, so when people need help, resources may be exhausted quickly. Disasters can disrupt or destroy employment, housing, and food supplies. For example, the BP oil spill in the Gulf of Mexico in 2010 destroyed many jobs in commercial fishing, some of which never returned. Country people have some familiarity with responding to the whims of nature, as they or their neighbors have experienced crop failures, droughts, fires, and storms. In such circumstances, there is a tradition of the community pooling resources to help their own. As is often the case, unless the disaster is localized, rural areas often wait longer for assistance to arrive. In 2005 Hurricane Katrina hit and devastated communities across almost a two-hundred-mile front, yet much attention was focused on getting aid to New Orleans. Rural communities in nearby Louisiana, Mississippi, and Alabama that had their whole infrastructure destroyed waited longer for help. Yet when formal help lagged, rural residents organized to provide assistance to one another by operating chainsaws to remove downed trees and using personal trucks to remove debris and haul food, water, and gasoline in for their neighbors.

EFFECTS OF SOCIAL POLICY ON RURAL COMMUNITIES

Virtually any social welfare policy, be it legislation, administrative regulation, or operating procedure, has the potential to play out differently in a rural community than in a larger city. The very uniformity across settings that a policy provides makes social welfare programs based on that policy easier to administer and gives those who use the services a degree of equitable treatment. Yet equitable treatment may not always be the most effective way to help people. Where the community and living conditions vary greatly, as they do between cities and the country, treating people the same way may have very different effects.

We often talk as if social policies unfairly disadvantage rural areas, and sometimes they do. But social policies can also have beneficial effects as well, and in other cases the effects of social welfare policy can just be different. For example, in the fields of mental and behavioral health, the US Department of Health and Human Services (2012) indicates that the Affordable Care Act, also known as Obamacare, will provide grants to help increase the number of professional social workers and psychologists who work with people in rural areas. This national policy should help address shortages in mental and behavioral health by adding more providers and potentially improving the range and quality of rural mental health services.

As many people know, or at least suspect, the US social welfare system that arises from social policy is far from perfect. Many people are excluded, assistance may be insufficient, society is primarily concerned with controlling costs, or the system may not be flexible enough to respond to changing conditions. Rural communities are all too aware of shortcomings in the economy, social welfare services, and the informal network of people and services that may help them cope with need. The history of numerous economic downturns, euphemistically called the business cycle, reminds us that the free market does not always work well. The Great Depression of the 1930s put people out of work and moved them into marginal existences, sometimes for a decade or more. Rural people were particularly hard hit during the Great Depression, and many who were engaged in agricultural work permanently lost their farms and livelihood. John Steinbeck's *The Grapes of Wrath* (1939/2002) provides an excellent portrayal of some of the struggles of rural families during this period. The farm crisis of the 1980s also hit many rural families and communities particularly hard—not only were farmers affected, but also suppliers and farm equipment and distribution businesses. These are not stories or memories that fade easily in smaller towns and rural areas.

The most recent economic downturn—sometimes called the Great Recession—began at the end of 2007 and has resulted in some long-term unemployment and displaced workers in both rural and urban communities. When the economic pendulum swings downward, many real people suffer. Some lose employment that families pursued for generations. The foreclosure of farms and the decline of family-based agriculture are excellent examples of the long-term effects of a declining economy on rural people. Hopefully our social welfare system can help take up some of the economic slack to soften the blow for people and communities facing hard times.

When the economy slumps, traditional sources of help, including family, church, and charitable agencies, can be overwhelmed in times of great need. Downturns hit small communities either hard or not at all because their economies tend to lack diversity. Effects of a single major employer closing or relocating can be devastating to everyone in a small town and can seriously deplete sources of employment, as well as informal and private assistance. Family members may move away to find employment and leave those behind with little immediate support. Immigrants who move into a small community may not have family living locally, and there may not be religious institutions to provide them with support until the population reaches critical mass. Indeed, in a small community there are many ways that traditional institutions and informal ways of receiving help either break down or fail to provide needed social welfare support. When that happens, people may have to turn to formal social welfare resources that are available.

The following presents two examples of how social welfare policies illustrate unanticipated rural-urban differences in the effects of programs. In 1996, the federal government implemented sweeping welfare reform in the Personal Responsibility and Work Opportunity and Reconciliation Act (Pub. Law No. 104–193, as cited in Pindus, 2001). This act replaced the Aid to Families with Dependent Children program with Temporary

Assistance for Needy Families (TANF) and moved from a framework of family support to one that was time limited and that emphasized recipients going to work (Popple & Leighninger, 2008). Yet as is often the case when a broad based national policy is put into place, the programs work differently in rural communities, and this is often not addressed in the program or policy.

As has been discussed earlier, the poverty rate is traditionally high in rural communities, and programs that serve the poor often have greater significance because of people's lower incomes. Those who want to find work and live in the country face greater commuting distances to employment sites and less reliable transportation for getting to work. Long distances, poor roads, and lack of mass transit create more barriers for rural job seekers in finding and keeping employment. Services that provide support for those seeking employment are more difficult to access in smaller communities because of the distances involved and the limited budgets of social welfare agencies. Common support services for poor people seeking work are things like day care, job training, education, health care, and emergency services that help provide a transition from welfare to work (Pindus, 2001; Ward & Turner, 2006). More difficulty in accessing support services makes it more difficult for rural TANF recipients to find employment and potentially creates less of a difference in income when they do. Because TANF is a national program, in many cases it does not take into account the barriers that rural participants face.

Despite these obstacles, evidence indicates that rural people have found ways to overcome structural barriers in "moving from welfare to work," so to speak, often by drawing on their own resilience, strengths, and resources. Reliance on the values of work and self-support provides a powerful motivation for seeking and accepting work when available, and the use of social capital in the community fills in some of the service gaps that exist (Pindus, 2001). While the resilience and resourcefulness of rural people is encouraging, it is often a necessity because otherwise they may be waiting for resources that may never come. Ultimately, the recipients who do leave TANF may be no better off, because they often lose food stamps, Medicaid, and child-care benefits (Klemmack, Roff, McCallum, & Stem, 2002). Effectively, they simply transition from the "assisted poor" to the "working poor." Of course, all rural TANF recipients who leave the program are not necessarily going to work. Perhaps family, neighbors, and friends help them survive. It does seem clear that key factors in helping rural families leave the TANF program are the informal resources and support found in small towns (Ward & Turner, 2006).

A second example of how social policy affects rural communities differently is found in health care. According to the American Hospital Association (2013), rural hospitals provide services to about fifty-four million people, nine million of whom receive Medicare benefits. Yet rural hospitals face financial pressures from rising costs. Shortages of health-care professionals, the small size of hospitals, rising liability costs, the need to purchase new electronic information systems, and poor access to the investment funds needed to update aging facilities make the operating costs of rural hospitals relatively high. Rural hospitals also tend to receive lower fees for services for many patients, given perceived considerations of operating costs and size of the population served. Given the need for outreach to dispersed populations, rural health care and hospitals face substantial travel costs and time commitments that workers often cannot recoup. Small-town hospitals also tend to serve patents that are older than the national average and where a higher-than-average proportion of people rely on Medicare benefits (American Hospital Association, 2013). Medicare policies generally make the lowest reimbursements for rural hospitals—the smaller the hospital, the lower the payment.

One interpretation of this is to assume that rural health-care costs are lower when, in fact, the opposite is true. Higher costs and lower reimbursements create great financial pressures for small rural hospitals, which makes it difficult for them to attract staff and update facilities and equipment. When financial pressures become too strong, local hospitals may be forced to close. When hospitals close, communities have difficulty attracting and keeping physicians, and this also increases travel time to hospital-based services (Reif, DesHarnis, & Bernard, 1998). Of particular concern is increased travel time to emergency rooms and differential access for vulnerable populations. Rural people are left with fewer health-care resources that are more difficult to access, especially hospital care. Health-care policies led to a widespread closing of rural hospitals in the 1980s, and although the rate of closings has slowed, financial pressures as a result of policy changes could trigger more closings.

More rural children receive public health coverage through Medicaid and the Children's Health Insurance Program (CHIP) than in cities (40 percent versus 32 percent) (Mueller et al., 2012). Medicaid is a major source of funding for rural health-care providers: one-third of rural physicians receive 25 percent or more of their income from the program. Should Medicaid and the CHIP be cut back, many cash-strapped rural counties would have to find the funds to provide indigent care. So any policy change in Medicare, Medicaid, or CHIP that would decrease the funding for rural services could have negative consequences for rural communities. This is an important policy consideration, as both federal and state governments are looking to reduce costs of these programs. But on the positive side, it is also possible that policy changes under the Affordable Care Act will infuse new life into rural health care once programs are fully implemented.

These examples help illustrate not only how broad social policy has a differential effect in meeting the needs of rural people but also the resilience of rural people in adapting and overcoming obstacles that confront them in their daily lives. The traditional values of hard work and self-reliance serve them well in this regard, as does the close-knit nature of the community, which tends to pull together and use its assets to help "their own." This is how rural communities have typically coped with need and social problems, and given the increasingly urban shift in the population, it may be how rural communities and people will have to continue to adapt to social policy in the twenty-first century.

IDENTIFYING AND ADDRESSING DISPARITY IN RURAL POLICY

Social welfare policy at any level—be it a grand approach, a program or group of programs, administrative rule, or a set of operating procedures—carries the potential to create some type of disadvantage for rural people and communities. How do social workers go about addressing these kinds of disparities in a meaningful way? The path to make things better lies in identifying the effect or disparity, taking action, and engaging in advocacy. Fortunately, a social worker is not a lone actor in this process, as resources exist to help identify important policy issues, and there are professional organizations that can provide support in efforts to make change.

Identification

Social workers who want to examine the effects of policy on rural communities will find that a simple Internet search reveals several organizations that explore the effects of social, economic, health-care, and communications policy on smaller communities. Some of these focus on a state or on specific aspects of rural life, but they can prove valuable sources of information for practitioners nonetheless. Policy centers and the research they generate can shed light on the current state of rural life, policies to address specific issues, and changes that have occurred over time.

Perhaps the best-known rural policy organization is the Rural Policy Research Institute (RUPRI), established in 1990 as a collaborative venture among the University of Missouri–Columbia, Iowa State University, and the University of Nebraska. RUPRI (2012) engages in research, policy analysis, dissemination of information, and outreach. The organization's mission is to provide objective analysis of the challenges and needs of rural America, and to generate discussion about the effects of public policy on rural people and communities (RUPRI, 2012). RUPRI helps sponsor and facilitate research and policy analysis and rural collaborations, and it provides policy-related information to federal and state governments. It is an excellent source of information about rural social welfare policy.

There are, of course, other rural policy organizations that provide excellent information and whose work has been cited in this and previous chapters. Some of these organizations include the Rural Assistance Center (2013), Health Resources and Services Administration (n.d.), the Carsey Institute (2013), the Muskie School of Public Service (2010), the Center for Rural Policy and Development (2012), and the North Carolina Rural Economic Development Center (2012). Sources like these can provide valuable information for assessing the potential and actual effects of rural social welfare policy.

Social work has even developed its own policy with regard to practice in rural communities and with rural people. The National Association of Social Workers' (2012) Delegate Assembly approved the rural social work policy statement that appears in *Social Work Speaks*, a collection of policy statements for the profession. The rural policy statement speaks to a number of inequities in society in which rural communities are especially disadvantaged. These include several issues that have been discussed in this and previous chapters. The areas of rural inequity in social policy outlined in the NASW Rural Social Work Policy statement are as follows:

- health care and health coverage
- poverty
- access to services
- mental and behavioral health
- shortages of professional staff
- the digital divide and access to telecommunications
- services for veterans

Ginsberg (2011) expands this list to include issues of housing, employment, and transportation. Locke and Winship (2005) add the use of illegal drugs and immigration, and Winship (2014) adds homelessness and housing. Social policy addresses all of these social problems to some degree, yet they remain persistent social welfare issues for rural communities, at least partly because policies and programs do not provide enough resources, culturally responsive approaches, or good access for rural residents. Also, the specific issues that take precedence and address needs of rural people vary from community to community, which is why social workers need to understand both the community and the social policy that serves the community.

What the NASW's (2012) rural policy statement adds to the discussion is a set of policy proposals for the social work profession that would improve the quality of service and better meet the needs of small communities. The policy recommends the following:

- advocacy for social work practice and legislation targeting rural clients

- developing culturally competent practice at the BSW and MSW levels
- further development on the applications of social work ethics in the rural context
- developing policies that attract and retain social workers in rural areas
- expansion of continuing education opportunities for rural social workers
- development and expansion of technology for rural social workers and clients

That the social work profession, which is essentially urban based, identifies a need to shape policy for rural practice is important because it recognizes that the profession's response to rural services could be strengthened. If elements of its policy are really implemented, significant improvement could be made. Still, many issues are of long standing, and it is important for rural voices to be heard more loudly and consistently to make progress.

Action and Advocacy

The task of rural social workers once social problems and services have been identified is how to translate this into action that will make a difference. This is where social workers' macro practice skills become valuable. Engaging the support of others is often vital to the effort. In 1933 Josephine Brown recognized the value of a rural social worker engaging the community in collective action:

> Only a few people in the county, possibly not more than one or two, may be convinced of the need to take action. But if these few have vision, determination, and courage, they may become leaders in a movement of great value to the whole community. . . . The work of ten or fifteen people whose interest is aroused to white heat will be far more effective at this point than that of a larger number whose concern may be less vital. (Brown, 1933, pp. 34–35)

Brown realized that rural social workers needed not only to deliver direct services but also to develop, create, and modify services. In her view, one of the most important functions of the rural worker was to convince people of a need, to mobilize support, to aid in the development of service, and to help in the organization and administration of agencies. In effect, Brown (1933) was recommending a healthy component of influencing, developing, and implementing social policy. Her points are as relevant today as they were eighty years ago when she wrote her book.

When social workers look to mobilize local support for programs and policies to empower rural residents, it is essential for them to identify potential allies and collaborators. Knowing the local community and the nature of a specific problem(s) are invaluable in engaging people to provide help and support. Concerned citizens may be engaged, and their influence may be felt in passion or in numbers. Social workers often seek out community leaders to become part of the change effort because of their ability to sway the opinions of others or the resources they control. Engaging leaders may also be important to gain tacit approval so that they will not oppose change—some leaders might resent not being consulted. Community leaders include politicians, clergy, businesspeople, financial leaders, and other people with strong reputations or connections. The nature of rural communities is such that leaders might not be as visible, and leaders may be influenced informally by someone they know and respect. As has been discussed earlier, in rural communities social connections are complex and deep, and gaining the support of one or more leaders can give change efforts broad credibility to make an effort successful.

On a farther-reaching level that affects both state and national policy, rural social workers probably have to reach beyond the local level to involve larger numbers of people. In this regard, rural information, advocacy groups, and organizations can be very helpful for reaching a broader audience and extending influence. In the social work profession the primary advocacy group for rural issues is the National Rural Social Work Caucus, which has existed since 1976 and was instrumental in the development and approval of the rural social work policy statement (NASW, 2012). The caucus influenced the NASW Code of Ethics to be more responsive to the needs of rural practitioners, generating information about rural communities and social problems, and developing knowledge about rural social work (Hickman, 2014; Locke, 2009; National Rural Social Work Caucus, n.d.)

There are, of course, other organizations that may prove valuable resources and allies in an effort to effect change in rural policy, including the National Association for Rural Mental Health, the National Rural Health Association, the US Department of Agriculture, the California Institute on Rural Studies, the North Carolina Rural Health Research and Policy Analysis Center, and others. The Child Welfare League of America has developed a rural resource page, and the Council on Social Work Education has a rural track in its annual program meeting. The specific kind of problems, services, and region may help social workers determine which organizations are most appropriate to engage. But in effecting policy change, numbers often speak loudly, and information is often essential to making productive change. Finding the appropriate organization and information can be a labor-intensive process, but it is often worth the effort.

CONCLUSION

A significant fact of rural life is that social and economic policy often affects small communities differently than larger cities. Sometimes the differences can be small; in others, they are much larger. With a tendency for social and economic policy to be made in urban areas, it is likely that new programs and practices may not give due weight to the needs of rural people and communities. Overlooking the needs of rural people is not new in social policy, but it is generally done without ill intent. Policy makers may not fully understand the nature of rural life and the conditions country people face. Or decision makers simply might not think about rural areas when developing policy, an out-of-sight, out-of-mind phenomenon. However benign the intent, the effects of policy are real and often place small communities at a disadvantage.

Currently, rural areas are affected by social welfare policy that creates challenges in terms of access to services and availability of specialized services. Yet many small towns have greater needs in areas like poverty, housing, and health. Indeed, social policy increases challenges for rural social workers, who must look even harder and be more creative in finding and developing the resources their clients need. Since policy affects which services are available, the amount and types of services, eligibility, and access to services, it is doubly important for rural workers to be involved in the macro side of practice even as they deliver direct services.

Even the social work profession is not immune from policies that occasionally make the rural perspective almost invisible. The profession retains an urban orientation today, as cities are where a majority of social workers are educated, live, and work. As a minority, rural social workers may be hesitant to speak up about the challenges that they face. More effort should be directed toward producing social workers for small communities and strengthening professional knowledge and skills in this field of practice. Small-town and rural social work is an important area of practice for which practitioners and educators should be eager to speak about and demonstrate their passion for change.

Rural social workers will be well served by keeping abreast of social and economic policies that have the potential to affect rural communities and clients. Analysis of policy in terms of effects, especially on the rural community, is something that they should do on an ongoing basis. If social workers do this early in the process of policy development, it might increase the possibility of them contributing their input. But to help shape policy that is most effective for rural areas and small towns, it is often necessary for social workers to get directly involved in policy making and policy implementation.

To change policy, it is helpful to collect relevant data and mobilize support. Much of this can be done at the local level, but sometimes involvement at the state or national level is needed. There are several organizations that focus on rural life and can be used as valuable sources of information and support. Obviously, there is no substitute for commitment to and passion for rural issues in motivating others to see the importance of incorporating a rural or small-town perspective into policy.

REFERENCES

American Hospital Association. (2013). *Rural health care*. Retrieved from http://www.aha.org/advocacy-issues/rural/index.shtml.

Barker, R. L. (2003). *The social work dictionary* (5th ed.). Washington, DC: NASW Press.

Belanger, K. (2008). *The welfare of rural children: A summary of rural challenges*. Retrieved from http://www.cwla.org/programs/cultural competence/welfareofruralchildren.pdf.

Bowman, B. (1995). *He's wetting on my leg, but it's warm and wet and feels good*. Lufkin, TX: Best of East Texas Publishers.

Brown, J. C. (1933). *The rural community and social casework*. New York, NY: Family Welfare Association of America.

Carsey Institute (2005). *Rural America depends on the food stamp program to make ends meet* (Policy Brief No. 1). Retrieved from http://www.carseyinstitute.unh.edu/publications/PB_foodstamps_05.pdf.

Carsey Institute. (2013). *Rural America*. Retrieved from http://carsey institute.unh.edu/policy/rural-america.

Center for Rural Policy and Development. (2012). *Welcome to the center for rural policy and development*. Retrieved from http://www.ruralmn.org.

Ginsberg, L. H. (2011). Introduction to basics of rural social work. In L. H. Ginsberg (Ed.), *Social work in rural communities* (5th ed., pp. 5–20). Alexandria, VA: Council on Social Work Education.

Health Resources and Services Administration. (n.d.). *Rural health resources*. Retrieved from http://www.hrsa.gov/ruralhealth/resources/index.html.

Hickman, S. A. (2014). Rural is real: History of the National Rural Social Work Caucus and the NASW professional policy statement on rural social work. In T. L. Scales, C. L. Streeter, & H. S. Cooper (Eds.), *Rural social work: Building and sustaining community capacity* (2nd ed., pp. 19–28). Hoboken, NJ: Wiley.

Klemmack, D. L., Roff, L. L., McCallum, D. M., & Stem, J. T. (2002). The impact of welfare reform on rural Alabamians. *Southern Rural Sociology*, *18*(1), 186–203.

Locke, B. L. (2009). The National Rural Social Work Caucus: 32 years of achievement. *Contemporary Rural Social Work*, *1*, 1–7. Retrieved from http://journal.und.edu/crsw/issue/view/22.

Locke, B. L., & Winship, J. (2005). Social work in rural America. In N. Lohmann & R. A. Lohmann (Eds.), *Rural social work practice* (pp. 3–24). New York, NY: Columbia University Press.

Lohmann, N., & Lohmann, R. A. (2005). Introduction. In N. Lohmann & R. A. Lohmann (Eds.), *Rural social work practice* (pp. ix–xxvii). New York, NY: Columbia University Press.

Mueller, K. J., Coburn, A. F., Lundblad, J. P., MacKinney, A. C., McBride, T. D., & Watson, S. D. (2012). *The current and future role and impact of Medicaid in rural health*. Columbia, MO: Rural Policy Research Institute. Retrieved from http://www.rupri.org/Forms/HealthPanel Medicaid_Sept2012.pdf.

Muskie School of Public Service. (2010). *Maine Rural Health Research Center*. Retrieved from http://muskie.usm.maine.edu/centers/mrhrc .jsp.

National Association of Social Workers. (2012). Rural social work. In *Social work speaks: National Association of Social Workers policy statements* (9th ed., pp. 296–300). Washington, DC: NASW Press.

National Rural Social Work Caucus. (n.d.). *The Rural Social Work Caucus 1976–1984: A history and descriptive analysis*. Retrieved from http:// ruralsocialwork.org/history.cfm.

Netting, F. E. (2014). Policy issues affecting rural populations. In T. L. Scales, C. L. Streeter, & H. S. Cooper (Eds.), *Rural social work: Building and sustaining community capacity* (2nd ed., pp. 223–225). Hoboken, NJ: Wiley.

North Carolina Rural Economic Development Center. (2012). *Rural policy*. Retrieved from http://www.ncruralcenter.org/index.php?option = com_content&view = article&id = 61&Itemid = 141.

Pindus, N. M. (2001). *Implementing welfare reform in rural communities*. Washington, DC: Urban Institute. Retrieved from http://www.urban .org/pdfs/rural-welfarereform.pdf.

Popple, P. R., & Leighninger, L. (2008). *The policy based profession*. Boston, MA: Pearson Allyn & Bacon.

Reif, S., DesHarnis, S., & Bernard, S. (1998). *Effects of rural hospital closure on access to care*. Chapel Hill, NC: Sheps Center for Health Care Research.

Rural Assistance Center. (2013). *Health and human services information for rural America*. Retrieved from http://www.raconline.org.

Rural Policy Research Institute. (2012). *About us—Purpose*. Retrieved from http://www.rupri.org/abtpurpose.php.

Steinbeck, John (2002). *The grapes of wrath.* New York: Penguin Books. (Originally published 1939.)

US Department of Health and Human Services. (2012, September 25). *Health care law increases number of mental and behavioral health providers* [Press release]. Retrieved from http://www.hhs.gov/news/press/2012pres/09/20120925a.html.

Ward, S., & Turner, H. (2006). *Work and welfare strategies among single mothers in rural New England: The role of social networks and social support.* Retrieved from http://www.rupri.org/Forms/WP06–04.pdf.

Winship, J. (2014). Living in limbo: Homeless families in rural America. In T. L. Scales, C. L. Streeter, & H. S. Cooper (Eds.), *Rural social work: Building and sustaining community capacity* (2nd ed., pp. 237–249). Hoboken, NJ: Wiley.

Sometimes Social Services in small communities are housed in nontraditional facilities: a rural community action office in a converted church (Texas).

CHAPTER FIVE

Social Welfare Services in the Rural Community

EVEN A CASUAL READING of the social work literature leads one to the conclusion that rural social welfare services are few and far between. Author after author recounts the scarcity of rural services and the major challenge this poses for social workers and clients. Rural people have earthy, down-home phrases that reflect scarcity: "empty as a church on Saturday night," "scarce as grass around a hog trough," and "scarce as hen's teeth." To anyone who has been in the country, these phrases capture the idea of something that is pretty meager.

This chapter examines social welfare services in small communities. Although a thorough consideration of all services is beyond our scope, the chapter does present examples of rural service programs. The services discussed here are mental health and substance abuse, health care, child welfare, domestic violence, and the emerging area of services for immigrants and migrants.

Just how scarce are these important services for rural people? At one time, an overall view of rural social welfare was that services were pretty bare. When Josephine Brown wrote her classic book *The Rural Community and Social Casework* in 1933 the argument could be made that rural services were scarce and sometimes nonexistent. But this was in the early years of the Great Depression, times were tough economically, and few of the social welfare programs of the New Deal had yet been put in place.

Most of the services that did exist were the work of private charities, but the money to support even those services had begun to dry up. So during this time, social welfare services were woefully inadequate to address the needs of rural communities.

The real question is whether things have changed so little in the more than eighty years since Brown wrote that we are still in the same kind of situation. Things have indeed changed in rural America in the twenty-first century, and it is important to assess what those changes have meant in terms of social welfare services and social work. The New Deal helped bring electricity to rural America and built a publicly funded network of social and economic support services that extended to the countryside. Programs like Social Security, Aid to Dependent Children, and child welfare services were then able to reach communities that had not experienced such support before.

Much of Leon Ginsberg's (1976) landmark book *Social Work in Rural Communities: A Book of Readings*, which provided the modern reintroduction of rural practice to social work, deals with topics related to services. Of the thirteen chapters in the book, eight deal with service-related topics, though from a decidedly community practice perspective, and five chapters focus primarily on social work education. The book was written when the long-term trend of rural people migrating to the city had reversed, and people were again moving back to the country. There was concern that the social services and skills of social workers would not be up to the task of supporting the growth of rural communities. But even in the mid-1970s there were clearly services available in rural communities, and many of the chapters focused on expanding services and extending their reach.

Since that time the rural social work literature has diversified considerably, expanding to include topics like special populations, social work ethics, and international content. Many authors continue to write quite a bit about rural services into the twenty-first century. For example, twelve of the twenty chapters in the fifth edition of Ginsberg's (2011a) *Social Work in Rural Communities* contain content that can be described as service related. One shift that has occurred is that much of the contemporary literature tends to focus on direct practice issues more than on community-based practice. This appears to reflect a general trend in social work to separate practice from the community development arena (Locke & Winship, 2005). Some might argue that this kind of shift does not serve social workers well who practice in rural communities. Twenty-first-century rural authors such as Scales and Streeter (2004; Scales, Streeter, & Cooper, 2014) have added a strengths perspective that examines booth existing services and informal resources as community assets.

What is clear is that in the twenty-first century social welfare services do exist and serve populations that need them. There is also general agreement that services are neither as extensive nor as specialized as may be needed. Service networks in rural areas do differ from those in the cities. The lower population densities of rural areas and the transportation networks to reach services often play out differently than they would in an urban community. Generally, rural social welfare service programs serve a larger geographic area than is typical for a metropolitan setting. This means that rural services may be further from at least some of the people who need them, and transportation to reach services could be a problem. Very few rural communities have mass transit systems, especially to reach towns that may be forty or fifty miles away.

The service and service delivery issues that face rural communities are not new. Josephine Brown (1933) wrote about how needed services may be some distance from clients and that transportation was a major barrier to accessing services. Today, the roads and communications are usually better, and there are more services available than in the 1930s. But the very nature of rural communities works against the social welfare service network being as strong as it may be in an urban area. Low population densities tend to make providing services in rural areas more expensive per capita than in a metropolitan setting. For political decision makers who are looking to cut costs and provide services economically, rural communities may not be high priorities. As governmental entities try to plan where to spend their limited service dollars, they generally turn to places where there are a lot of people, and those are the cities. There may also be some old prejudices and mythology at play if decision makers think of rural communities as idyllic places with few problems.

Services are often planned on a per capita basis, and as a result rural areas tend to receive less funding for services. Moreover, in a rural area funding has to be spread over a wider geographic area. So it is usually the case that needed services may be available but not be found locally. Instead, services may be offered at a regional center that requires clients to travel to reach it. In some very rural or frontier areas these distances may be prohibitive, and so there are effectively few services available. This tends to be a more significant issue in regions with a lot of wide-open space, like Alaska, North Dakota, Montana, and New Mexico. An important example of this is services to veterans. Approximately 3.3 million veterans, about 41 percent of those who are enrolled in the VA health system live in rural areas, and the distance from service centers often means that they do not get access to the services and care they need (White House Rural Council, 2011).

While some of the basic social welfare services may be available, accessing specialized services may be a different issue altogether. Specialized services tend to serve a much smaller segment of the population, and they also can be expensive to deliver. Consequently, they are generally offered in a central location where they can serve larger numbers of people from several communities more efficiently. For example, inpatient mental health services are used to treat only certain types of chronic or acute conditions, and they are more expensive than outpatient services. A single rural area may not have enough people with the requisite conditions to fully utilize a facility, but several communities together might. As a result, regional service centers tend to be established to serve smaller communities. In many ways this advantages those communities that are closer to the service center and disadvantages those who are more remote.

What this may mean for rural social workers and clients is that needed social welfare services may not be available in their community. The challenge then becomes one of accessing the services that are available and addressing the barrier of distance. These are all too real, significant parts of rural social work, and sometimes it is possible to overcome them. In such instances, social workers need to be both creative and flexible in trying to help empower their clients in their home communities. In so doing, rural workers can take one of three approaches to try to address the insufficient local resource situation: (1) finding and employing informal resources, (2) developing creative combinations of services that exist, and (3) engaging in community development to enhance the supply of resources. Any and all of these are part of rural social work.

When one speaks of the assets of small towns and communities, the discussion is usually about the local people and organizations. These assets have traditionally filled the gap when formal social welfare resources were unable to do so. Some examples of informal resources include working with friends, family, or neighbors to provide services like day care or foster care, meals for the elderly, or rides for clients to keep medical or agency appointments. Churches and local civic organizations can also be mobilized around specific projects, such as a family who needs assistance because their home was destroyed by a fire or a tornado, or providing transportation to someone who needs medical treatment.

But informal services, though valuable, are usually specific to the community or even to an individual, and as such, they require rural workers to discover and learn about these resources. And there are certainly limitations as to what informal services can provide. But the use of informal, nonprofessional services is a very important part of rural work. Because of their unique nature, most informal resources are too distinct and diverse to discuss in this chapter except in a very general way. As a consequence, most of the remainder of this chapter centers on the kinds of formal services that exist in rural communities.

Despite the many service-related challenges that are found in practice, rural social workers and their agencies have found ways to adapt and provide many needed services. Rural workers have done this by being independent, creative, adaptable, and willing to look for solutions when just getting by and doing what has been done in the past would be much easier. Agencies have adapted and provided outreach to be more helpful to their communities. But most of all, in various ways rural helping professionals have shown leadership in responding to community needs. The remainder of this chapter looks at some of the types of service programs that have been developed and implemented for small towns and rural areas.

MENTAL HEALTH AND SUBSTANCE ABUSE

Although the rates of mental and behavioral health issues do not differ significantly between rural and urban areas, the experiences of the two populations differ quite a bit with respect to treatment services. The primary difference is that it is more difficult for rural people who experience mental health or substance abuse issues to get treatment that might help them (Conway, BigFoot, & Sandler, 2011). Rural residents are less likely to receive any treatment for their behavioral disorders, and the quality of care for those who do may be poorer than people who live in metropolitan areas (Office of Rural Health Policy, 2011). Rural veterans with mental health disorders tend to be sicker than their urban counterparts, yet they receive services less often (National Association of Social Workers, 2012). However, in terms of mental health, rural people have higher rates of some conditions. For example, rural residents tend to experience more depression, suicide, and substance abuse than those in the city. They also have more behavioral risk factors such as smoking and obesity (Conway et al., 2011; Stone & Fredrick, 2011).

Similarly, substance abuse rates are also much the same in rural and urban areas, but there are fewer rural treatment resources for substance abuse. There are increasing concerns about illegal drug use in rural areas, and often these problems are addressed by the criminal justice system instead of treatment (Johnson, 1998; Locke & Winship, 2005; Rural Assistance Center, 2012b; Substance Abuse and Mental Health Services Administration, SAMHSA, 2007).

Transportation is a barrier to accessing drug treatment services, as it can be difficult in rural areas to have transportation that gets people to where services are offered. Simply, it can be many miles, sometimes over difficult roads, to reach treatment. Other barriers to receiving treatment include relatively few rural substance abuse treatment programs and the stigma of substance abuse. These all tend to reduce the likelihood that people receive treatment. There is community scorn that goes with being identified as mentally ill or as a drug user, and most rural residents want to avoid that scorn. There are many colloquial terms for someone who might be seen going to the mental health center, such as "he has a hole in his screen door," "she's a few pickles short of a barrel," or "his Christmas lights are missing a few bulbs." Substance abusers might be called "pot heads" or "speed freaks," or be described as "drunk as a skunk in a trunk," "smoking left-handed cigarettes," "three sheets to the wind," or as having "bottle fever." These are phrases people use when they don't want to speak directly, and none of them is particularly flattering. Being viewed in these ways can frame a person as a community outcast or an object of pity. Indeed, there are many factors in rural areas that make it difficult to get appropriate services for substance abuse or mental illness.

There is also evidence of an increased flow of drugs into rural communities. The manufacture of methamphetamine has become a viable source of income, if a dangerous cottage industry; the cultivation of marijuana has created a new cash crop; and drug dealers, large and small, have opened up new markets in rural communities. In fact, the cultivation of marijuana has grown so extensive that some people contend that it is now the nation's biggest cash crop (Bailey, 2006). As traditional sources of income decline, the cultivation of crops like marijuana and the production of methamphetamine provide lucrative income sources. Given the movement of drugs into rural areas and the traditional reluctance of rural people to seek formal services, it is not surprising that in rural communities a higher percentage of referrals for treatment were from criminal justice sources than from family, friends, or self-referrals (SAMHSA, 2012).

Several contemporary trends in the mental health and substance abuse field have created special problems for rural communities. The problems often stem from adopting models of mental health services developed for metropolitan areas and applying them as broad policies without first evaluating their effects on rural communities. Several policies have been implemented with the intent of cutting or containing the cost of services. Rural mental health services have traditionally been underfunded (Scheyett & Fuhrman, 1999), and further cost cutting that fails to address the needs of rural people can and does lead to lower service use and serious underserving of the behavioral health needs of people in small towns and rural areas.

For example, a trend in mental health and substance abuse treatment is the move to managed care (Scheyett & Fuhrman, 1999). The idea behind managed care is that by controlling the services delivered, increasing efficiency, and fees paid for services, cost efficiencies can be achieved and overutilization of resources reduced, thus producing significant savings. But managed care works best in urban settings where there are large and concentrated populations, coordinated service systems and information, and multiple service providers and competition. None of these characteristics describes rural communities. Rural providers often depend more on public funding than urban services do. For example, programs like Medicare and Medicaid help fund rural services, and cutting costs associated with these programs can make it more difficult for providers to offer services, especially where there are few service providers, low population densities, and large service areas. These factors often contribute to an increased cost per unit of service. Of course, many rural people have little or no private insurance coverage, which makes it difficult for them to receive any services at all. The recent expansion of health insurance may help improve access to health care, but it is too early to tell. However, many rural people are still opposed to the recent Affordable Care Act, or Obamacare, and it may take some time for them to overcome resistance to participation in the program.

In terms of treatment, the market forces and economies of scale that are the key assumptions of managed care strategies are not rural-friendly. According to the National Rural Health Association (1999), a significant number of rural counties do not have any mental health services; thus, there is no competition or alternative service to drive down prices. Even if there were more agencies, rural communities do not have enough professional mental health personnel to provide services in those agencies that do exist. Mental health agencies in rural areas have a hard time attracting and retaining professional staff, and they are especially short of specialists (Stone & Frederick, 2011).

The move to deinstitutionalize residents of state mental hospitals and return them to the community for treatment, though commendable, has had a significant effect on rural communities. Many rural communities used state hospitals as a treatment resource because they did not have or could not afford adequate mental health services. Deinstitutionalization and the closing of state hospitals has served to keep the mentally ill in their own community, where there may not be resources to serve them. A result of nationwide deinstitutionalization of the mentally ill, for example, is that people typically end up in general hospitals, jails and prisons, and nursing homes, which may not be set up to provide the services they need (Advocacy Treatment Center, n.d.). It also means that some mentally ill people who are not elderly or do not present criminal justice or health problems may receive little or no services at all. With community mental health services strapped with declining funding, many have shifted services away from low-income clients who receive Medicare or Medicaid to fee-generated services based on private insurance and ability to pay. As Randall and Vance (2005) indicate, cuts in public funding, staff downsizing, and an inability to keep up with current research-based treatments have all seriously impaired the ability to provide services for the chronically mentally ill in rural areas. All of these increase the possibility that mentally ill people and substance abusers in rural areas will receive less service or no services. Indeed, for people in rural areas, mental health and substance abuse services already have begun to shift from the mental health system to the criminal justice one.

Although so far this paints a pretty bleak picture of options for rural clients who have mental illness or substance abuse issues, there are things that social workers and agencies can do to help provide encouragement. A model of treatment that has been suggested as an approach for rural communities is assertive community treatment (ACT), in which multidisciplinary teams with low caseloads provide intensive case management and coordinate both treatment plans for mentally ill individuals and substance abuse treatment for the dually diagnosed (Randall & Vance, 2005). But as Meyer and Morrissey (2007) suggest, the realities of rural communities have forced adaptations of the model that tend to reduce the size of treatment teams, create a less diverse staff, and offer less intensive service that may reduce the effectiveness. In general, if treatment teams must travel a lot to reach clients, then they will be able to assist fewer clients because of travel time. Still, the ACT model can help bring more services to remote clients.

Another outreach method that holds promise is the use of telemedicine, or real-time, two-way interactive telecommunication between patients and health-care providers, to reach out to clients in distant communities. Telemedicine holds promise, but smaller communities still may not have the communications infrastructure to support it. At this point, there are still rural areas with poor connections to communications networks, and communications technology is expensive. Once again, it becomes an argument about cost-effectiveness, as to whether there are enough people who need services to avoid making their cost prohibitive. For now, telemedicine may bring services closer to clients, but they might still have to travel. In any event, some mental health and substance abuse treatment staff will still need to travel to clients.

There is also the old-fashioned outreach model, in which regional service providers establish satellite clinics or develop some type of mobile unit that can travel from community to community. Depending on the size of the population served, the facility may be staffed only periodically, perhaps two days a week or less. This provides some outreach, and depending on the schedule, a schedule of services might be predictable. This type of arrangement may provide earlier intervention than waiting for patients to travel to distant health care facilities for services. These outreach services can still be expensive, though, and clients may have to travel for specialized services.

To be most effective, mental health and substance abuse services must be adapted to the community and employ available resources. An example of this might be to develop sensitivity to the local culture and work with local people to develop culturally sensitive treatment practices, possibly even incorporating folk medicine, in addition to the traditional evidence-based approach (Conway et al., 2011). For example, Native American and Hispanic populations may benefit from the involvement of shamans or *curanderos*, respectively, in the treatment process. In another example, Furstenberg and Gammonley (1999) discuss the use of local companions with older people receiving outpatient mental health services in rural North Carolina. The program matched lay retired people with mental health consumers to augment traditional services, and it achieved good results. The use of community volunteers helped extend and enhance the treatment experience of the mentally ill.

Another approach that Randall and Vance (2005) suggest is to engage in service coordination. This can be effective when a service area covers several communities in a geographic region. Providers in one area may not be used to working with agencies in other communities, and basic service coordination could extend the services for the region. In any event, social workers who work across communities must establish credibility with the people in each one. In other words, just because an agency or service is accepted in one community does not mean that it will be accepted even in nearby communities.

In any event, social workers who deliver mental health or substance abuse services need to be creative and flexible in responding to the needs of clients and overcoming some of the challenges of rural practice. Some community practice in extending, coordinating, and enhancing service may also be needed, in addition to good clinical skills in order to engage in behavioral health. But then, good rural social workers should always be creative and adaptable, and think as generalists.

RURAL HEALTH CARE SERVICES

The availability of quality health care is important for rural people. Approximately one-third of rural residents are in poor health, and about half have a chronic health condition (Cashwell & Starks, 2011). Yet people who live in rural communities tend to have less contact with physicians and health care than city dwellers. Casey, Blewett, and Call (2004) have suggested that many unmet rural health-care needs are a result of inadequate health insurance, low income, and cultural barriers. Yet Medicare payments to rural hospitals are less than those for urban hospitals, which may be a factor in the closing of 470 rural hospitals over the past twenty-five years (NASW, 2012).

Many of the same issues that face social workers in the areas of mental health and substance abuse also apply to work in the health-care field. The main problems that rural communities face in getting health care are access, availability, image, and breadth of coverage (Cashwell & Starks, 2011). Once again, the issue of managed care, shortages of professional staff, low population density, and distance all affect the range and quality of rural services. With rural health care, unlike with rural mental health care, there is typically not community stigma associated with physical illness. But people may still have some reluctance about being seen undergoing some types of treatment, and they may not want the whole community to know the specific nature of their illness. There is, however, still some public stigma in using public funds to pay for health care, which may tend to inhibit the use of some health-care services such as public clinics or hospitals.

When we talk about health care, we are referring to services that provide prevention, primary care, outpatient care, hospital care, follow-up care, emergency care, and dental services. Rural people experience difficulties accessing these services for several reasons. For example, access may be restricted by the availability or unavailability of services in an area. One population that has been identified as underserved by the rural health care is veterans (NASW, 2012). Forty-four percent of military recruits come from rural areas, and often they return to live there. They can have greater health needs than the average population, but they have less access to health care (NASW, 2012).

There is also a shortage of health-care professionals to serve rural areas. For example, Cashwell and Starks (2011) observed that only 9 percent of physicians practice in a rural setting. The effect of this is that health care has been moved to regional centers, typically to larger towns in a region. While this provides services for the region as a whole, the health care may still be difficult to access because of travel times or distance to the regional center. Time and distance can be critical, especially when emergency services are concerned, as extra time may mean life or death.

Access to health care may be restricted for other reasons. Local health-care centers may be small or lack comprehensive services. They may be able to diagnose, but for treatment patients may need a referral to a larger facility, which would make treatment even more difficult to access. Not having the needed range of services could cause local people to bypass a regional center altogether, thus lowering the utilization rate of the facility and increasing the operating costs even more. The smaller size of rural facilities may result in a reduced capacity to serve the local population, and people may have to be wait-listed. If the wait is too long, folks may give up seeking services and leave their condition untreated. In contrast, staying too long on a waiting list could result in serious complications and even more extensive services being needed. Neither of these is a good option for a person's health.

Access to health care in rural communities can also be an issue, for slightly different reasons. Many rural people do not have adequate health insurance, which makes them reluctant to seek out health care. Lack of insurance and ability to pay for health care are common problems among the poor, as well as for the working poor in rural communities. Salaries and family incomes tend to be lower in rural areas than in the cities, and many jobs do not provide health insurance coverage. Many people who lack insurance coverage or use public insurance are minorities, and there are significant health disparities among groups. Also among the limited health-care options facing smaller communities are facilities and providers who elect not to accept public programs like Medicaid. This further restricts an already-limited health-care market in a rural community.

Rural people who fear being unable to pay for health care or being denied services may put off getting health care until it is absolutely necessary. Inability to pay for services creates internal conflict because it implies that the person is not self-sufficient and needs to accept charity. This is not unique to rural people, but it is probably accentuated by the stronger emphasis on self-support value and by higher-than-average poverty rates in rural areas. So people avoid getting formal health care, or they may substitute folk remedies and just hope that things work out. However, if people wait until a condition gets more serious before seeking medical attention, it means that hospital emergency rooms often become their source of primary care. This is not uncommon among the poor or the uninsured, but it does tend to make health care very expensive and overcrowd emergency rooms. In some rural communities the emergency room isn't an option if it is too far away.

An example can help illustrate the challenges found at the intersection of availability and access to health care. The rural county Madison has a small regional medical center, with two hospitals and several health-care providers. But many health-care resources for indigent patients and recipients of Medicaid and Medicare are limited because some providers would not treat patients unless they could pay through private insurance or personal funds. For indigent pregnant women, no provider in the community was willing to provide prenatal care or deliver children. The county hospital would deliver children in emergencies. Most cases were not considered emergency services, and thus not covered by the county hospital. So patients could not get prenatal care or delivery services if they couldn't pay. Ultimately, the designated facility for serving those patients was 180 miles away, and the trip there took more than three hours. The basic issue in this case is payment, but obviously health complications can develop for many people in this situation.

Another reason people may not access health care much in rural areas is because of a traditional reliance on folk medicine. Some of these cures rely on roots, herbs, and oils, and they might be administered by a folk medicine practitioner. Some rural groups retain at least some folk healing practices as an alternative to traditional medicine, such as castor oil as a purgative, catnip and chamomile for colic, tobacco for drawing out poison from insect stings, willow bark for headaches, sassafras for internal illnesses, whiskey for teething, and brown sugar and turpentine for the flu (Cavender, 2003). Some of these practices have therapeutic value, but unwavering belief in their efficacy may prevent very traditional rural people from using health care when they need it most.

Today, rural health care provides quality services, and providers meet accepted professional standards. Yet the myths persist that somehow rural health care is subpar—perhaps because salaries are higher and better-known medical facilities are in urban areas. So, in general, many rural residents have the attitude that for routine health care, local facilities are fine, but for something serious, the city is the place to go. That is a realistic perspective with specialized services, because they are more widely available, but it does not reflect general opinion that rural health care is not up to snuff. They seek treatment in a larger city because of the wider range of treatment options.

In rural areas, another health-care consideration is that some health problems may be environmental in nature, and therefore a broad public health concern. For example, agricultural workers frequently work around pesticides and herbicides that may have long-term toxic effects on the body and produce a number of aliments. Some types of fertilizer and even animal litter can be toxic in high quantities. Mining and oil and gas production sites leave behind chemicals that can cause health problems through direct contact with them, breathing their fumes, or contaminated drinking water. Chemicals can seep into the groundwater and be consumed by people over a long period of time. Workers can be exposed to hazardous bacteria at meat-processing plants. Natural agricultural waste may have toxic effects that result in illness. For example, broiler litter—the droppings in chicken houses—contains a number of toxic chemicals that can lead to health problems, as well as air and water pollution. Social workers in the area of health care should be alert to cases of similar illnesses in people living in an area so that they can identify, investigate, and address possible public health issues.

In looking at rural social work practice in the health-care field, some significant ideas for improving services come to mind. A first step is to develop knowledge of the local people, including minority and oppressed groups. Clients' beliefs about disease and illness, their view of treatment, and their use of folk medicine are all very useful in helping workers start where the client is, in building relationships, in making assessments, and in developing interventions. Secondarily, developing knowledge of the people, organizations, and informal resources that can provide sources of support can be helpful in developing solutions. For example, knowing folk medicine practitioners who might work alongside traditional medicine could be useful for working with clients who have strong beliefs in the use of folk medicine. It is also important to identify family members who can provide personal care, do chores and other tasks, and provide transportation to fill gaps when formal resources may not exist or be limited. Churches, for example, can help address spiritual aspects of healing and also assist with transportation.

Rural social workers may have to fill many roles in providing health-related services. For example, Smith, Glasser, and Korr (2011) discussed the value of psychosocial services as important for cancer patients in rural areas, including assessment, distress screening, problem solving, cognitive behavioral therapy, and patient advocacy. Cashwell and Starks (2011) also highlighted some of the macro practice aspects of rural work, including seeking grants, coordinating formal and informal resources, mobilizing community support, and facilitating collaboration.

CHILD WELFARE

Child welfare and child maltreatment are significant social problems and the provision of services to protect children and assist families in need is a traditional arena for social work practice. According to the Children's Bureau (2011), in 2011 there were 3.7 million children who were the subject of a maltreatment report. Not all reports were substantiated, but about one in five (19.5 percent) were found to be either substantiated or indicated (Children's Bureau, 2011), a sign of serious issues that required intervention.

In terms of rural communities, the manner in which child abuse data have been collected has created some difficulty in making some comparisons between rural and urban areas. However, the most recent National

Incidence Study of Child Abuse and Neglect indicated that maltreatment is greater in rural communities than in urban ones (Child Welfare Information Gateway, 2012). In virtually every category of maltreatment, rural communities experience rates that exceed those of the cities. Data from prior years have been less clear, but they suggest that the rate of child abuse in rural areas appears to be at least as high as that in urban communities (Belanger, 2008; Ginsberg, 2011b; Walsh & Mattingly, 2010). In any event, child maltreatment is always a serious social problem to be addressed wherever it occurs.

Because of state and federal funding, child protection and foster-care services extend to all regions of the country, including rural areas. How well such services reach rural communities varies considerably in terms of both access and adequacy, and depends on the community and the region, but rural agencies and workers face some challenges not typically found in the cities. The consistent rural factors of distance, population density, shortage of professionals, and availability of specialized services often create barriers rural child welfare workers must address.

Information about social work practice in rural child welfare is somewhat sparse, and clearly, we need to know more about this important field to understand both the successes and the challenges, and to enhance policy and services for families and children (Belanger, 2008). One thing we do know is that rural child welfare practice is more likely to be generalist, covering a broad range of services instead of specialized ones (Child Welfare Information Gateway, 2012). There are simply not enough workers available to support workers' field specialization. However, one area of concern for rural child welfare is the professional workforce available to provide services. Providing effective services for children in a rural setting requires professional education and training for evaluations and appropriate interventions (Leistyna, 1980). But nationwide, child welfare agencies have difficulty in attracting and retaining qualified workers to provide child welfare services (Zlotnik, 2003), and in rural communities there are fewer workers with social work degrees (Child Welfare Information Gateway, 2012). This is unfortunate, because many child welfare agencies prefer that social workers have professional training, which often generates a greater commitment to the field and longer retention (Whitaker, 2012).

Another challenge workers face in this area is isolation: many social workers are isolated in large geographic service regions (Sudol, 2009). Thus, resources are stretched over long distances, and workers have extended travel times to reach clients. This means that a greater portion of rural workers' time is spent on travel rather than directly providing services. And supervision, which is an important source of support, is more difficult to get in a rural setting (Child Welfare Information Gateway, 2012).

Another practice issue is that children in rural areas might encounter factors that affect their safety, permanence and stability in care, and well-being, but without the same access to supportive services that many urban children have. Smaller towns have few treatment options for substance abuse, mental health, and specialized placement facilities for children. Treatment options for children with special health or behavioral needs are especially limited. Support services for children and families are important resources for keeping children in their own homes and strengthening families. These supports reduce a need for foster care and shorten the length of time in care once children are placed there by building a safer home environment as quickly as possible. Support services are essential for family preservation to work effectively because they affect whether a child is placed in foster care and can remain at home once returned (Belanger & Stone, 2008). Unfortunately, rural communities often do not have enough support services to meet such needs.

When rural children are placed in care outside of their homes, they often are placed far from their home communities, and so they have more limited family contact and family preservation efforts suffer. For example, parents with mental health issues may have children removed and placed out of the home because there are insufficient treatment services available to them. Neither children nor families benefit from this, and the community suffers because of the extra expense of maintaining children in foster care. One way to maximize limited resources for rural children and families is for smaller communities and agencies to coordinate activities, services, and resources (Leistyna, 1980; National Child Welfare Resource Center, 2003; Sudol, 2009). Through coordination and cooperation, small communities can work together to share existing resources across geographic boundaries, make limited specialized resources more available, and extend the reach of their services.

Undoubtedly, another factor that works against families, children, and rural communities is the higher-than-average rate of poverty (Belanger, 2008). Child maltreatment rates are generally higher among poor families. Poor families have fewer resources with which to support their families, which potentially increases the likelihood of some types of child maltreatment, especially neglect. For example, poor families are more likely to live in substandard housing, to have difficulty clothing and feeding their children, and less likely to provide parental supervision. For working parents with marginal income, it is unlikely that they will be able to afford either child care or babysitting during work hours. Day-care centers are more limited in rural areas, and people are more likely to work nontraditional hours, further limiting access to day care (Friedman, 2003). In some small communities, quality day care may not be available at all. Thus, working parents may have to sometimes leave children unsupervised while they try to make ends meet.

A significant issue in foster care nationwide is the disproportionately high rate of minority children who are placed there. For example, African American and Hispanic children tend to be placed in out-of-home care at higher rates than Caucasian children. Rural communities that face high poverty and do not fully accept members of minority groups face an especially high risk for foster-care placement of poor and minority children. Family and community resources also seem to be a factor in such placements, and poor families with limited resources may not be able to provide assistance to their relatives in need.

In rural communities, some characteristics and traditional values may make child welfare services more difficult to provide as well. Ginsberg (2011b) suggests that domestic violence, including child maltreatment, may be more hidden in smaller communities because of a lower concentration of housing. These conditions make it less likely that people will observe and report cases of suspected maltreatment. In addition, people might fear that a family's rights will be violated by outside organizations, and so they are deterred from reporting maltreatment (Sefcik & Ormsby, 1980). Many rural communities still believe in "sparing the rod and spoiling the child," and they interpret it literally. This is another factor that may make people reluctant to become involved in what they see as essentially a family matter. The trend in several states to centralize the reporting of child maltreatment may also reduce reporting maltreatment in rural areas, especially if community members do not trust calling a toll-free number in a distant, often urban community. Traditional values that reinforce the idea that family problems, including maltreatment, belong in the family can be quite strong, producing reluctance to make a formal report, except under extreme circumstances. Moreover, law enforcement and medical personnel may be reluctant to intervene because they know a family or expect family matters to be handled internally. Child welfare workers may face pressure to avoid intervention with some families because of who the families are and their relative power in a community. Without enough information or available services, rural agencies may end up leaving more children in potentially dangerous situations (Child Welfare Information Gateway, 2012).

Despite all these challenges, rural child welfare agencies have shown an ability to adapt to local realities and enhance their services. Rural agencies have used coordinated wraparound services to improve what they do (Child Welfare Information Gateway, 2012). Developing wraparound services and integrating child welfare with health care and other human services is one solution. Rural services have also benefited from decentralization of services at the local level, allowing delivery of education and preventative services and work with community resource centers (Child Welfare Information Gateway, 2012). Examples of this include the RURAL program in California, which provides competency-based training to workers in managing barriers to service access, in strengthening families, in improving access to faith-based and community services, and in working with state, local, and tribal governments (Denniston, 2008). Also, the HERO Project in Hale County, Alabama, works to coordinate community services and provide a forum for identifying community issues and devising solutions (National Child Welfare Resource Center, 2003). To reduce problems of distance and access, some pilot programs in rural child welfare have used virtual home visits via Skype connections (Family Center on Technology and Disability, 2010).

How to effectively deliver child welfare services to rural communities is a challenge that many small towns and rural areas face today. It is clear that at least some effort must be put into the community aspects of practice to develop ongoing collaborations and communication with local social welfare agencies. Creative solutions for outreach for services and supervision also must be devised. Child welfare agencies must also recruit, attract, and retain workers who are multiskilled and have a professional background in generalist approaches. It is also essential that workers are sensitive to the rural culture and able to learn the local culture. Given the isolation of many rural social workers, it is a plus that they have a degree of autonomy, creativity, and flexibility. There are many formidable challenges, yet many agencies and communities successfully find a way to adapt and provide high-quality services.

DOMESTIC VIOLENCE

Domestic violence is a serious social problem in the United States, yet there remains much to be learned about it. Much of what we know about domestic violence comes from case studies and anecdotal reports. Reliable figures on the extent of domestic violence are difficult to pin down, as public reporting to a central source is inconsistent. Much of what we know of the prevalence of domestic violence comes from social surveys that rely on different methodologies and definitions of the problem. Thus, figures on domestic violence vary considerably. For example, one source indicates that 22 percent of women have been assaulted by a partner at some point in their lives, and that 1.3 million women and 835,000 men are physically assaulted in the United States annually (Rural Assistance Center, 2012a). Another source estimates that between 4 million and 6 million women are affected by domestic violence each year (Turner, 2005). It is clear that more research is needed on the topic of domestic violence, especially in regard to rural areas (Rural Assistance Center, 2012a).

The extent of rural domestic violence is particularly unclear. We do know that in the rural context, there are several barriers that need to be addressed in providing domestic violence and related services to clients. Turner (2005) indicates that rural victims of domestic violence confront unique barriers to leaving an abusive situation, including geographic isolation, lack of transportation, and lack of community resources. Chiarelli-Helminiak and Bradshaw (2011) identify essentially the same barriers for rural women, and they add high rates of poverty. In writing about indigenous women in Alaska, Shepherd (2005) identified additional barriers, including few law enforcement officials, lack of transportation, severe winters, extended family networks, language barriers, ties to the land, cultural history, and even availability of weapons. What can be concluded from this is that there are a variety of contextual factors that keep rural victims of domestic violence in a relationship and may impair their motivation to seek services, as well as their ability to receive and benefit from services. Just which barriers exist depends somewhat on the individual, the community, geography, culture, and the family network.

There are domestic violence services and shelters in rural communities across the country, but shelters and domestic violence services face major challenges in terms of access. Low population densities combined with geographic isolation often result in considerable separation between people and the services they need. Given the need and geographical expanses, rural domestic violence shelters and services often end up serving multiple counties in a region. To access services, domestic violence victims need to get to service centers, which are typically located in a larger town in the region. Consequently, they often need reliable transportation to access the services. Distance, road conditions, and even weather can affect just how easy that access might be. Severe winters and storm conditions can shut down travel for a considerable time, and the combination of long distances and poor roads can make travel very difficult. For a shelter that serves a large geographic area, considerable community outreach is often necessary, especially in outlying areas, to inform people that services exist, what the services are, where they are located, and how to access them.

In some small communities people are isolated and uncertain about reaching out for help. Victims might be surrounded by family members and friends of the perpetrator. There is little confidentiality because everyone knows everyone, and there is reluctance to reveal family problems. Rural communities are often not supportive of victims, and they often deny the existence of domestic violence (Johnson, 1998). There may be few law enforcement personnel in rural areas, and response times may be exceedingly slow. Law enforcement may also tend not to take domestic violence seriously, perhaps viewing it as a family problem. Or law enforcement officials may know the perpetrator and call on the "good old boy system" to protect him.

Domestic violence tends to generate stigma and embarrassment for victims in small towns, which makes victims reluctant to reach out for help. There may also be cultural factors that keep victims from getting informal support from family and friends. The attitude "you made your bed, now lie in it" may come into play.

Realistic concerns about confidentiality and safety may arise about domestic violence services. Many shelters keep their locations confidential for security reasons to keep perpetrators from tracking victims down and harassing or hurting them. Such locations are rarely confidential in small towns, and if victims do not feel secure about being in a safe place, they are often reluctant to reach out for help. For example, in two rural communities in which I lived, locals could give most anyone directions to the shelter safe house even though its location was "confidential."

Seeking services from a rural domestic violence shelter may mean that a person would have to leave his or her home community and relocate to another, and this is where the rural value of connection to the land comes into play (Shepherd, 2005). If the person has strong roots in his or her home community and believes that services involve moving to another, that person will be less likely to seek out services. Low incomes and poverty in rural areas may also constitute a barrier to services. A victim of domestic violence with low income may have fewer resources, such as transportation, for seeking out services. The availability of options for family income if the victim leaves the perpetrator may be much more limited in a rural setting, depending on the area's economy. Language can certainly be a barrier to seeking services, as victims may have difficulty communicating their situation and needs, and/or they may be uncertain as to how outsiders view or understand their culture.

So, what kinds of services can rural social workers expect will be needed to serve domestic violence victims? Turner (2005) indicates that for many rural communities, having a shelter is ideal. But not all rural communities can support a shelter, and the need for one would have to be assessed by each community. If a shelter is needed, then community development could be used to establish it. Shelters are costly, and a needs assessment would have to be undertaken with the full understanding that even if a shelter were to exist, some rural people might be reluctant to use it. However, many rural communities could benefit from supportive services, if not a shelter, for domestic violence victims (Turner, 2005).

At a minimum, domestic violence services might include a twenty-four-hour crisis line, information, case management, coordination of community services, temporary emergency housing, services for batterers, and community education (Chiarelli-Helminiak & Bradshaw, 2011; Shepherd, 2005; Turner, 2005). Rural social workers might have to engage in advocacy with existing service agencies to address the many barriers that domestic violence victims face in receiving services. Workers might need to engage informal community resources, such as concerned individuals, civic organizations, and churches.

SERVICES FOR IMMIGRANTS

As discussed earlier, a primary area of growth in rural communities is a result of in-migration. Much has been written about services to Hispanics, especially migrants and immigrants in rural areas, although they are by no means the only group migrating to rural areas. At this point, there is little written about social welfare services programs addressing the needs of immigrants other than Hispanics, such as Asians.

Hispanics account for one of the fastest-growing populations in the United States. As of the 2010 census, they accounted for about 16 percent of the population (US Census Bureau, 2011). The past ten years have seen dramatic increases in rural areas of Hispanic residents—many of whom are undocumented immigrants—which has been a major contributor to the increased rural population. Between 2000 and 2006 alone, the Hispanic population of rural communities experienced an estimated 22 percent growth (Mather & Pollard, n.d.). Many communities that previously did not have Hispanic residents saw significant in-migration. As job opportunities opened up in construction, agriculture, services, and other sectors, Hispanics began to move past traditional southern border regions of the United States into the middle of the country.

On the basis of recent trends in Hispanic immigration and projections of future immigration, rural social workers have increasingly identified Hispanic immigrants to the United States as an underserved population and have begun to focus on providing services to meet their needs. For example, since 1990 there has been a trend toward decreasing social integration of immigrants as in rural communities that appears to correspond to the number of recent arrivals (Koball, Capps, Kandel, Henderson, & Henderson, 2008). In other words, the greater the number of immigrants to a rural community, the less likely they are to be integrated into that community. Much of this appears to be about language, as many communities who experience high immigration have few people fluent in Spanish or other languages to work with those who might not speak English well. It is also difficult for existing residents to understand or appreciate the culture of new immigrants if they cannot communicate with them well. And then there is the fact that rural communities are not noted for their tolerance of newcomers or outsiders. There is also the fear that recent trends in state laws identifying undocumented immigration as a crime and the exclusion of Hispanics from the traditional service delivery system will further disadvantage them in society.

For migrants and immigrants who do not have a legal immigration status, there is fear of detention, deportation, and possible separation from their family. In addition, they are often barred from receiving public benefits. All these things discourage the use of services and health care in small towns and rural areas. But there are examples of programs specifically designed to help reduce these kinds of barriers. For example, Dollar, Reid, and Sullivan (2009) discuss a multistage health program called Salud para la Vida (Health for Life) that was developed in rural Missouri. The program provided education to health profession students about rural and Hispanic cultures, and helped them develop medical Spanish skills and cultural competency. It also delivered culturally appropriate preventative health and clinical follow-up for low-income Hispanics. The program used a multicultural approach to bridge the language and cultural gap between new immigrants and rural residents (Dollar et al., 2009). Such an approach also provides for better outreach and follow-up services, and the program reported successful results in providing health care to this underserved group.

In another program example, Rodriguez, Cooper, and Morales (2004) outline the use of community practice to organize residents of a *colonia* in rural Texas to form an ongoing community spokesgroup to engage in advocacy for underserved community residents. The program, Hispanic Alliance for Community Enrichment (or HACER, which means "to make" or "to do" in Spanish), a voluntary coalition of churches, law enforcement, education, and social service agencies organized by a social worker, helped address issues like road maintenance, restoration of school bus service, work with stores to carry culturally relevant items, and work with city government to better address the needs of this population.

In the twenty-first century it no longer is clear, as it was once, where one might find significant groups of immigrants who may need services. The Salud para la Vida program is in an area near the middle of the country, and the HACER program is in a region of Texas that had traditionally not experienced significant Hispanic immigration. Even in rural areas of the US South, services for immigrants are being established. For example, in my county in Alabama, services are being established for both Hispanic and Southeast Asian immigrants.

Many of the newly established programs to serve immigrants and migrants are either funded through grant funds or established by churches and not-for-profit agencies. For example, in my county, rural services for Hispanic immigrants originated with the Catholic Church, Catholic Charities, and a Catholic hospital. There is also a rural health clinic that serves many people of Southeast Asian descent. Given that there still is societal bias against new immigrants, states and local communities, especially rural ones, are unlikely to offer much to help until they can no longer ignore the presence and needs of immigrant populations within their communities. This means that rural social workers will need to be alert to new minority groups entering the area and their needs. And workers may need to spend a portion of their time on community education and advocacy on behalf of immigrants. Community practice skill may need to be used to solicit grant funding, coordinate existing and develop new resources, and mobilize informal sources of support. It certainly appears that developing culturally appropriate services for new rural immigrants will be an important field for practice in the future.

CONCLUSION

Popular beliefs to the contrary, social welfare services are present in rural communities in some form, but that certainly does not mean that the available services are ideal. Rural communities frequently face a number of barriers to providing services that reach people who need or benefit from them. Small towns and rural areas tend to have significantly lower concentrations of people than one would find in a city. The result is that providing services in rural areas tends to be more costly, services are spread over a wide area, and they often are not found where clients might need them.

The common problems encountered by rural social workers, agencies, and communities typically fall into one of five categories. The first problem is access to services. The expanse of the countryside and a service area can mean that needed resources are located some distance from those who need them. Rural services tend to be found in larger towns that serve as regional centers, but people in rural areas have to find a way to get there. Travel over country roads, long distances, and weather and geographic barriers for people who have less-than-reliable transportation may mean that services are effectively unavailable. A second problem is availability of specialized services. Rural people who have special needs may not find service available locally. Children who have behavioral or mental health problems may find services locally, but perhaps not the service that best addresses their need. Getting specialized treatment can require long commutes, perhaps hundreds of miles, to get the appropriate treatment.

A third problem with rural service is funding. In today's society, where social welfare funding is a target for budget austerity, money flows more readily to communities where the most people live and where services are delivered more efficiently. With lower populations and higher costs per unit of service, rural agencies are often chronically underfunded. A fourth problem facing rural services is attracting and retaining professional staff to deliver services. Often larger communities offer more opportunities, better salaries, and a different lifestyle, which makes it difficult to build and maintain appropriate levels of professional staff. A fifth and final service barrier is the traditional value base of many rural communities, which emphasizes personal responsibility, self-reliance, and use of informal resources. These values make people reluctant to access formal services for a variety of reasons.

These challenges for rural social workers and services can be formidable. Yet social workers, agencies, and communities have adapted to serve people in need. New technology offers some promise for outreach, but there is no substitute for good community work to coordinate and build on what is available to build support for needed services. Generalists can provide direct services as well as leadership in community development. Instead of focusing on what is not in a community, successful workers and programs concentrate on the assets available, are creative in developing new approaches, and are culturally responsive to the community. More creative approaches to services are needed to face the challenges of service delivery in the twenty-first century.

REFERENCES

Advocacy Treatment Center. (n.d.). *Deinstitutionalization*. Retrieved from http://www.treatmentadvocacycenter.org/a-failed-history.

Bailey, E. (2006, December 18). Marijuana is top US cash crop, pro-legalization analyst says. *Seattle Times*.

Belanger, K. (2008). *The welfare of rural children: A summary of rural challenges*. Retrieved from http://www.cwla.org/programs/cultural competence/welfareofruralchildren.pdf.

Belanger, K., & Stone, W. (2008). The social service divide: Service availability and accessibility in rural versus urban counties and impact on child welfare outcomes. *Child Welfare, 87*(4), 101–124.

Brown, J. C. (1933). *The rural community and social casework*. New York, NY: Family Welfare Association of America.

Casey, M. M., Blewett, L. A., & Call, K. T. (2004). Providing health care to Latino immigrants: Community-based efforts in the rural Midwest. *American Journal of Public Health, 94*(10), 1709–1711.

Cashwell, S., & Starks, S. (2011). Rural health care: Access, disparities, and opportunities. In L. Ginsberg (Ed.), *Social work in rural communities* (5th ed., pp. 347–366). Alexandria, VA: Council on Social Work Education.

Cavender, A. (2003). *Folk medicines in southern Appalachia*. Chapel Hill, NC: University of North Carolina Press.

Chiarelli-Helminiak, C. M., & Bradshaw, J. M. (2011). Victims of interpersonal abuse in rural communities. In L. Ginsberg (Ed.), *Social work in rural communities* (5th ed., pp. 327–346). Alexandria, VA: Council on Social Work Education.

Children's Bureau. (2011). *Child maltreatment 2011*. Retrieved from http://www.acf.hhs.gov/sites/default/files/cb/cm11.pdf#page=28.

Child Welfare Information Gateway. (2012). *Rural child welfare practice*. Retrieved from https://www.childwelfare.gov/pubs/issue_briefs/rural.pdf#Page=3&view=Fit.

Conway, P., BigFoot, D. S., & Sandler, E. P. (2011). Resiliency and behavioral health challenges among American Indians and Alaska natives in rural communities. In L. Ginsberg (Ed.), *Social work in rural communities* (5th ed., pp. 249–269). Alexandria, VA: Council on Social Work Education.

Denniston, J. (2008). *RURAL project*. Retrieved from http://library.childwelfare.gov/cwig/ws/library/docs/gateway/Record?rpp=10&upp=0&m=1&w= +NATIVE%28%27recno%3D61472%27%29&r=1.

Dollar, S., Reid, H., & Sullivan, L. (2009). Better health through the Salud para la Vida project. *Contemporary Rural Social Work*, 1. Retrieved from http://journal.und.edu/crsw/article/view/372.

Family Center on Technology and Disability. (2010). *A new approach to early intervention: Virtual home visits*, *104*, 1–22. Retrieved from http://www.fctd.info/assets/newsletters/pdfs/275/FCTD-News-Feb2010.pdf.

Friedman, P. (2003). Meeting the challenges of social service delivery in rural areas. *Welfare Information Network*, *7*(2). Retrieved from http://www.financeproject.org/Publications/meetingthechallengeIN.htm.

Furstenberg, A., & Gammonley, D. (1999). Building support for rural elderly people with mental illness: The Carolina companions project. In I. B. Carlton-LaNey, R. L. Edwards, & P. N. Reid (Eds.), *Preserving and strengthening small towns and rural communities* (pp. 196–208). Washington, DC: NASW Press.

Ginsberg, L. H. (1976). *Social work in rural communities: A book of readings*. New York, NY: Council on Social Work Education.

Ginsberg, L. H. (Ed.) (2011a). *Social work in rural communities* (5th ed.). Alexandria, VA: Council on Social Work Education.

Ginsberg, L. H. (2011b). Introduction to basics of rural social work. In L. Ginsberg (Ed.), *Social work in rural communities* (5th ed., pp. 5–20). Alexandria, VA: Council on Social Work Education.

Johnson, H. W. (1998). Rural crime, delinquency, substance abuse and corrections. In L. H. Ginsberg (Ed.), *Social work in rural communities* (3rd ed., pp. 249–264). Alexandria, VA: Council on Social Work Education.

Koball, H., Capps, R., Kandel, W., Henderson, J., & Henderson, E. (2008). *Social and economic integration of Latino immigrants in new rural destinations*. Retrieved from http://www.mathematica-mpr.com/publications/PDFs/LatinoImmigrants_isbr2.pdf.

Leistyna, J. A. (1980). Advocacy for the abused child. In H. W. Johnson (Ed.), *Rural human services: A book of readings* (pp. 92–96). Itasca, IL: Peacock.

Locke, B. L., & Winship, J. (2005). Social work in rural America. In N. Lohmann & R. A. Lohmann (Eds.), *Rural social work practice* (pp.3–24). New York, NY: Columbia University Press.

Mather, M., & Pollard, K. (n.d.). *Hispanic gains minimize population loss in rural and small-town America*. Washington, DC: Population Reference Bureau. Retrieved from http://www.prb.org/Articles/2007/HispanicGains.aspx.

Meyer, P. S., & Morrissey, J. P. (2007). A comparison of assertive community treatment and intensive case management for patients in rural areas. *Psychiatric Services*, *58*(1), 212–217.

National Association of Social Workers. (2012). Rural social work. In *Social work speaks: National Association of Social Workers policy statements* (9th ed., pp. 296–300). Washington, DC: NASW Press.

National Child Welfare Resource Center for Organizational Improvement. (2003). Interagency collaboration in rural areas. *Managing Care for Children and* Families, *4*(2). Retrieved from http://muskie.usm.maine.edu/helpkids/rcpdfs/MCIV2.pdf.

National Rural Health Association. (1999). *The scope of mental health issues in rural America.* Retrieved from http://www.globalaging.org/ruralaging/us/mentalhinra.htm.

Office of Rural Health Policy, US Department of Health Resources and Services Administration. (2011). *Rural behavioral health programs and promising practices*. Retrieved from http://www.hrsa.gov/ruralhealth/pdf/ruralbehavioralmanual05312011.pdf.

Randall, E., & Vance, D. (2005). Services for the chronically mentally ill in rural areas. In N. Lohmann & R. A. Lohmann (Eds.), *Rural social work practice* (pp. 171–186). New York, NY: Columbia University Press.

Rodriguez, R., Cooper, H. S., & Morales, L. (2004). Working with Mexican immigrants in rural East Texas. In T. L. Scales & C. L. Streeter (Eds.), *Rural social work: Building and sustaining community assets* (pp. 34–42). Belmont, CA: Brooks-Cole/Thomson.

Rural Assistance Center. (2012a). *Domestic violence frequently asked questions.* Retrieved from http://www.raconline.org/topics/public_health/dvfaq.php#ruraldv.

Rural Assistance Center. (2012b). *Substance abuse.* Retrieved from http://www.raconline.org/topics/substanceabuse/.

Scales, L. T., & Streeter, C. L. (2004). *Rural social work: Building and sustaining community assets.* Belmont, CA: Brooks-Cole/Thomson.

Scales, L. T., Streeter, C. L., & Cooper, H. S. (Eds.). (2014). *Rural social work: Building and sustaining community capacity.* Hoboken, NJ: Wiley.

Scheyett, A., & Fuhrman, T. (1999). Managed behavioral health care in a rural environment: Carolina alternatives. In I. B. Carlton-LaNey, R. L. Edwards, & P. N. Reid (Eds.), *Preserving and strengthening small towns and rural communities* (pp. 119–133). Washington, DC: NASW Press.

Sefcik, T. R., & Ormsby, N. J. (1980). Establishing a rural child abuse treatment program. In H. W. Johnson (Ed.), *Rural human services: A book of readings* (pp. 97–104). Itasca, IL: Peacock.

Shepherd, J. (2005). Where do you go when it's 40 below? Domestic violence among rural Alaskan Native women. In L. Ginsberg (Ed.), *Social work in rural communities* (4th ed., pp. 283–300). Alexandria, VA: Council on Social Work Education.

Smith, S. N., Glasser, M., & Korr, W. S. (2011). Rural oncology social work: Culture, context, and care in the rural setting. In L. Ginsberg (Ed.), *Social work in rural communities* (5th ed., pp. 385–398). Alexandria, VA: Council on Social Work Education.

Stone, G., & Frederick, B. (2011). Assessing clinical social work practice in rural mental health settings. In L. Ginsberg (Ed.), *Social work in rural communities* (5th ed., pp. 367–384). Alexandria, VA: Council on Social Work Education.

Substance Abuse and Mental Health Services Administration. (2007). *Rural substance abuse: Overcoming barriers to treatment*. Retrieved from http://www.samhsa.gov/SAMHSA_News/VolumeXV_4/article 1.htm.

Substance Abuse and Mental Health Services Administration. (2012). *Rural substance abuse treatment admissions significantly more likely than urban counterparts to be referred by criminal justice system*. Retrieved from http://www.samhsa.gov/newsroom/advisories/1208 145516.aspx.

Sudol, T. (2009). *Information packet: Rural issues in child welfare*. New York, NY: National Center for Family-Centered Practice and Permanency Planning. Retrieved from http://www.hunter.cuny.edu/soc work/nrcfcpp/info_services/Sudol_nfo%20Pack_Rural%20Issues _Aug%202009.pdf.

Turner, W. (2005). Identifying the needs of battered women in a rural community. In L. H. Ginsberg (Ed.), *Social work in rural communities* (4th ed., pp. 223–234). Alexandria, VA: Council on Social Work Education.

US Census Bureau. (2011). *The Hispanic population 2010*. Retrieved from http://www.census.gov/prod/cen2010/briefs/c2010br-04.pdf.

Walsh, W. A., & Mattingly, M. J. (2010). *Rural families with a child abuse report are more likely headed by a single parent and endure economic and family stress* (Issue Brief No. 10, Carsey Family Institute, Durham, NH). Retrieved from http://carseyinstitute.unh.edu/ publications/FS-Mattingly-Childabuse.pdf.

Whitaker, T. R. (2012). Professional social workers in the child welfare workforce: Findings from NASW. *Journal of Family Strengths*, *12*(1), 1–14. Retrieved from http://digitalcommons.library.tmc.edu/jfs/vol 12/iss1/8/.

White House Rural Council. (2011). *Rural veterans and the tyranny of distance*. Retrieved from http://www.whitehouse.gov/blog/2011/08 /03/rural-veterans-and-tyranny-distance.

Zlotnik, J. L. (2003). The use of title IV-E training funds for social work education: A historical perspective. *Journal of Human Behavior in the Social Environment*, *7*(1–2), 5–20.

Rural communities have come together in central spots for social interaction and to help others informally for a long time. Photo from Colorado in the 1890s.

CHAPTER SIX

History and Development of Rural Social Work

AH, THE RURAL LIFE. In so many ways life in the country has often been described in pleasant and idyllic terms and the tranquility, beauty, and healing qualities of the countryside have been celebrated. Urban dwellers long for the weekend escape or the summer trip that takes them away from noise, crowds, and congestion and into the simplicity of nature and a style of life that doesn't include rush hours, crowded schedules, waiting in line, and a quest for the newest and most desired consumer items. Yes, in many ways our images of rural life are ideal. The subject of this chapter is how we arrived at this point of the ideal view and how rural social work came to exist, how an interest in rural social work eventually developed, and how both ideal and pragmatic views influence rural social workers and the services they deliver.

We have idealized country life so much that we have even mythologized it. Country life is uncomplicated, basic, a return to our roots, and free from the grime and vice of the city. But those myths have usually ignored the brutal realities that can come with rural life. The ideal image of rural existence fails to reflect the unreliability of crops and employment, the low pay, the hard and dangerous work, and the long days in the blazing sun or winter's snow to, for example, complete a harvest or cut lumber. The virtues of rural life and people have been part of folklore in the United States for almost two hundred years, and those virtues are sometimes only loosely grounded in reality.

Yet we still cling stubbornly to our ideals and myths. We like the beauty of the country, we yearn for the country lifestyle—but we often overlook the real needs of rural people. The stereotypes about rural life keep us from seeing what we need to see. Rural life can be hard, and rural people struggle to make ends meet. Crime, violence, and poverty exist in the city—the media reminds us of this frequently. But we do not see or believe such things exist in the country as we speed past to our destination. And crime cannot exist in places where people still don't lock their doors, can it?

The media allows country folks to see and aspire to the same "good" life as that of the city dweller, but they may be denied the opportunity to participate in the same ways because of limited income or because those attractive goods and services have not reached their area yet—and they might not ever if it isn't profitable.

Despite the myths, we have long known that rural areas have higher-than-average poverty rates, and rural populations tend to be more advanced in age than urban populations. We also know that fewer social welfare services exist for rural people and that, over time, services have shifted with the population from rural to urban communities (Stuart, 2004). The confluence of these forces puts rural people at a disadvantage in receiving help from social welfare services, often when help is really needed. Still, rural people are often "out of sight, out of mind" for policy makers in states with increasingly urban populations. Thus, the ideals of the pastoral, beautiful country persist, getting in the way of helping rural people.

Even a casual review of US social welfare history tells a familiar story of the rise of professional social work. With the growth of large-scale industrialization, living and working conditions in rapidly growing cities became so appalling that social reformers began to address the needs of the poor in the late nineteenth and early twentieth centuries. Charity organization societies and later settlement houses arose in major cities as significant social and philanthropic reforms to deal with the needs of the indigent. It is from the charity organization societies and settlement houses that we can trace the origins of modern social work.

But what was social welfare like in rural America during this period? Most texts tell us very little. Even in the early decades of the twentieth century, vast sections of the country did not have cities of significant size, and most of the population was rural. The South, the West, and much of the Midwest were almost entirely rural. How did these areas address social welfare for their needy people? How did social work, which was primarily an urban-based endeavor, come to the countryside? The answers to these questions still have relevance for modern social workers and the shaping of rural practice.

ORIGINS OF THE RURAL MYTH

Prevailing beliefs about the country and the people who live there have had a profound influence on social policy in rural communities. Yet the popular view of rural life has at times been more myth than reality (Chambers, 1980). The pace of rural change might be a bit slower than in the city, but change continues even today. To better understand rural social work, an understanding of how it developed and grew is helpful.

In the eighteenth and nineteenth centuries, land was a source of opportunity, status, wealth, and political power. Most residents of European descent in North America settled near the coast and rivers that flowed into the ocean. But most desirable land in settled areas of the country was already spoken for, and if people of limited means wanted land, they had to go west (Guinn, 2011). Also, settlers of European descent had little respect for Native Americans and their culture, religion, and lifestyle, and many settlers had no qualms about claiming title to Native American–held land or seizing land that Native Americans had not developed (Donovan, 2008). The settlers often had few reservations about killing people they considered "savages" (Donovan, 2008).

The primary occupation for most people going west was exploiting the land. In the eighteenth and nineteenth centuries, farmers were the most common settlers of new lands, but there were also those who trapped, hunted, traded, mined, and cut lumber. All of these occupations were labor intensive and required hard work to be productive. Land had to be cleared, prepared, and planted, and crops harvested. Hunting and trapping were equally demanding and potentially dangerous. The early pioneers needed to cooperate, and the failure of one often meant the failure of others (Guinn, 2011).

But there was typically much more available land than labor. Some of the movement in the nineteenth century was into the South, as new lands became available. For those who could afford it buying slaves or getting indentures helped to secure a steady supply of help. Indeed, much of the agricultural wealth generated was based on slave and indentured labor. Cash crops like cotton, tobacco, and sugarcane usually required so much labor that people justified slavery to keep their businesses and farms afloat. This was big business, and by the start of the Civil War there were some four million slaves in the United States (Gallagher, 2011). Many family farmers in the South could not afford to purchase slaves and depended on family and neighbors to provide extra help in building houses and barns, and for the harvest. It was common for extended families to live near one another and help out when needed.

In the nineteenth century, beyond families, rural communities were small, and of necessity they became close knit. People knew their neighbors and often had to rely on them for help from time to time. Each person had to contribute to the community good (Guinn, 2011), through his or her profession or in other ways. Travel and communication were slow, and people often relied on informal networks to get the most current news and information.

Moving beyond the boundaries of settled areas offered people a lot of freedom, and perhaps excitement and danger. Frontier life was hard and often brutally short. And frontier dwellers were often viewed as an odd collection of uncouth social misfits—alcoholics, social isolates, criminals, fugitives, debtors, escapees from social stigma, and the mentally ill. It was easy to hide and assume a new identity out west, as a song popular at the time, "What Was Your Name in the States?" indicated (Guinn, 2011). Everyone realized that many went to the frontier because they had failed in "more civilized" society, and many of those in society were glad to be rid of them.

It was not until the early 1830s that public interest turned to the frontier and the exploits of those who lived there. Andrew Jackson's presidency led the way for a popular movement to extol the virtue of the common man and westerners. The lionization of the common man and the westerner developed as lands were opened to settlement through the forcible removal of Native Americans, with the Indian Removal Bill. Popular media began to fictionalize folk heroes in western terms, claiming incredible exploits—the bigger the better (Guinn, 2011). Writers like James Fenimore Cooper (Guinn, 2011) and characters like Jeremiah Kentucky and Nimrod Wildfire emerged to exemplify the western folk hero (Davis, 1998). They were soon supplanted by Davy Crockett, who quickly became a folk hero. This began a tradition of the self-reliant, fair-minded, independent rural hero who could accomplish almost anything and tame the land (Davis, 1998).

Land speculators anxious to make money by attracting new settlers were quick to exploit clever advertising to make rural life appealing. Claims of beautiful scenery, fertile land, good water, cheap prices, and growing communities appealed to those who wanted a better life. Often the stories were much more pleasant than the reality. And this land had to be taken, usually forcibly from the Native Americans who lived there. Battles were sometimes fictionalized and heroes made of those who defeated the Native Americans. Usually, the Native Americans who remained were displaced to poorer lands farther west with little, if any, compensation.

Out of the folk hero and idealized and fictitious portrayals of country life, a rural image began to emerge. Stories that sold books and land were good business and drew settlers westward.

INDUSTRIALIZATION AND THE RISE OF SOCIAL WORK

Industrialization began in the United States in the early nineteenth century, but it was the Civil War in the 1860s that greatly accelerated industrial capacity. The demand for war material was insatiable in the North, as uniforms, weapons, shoes, and food had to be produced in great quantities. New and bigger businesses and industries grew overnight. Capital was available for expansion and production, but cheap labor to make factories run was difficult to find, especially with so large a portion of the labor force in the military. The war spurred industrialization in the South as well, but by the war's end most of that industry would lie in ruins.

Immigration from Europe provided a source of labor that was both cheap and replaceable. Poorly paid immigrants packed into tenements in neighborhoods near factories. There was little planning to handle this growth and living conditions became overcrowded, ridden with disease and crime, foul smelling, and vile. Work was often dangerous, and all members of a family would sometimes have to work just to live. One observer in the mid-nineteenth century described the poor areas of the city in this way:

> The filth of the streets is composed of house-slops, refuse vegetables, decayed fruit, store and shop sweepings, ashes, dead animals, and even human excrements. The putrifying organic substances are ground together by the constant passing of vehicles. When dried by the summer's heat, they are driven by the wind in every direction in the form of dust. (Schecter, 2005, p. 109)

Given these conditions, small wonder that urban residents believed that the country provided a healthier, more beneficial environment.

Many immigrants were moving west if they could, often to escape the wretched living conditions in the cities. Many were from rural roots in their home countries and were returning to the work they knew. All they needed was enough money and resources to buy land and move westward. Once they arrived in the country, though, families still regularly fell into need. There were crop failures, human disease and epidemics, hostile neighbors, and natural disasters. When families fell into need, generally the extended family, community, or church was the source of temporary relief.

An early effort at rural social welfare was the creation of the Freedmen's Bureau, which existed from 1865 to 1872. This US federal agency was established in the aftermath of the Civil War to provide for the needs of African American former slaves. Many former slaves lived primarily in the rural South and were left without a means of livelihood in the aftermath of the war, given the devastation of the Southern economy. The Freedmen's Bureau led a major relief effort aiming to bring the freedmen (and women) to full citizenship. The bureau distributed food and clothing, operated hospitals, helped locate family members, promoted education, helped legalize marriages, provided employment and legal representation, investigated racial confrontations, settled freedmen on abandoned or confiscated lands, and worked with African American soldiers and sailors and their heirs to secure back pay, bounty payments, and pensions (National Archives, n.d.).

In the cities social reformers in the mid-nineteenth century developed private agencies to do charity work with the poor. Private groups developed charity organization societies in the 1870s to help those considered most deserving. In the 1880s settlement houses were organized to provide services and create social and economic change in society. Essentially, these were urban efforts, with scant thought given to the rural areas, which were still seen as pristine and unspoiled by modern development.

COUNTRY LIFERS AND THE EARLY CONCERNS ABOUT RURAL COMMUNITIES, 1900–1920

A series of events occurred in the late nineteenth century to dispel some of the myths about rural areas, bringing the needs of rural people into the spotlight and generating an interest in rural social work. One of these events was the closing of the frontier. In 1890 the US government declared that there was no more frontier left to settle and that the frontier was effectively closed, indicating that the era of cheap available government land was over (Guinn, 2011). The days of buying cheap new land and moving west were effectively over. An economic depression hit hard in 1893, one of the worst in US history (Whitten, 2010) (it was known as the Great Depression until the Depression of the 1930s hit). Farming was particularly hard hit, as many farms, especially in the central part of the country, were heavily mortgaged. Lower prices for crops meant that many farms could no longer remain solvent, and many rural people lost their land or struggled to make ends meet. With no systematic social welfare assistance there was widespread hardship, and many rural families were forced to move to cities.

Social reformers in the early twentieth century began to notice the needs of people in the countryside. Farming, the mainstay of rural life, was on the decline; by 1890 agriculture accounted for only 40 percent of the economy. Although more than half of the US population still lived in rural areas, there were clear indications that rural people would be in the minority within a few years. In the early twentieth century, it appeared to many people that modernization was a distinctly urban phenomenon. The telephone had revolutionized communication, and electricity had replaced kerosene and gas lamps. Transportation had improved, with more railroad mileage and access to automobiles. There were improvements in running water, sanitation, and education. But for most rural communities, many of these modern conveniences had not yet come their way.

In the early twentieth century the country life movement arose, in response to a concern about the needs of rural communities (Martinez-Brawley, 1980a). The country life movement was essentially a social movement concerned with improving the quality of rural life, and the origins of rural social work are often traced to early "country lifers" (Swanson, 1980). The country lifers raised concerns about the conditions of rural life, suggesting that quality of life in the cities was drawing away the best, brightest, and most talented young people from rural communities, thus depriving rural areas of youth, talent, and to some degree their future. National attention was centered on the cities, thus disadvantaging the countryside, at a time when rural areas needed help. The idea was to bring scientific methods into agriculture to promote the rural economy, and to engage in rural community development through existing organizations in order to strengthen country life.

As a result of these efforts, President Theodore Roosevelt created the Country Life Commission, raising rural issues to the national level. The commission's report in 1909 recommended agricultural extension services, stronger agricultural economics, better highways, and improved rural education and health care. Existing rural churches, schools, civic groups, and community services were to be used as vehicles to improve life in small towns and the country (Swanson, 1980). The country life movement created a focus on rural issues through community improvement, which eventually helped spur the growth of rural social work.

Interest in rural issues, especially rural social welfare issues, increased dramatically from the 1900s to the 1930s, as indicated in table 1.

Increased interest in the welfare of rural people and communities in the early twentieth century also saw development of organizations and services that led to the growth of rural social work. For example, rural

TABLE 1
References to the Word *Rural* in Social Work Literature, 1874–1930

Period	*References in text*	*References in title*
1874–1890	78	0
1891–1900	75	1
1901–1910	169	4
1911–1920	1,653	58
1921–1930	1,843	49

Source: Proceedings of the National Conference on Social Work
Note: The proceedings of the National Conference on Charities and Corrections (renamed the National Conference on Social Work in 1917), a major social welfare forum for the time, were searched for the term *rural* for the years 1874 through 1930.

settlements were early efforts to expand traditional social welfare services to small towns and rural areas. Social settlements were efforts at social reform begun in urban areas; they provided a variety of local, site-based social welfare services in impoverished areas (Galen & Alexander, 2011). The Hindman Settlement, founded in 1902, and the Pine Mountain settlement schools, established in Kentucky in 1913, are examples of early rural settlement activity (Galen & Alexander, 2011). While rural settlements strove to adapt settlement-house concepts to the rural community, the settlements were not considered a mainstream part of the movement because they were rural. Yet rural and urban settlements often focused on similar issues, such as recreational opportunities, exploitation of child labor, provision of health services, and school attendance. Rural settlements received little attention in the social welfare literature of the period, and today rural settlements are uncommon, and the past contributions of such settlements remain largely ignored even today (Galen & Alexander, 2011).

Local branches of the YMCA and YWCA, initially established in urban areas, were also developed for rural areas. Rural Ys attempted to build good character and Christian values among the people they served, and they strove to improve the lives of wageworkers, such as miners, railroad workers, and loggers, as well as farm families. Yet the YMCA and the YWCA remained essentially urban movements (Winter, 2002), and the organizations never truly embraced rural services. But rural Ys still were local organizations that helped provide services and leaders for rural social work.

THE GROWTH OF RURAL SOCIAL WORK PRACTICE AND THE GREAT DEPRESSION, 1920S AND 1930S

Rural social work appears to have developed from the efforts of the American Red Cross during and after World War I, and from services being regionalized at the county level in rural areas. During World War I the Red Cross's Home Service workers became involved in providing assistance to families of armed service members. The federally funded War Risk Insurance program was designed to ensure that families of service members were provided with economic support and benefits, especially in the case of disability or death. Then, as now, many service members who enlisted were from rural areas, and their enlistment in the military deprived their family of a major source of income. This support from War Risk Insurance helped ensure more enlistments and less resistance to conscription. War Risk Insurance was an important social welfare program for families. The phrase "bought the farm," to mean that someone died, might date to this period, referring to how insurance could help a family pay off the mortgage (Urban Dictionary, n.d.).

The Home Service of the Red Cross provided assistance to many rural families who were not sure how to apply for War Risk Insurance benefits or resolve issues that arose with insurance (King, 1980; Persons, 1980). The Red Cross programs provided valuable experience for a number of social workers who would later go on to leadership positions in rural social work and in the profession (Locke & Winship, 2005). Red Cross workers established local chapters in rural areas, acted as case managers, coordinated with local agencies, and organized the work of volunteers helping families of servicemen. The Red Cross continued the Home Service in rural areas after the war, often working to help veterans reintegrate, using a regional service model. Reintegration was an important concern, as before the war, many service members had never left the county of their birth. As a popular song of the time aptly put it, "How ya gonna keep 'em down on the farm (after they've seen Paree)?" Assistance was also provided to soldiers who were disabled in service-poor rural areas. Red Cross services continued into the 1920s and helped serve as a nucleus for rural social work development.

The 1920s also saw serious efforts to provide social welfare services on a regionalized level for rural communities (Martinez-Brawley, 1980b, 105). Social workers began to use systematic survey data of social conditions to influence county and state governments to address social conditions that had been ignored in rural communities. The growing concern about services for rural communities may have been influenced by volatile economic conditions, such as the depression of 1920–21. Declines in agricultural prices hit rural communities and farmers hard, resulting in a need for services (and again when this occurred just before the Great Depression in the 1930s). Interest also emerged in developing standardized models for rural services in areas like child welfare and juvenile justice. For example, county welfare boards were established in North Carolina and there was a push for public child welfare services in Oklahoma (Martinez-Brawley, 1980b).

In the 1920s, early rural social workers were interested in defining principles for the application of social casework in rural communities. Only ten years after Mary Richmond (1917) had written her landmark text, *Social Diagnosis*, Matthews (1927/1980), writing in *Social Forces*, suggested that rural social workers use Richmond's work and that of the existing professional journals *Family* and *Survey* as guides to adapting to the conditions of rural practice. Leading educator E. C. Lindeman (1924) added:

> First, social work is for the present indigenous to the city; its rural applications are in reality extensions from urban to rural groups. But a process of social adjustment cannot proceed by external means. If the technique of social adjustment is to become a part of rural culture, that technique must evolve from within and not from without. (p. 39)

Richmond's (1917) work, the best professional model at the time, could be adapted well, as it highlighted the importance of a balanced approach centering on the person in the environment.

Rural social workers of the 1920s used volunteers to extend their efforts and worked with existing local organizations. Many programs offered by local organizations provided character-building programs and were implemented by service organizations and clubs. Young adults and children were their primary clients. Major agents of the rural service network included churches, the YMCA and YWCA, 4-H clubs, and other agricultural clubs (Drew, 1922; Johnston, 1980; Martinez-Brawley, 1980b; Middleton, 1919). All of these focused on building and strengthening ideas of moral behavior, self-governance, leadership, and democracy.

Rural communities did not fare well economically in the 1920s (Martinez-Brawley, 1980b), as the prosperity of the Roaring Twenties was primarily an urban phenomenon. Farm prices remained low, and at times the value of crops fell below the price of production. Farm foreclosures became common. Some farmers were able to get by growing most of what they needed to eat, but they were still extremely cash poor. Mining and timber were also hit by depressed prices, and resultant unemployment.

The stock market crash of 1929 provided a harsh transition to the 1930s. Unemployment rose in all areas, as demand and prices fell for farm, mining, and timber products. Many farms were repossessed when farmers were unable to make mortgage payments. A serious crop-destroying drought also began in 1930 in the US Great Plains and the plains of Canada. The parched soil calcified and was driven by winds into great dust storms, known as the Dust Bowl, and with the topsoil gone, there was little hope of farming the land (Egan, 2006). As a result, many rural people were set adrift to look for work in an economy in which unemployment rose as high as 25 percent overall, and was significantly higher in some areas. As they moved to cities or other rural areas, these unwelcome migrants experienced a great deal of prejudice. They were called Okies, an extremely derogatory term for migrant farm workers assumed to be from Oklahoma, and worse. And rural communities suffered from their poor economy and loss of population.

During the early 1930s, more than fifty articles on rural topics were published in social work magazines and journals (Davenport & Davenport, 1984). However, it was Josephine Brown's groundbreaking book in 1933, *The Rural Community and Social Casework*, the first comprehensive approach to social work with rural communities, that firmly established the foundation of rural social work practice (see Locke & Winship,

2005). Brown's book established many concepts and practice principles that still guide rural work today (Davenport & Davenport, 1984), including a generalist method (social casework combined with community organization), the use of clients' strengths, and the need to develop existing community resources.

The 1930s were a period of governmental focus on regulating agriculture and providing relief efforts in rural areas (Martinez-Brawley, 1980b). The federal government also tried to improve the quality of rural life by bringing electricity to the countryside through low-cost financing to electrical co-ops (Brown, 1980). With the onset of the Great Depression, though, efforts to help rural people and communities shifted from a local to a state system of administering federal and state funds for community development, and much of this came though the Federal Emergency Relief Administration (Atkinson, 1980). There was also much discussion in social work of developing rural services targeting problems like child welfare and public health (Abbott, 1980; Sanderson, 1980). Implementation of the Social Security Act and other federal relief efforts changed the shape of rural social welfare in rural communities during the 1930s. Services were increasingly publicly funded, and the shift from private to public funding increased the numbers of workers and the services available (Twente, 1980). As rural social work expanded, social workers faced the challenge of working with people and problems that had not been attended to in earlier years.

RETREAT FROM RURAL ASSISTANCE: THE 1940S AND 1950S

During the 1940s and 1950s interest in rural social work and social welfare dwindled considerably (National Rural Social Work Caucus, n.d.), as concerns about the Great Depression subsided and the country entered World War II (Locke & Winship, 2005). Martinez-Brawley (1981) noted that by the end of the 1940s, interest in rural social work had waned to the point that few references to it could be found in the professional literature. The proceedings from 1940 to 1960 of the National Conference on Social Welfare bear this out. In 1940 there was a rural social welfare section in the conference, with two sessions and 244 listings in the index to rural work. By 1943 the emphasis had shifted to single presentations on specific rural services, and the number of uses of the term *rural* in the index had dropped to 110; by 1945 presentations with a rural focus had ceased and references dropped to 20. Rural presentations did not reappear at the conference until 1970.

Undoubtedly, World War II and the Korean War took precedence as public attention was focused on efforts to support the wars. Increased urbanization following World War II and the growth of manufacturing also focused the nation's attention on managing these new issues. Social work and the needs of rural communities took on decidedly fewer resources and professional literature about rural social welfare and social work almost disappeared.

THE RENAISSANCE OF RURAL SOCIAL WORK: THE 1960S AND 1970S

For most of the 1960s, interest in rural social work languished as the profession continued its urban orientation to practice. By the end of the decade, rural social work seemed almost forgotten, as little had been written about it for decades. Apathy for rural social work was such that Buxton (1976) wrote "Social work in rural areas has been given little attention in past years. The national emphasis has been on urban problem, and skills have been developed essentially to deal with these" (p. 29).

As the percentage of the country's population that lived in cities continued to grow, an emphasis on urban work seemed justified. Social workers were still doing rural work, but it appeared to most people that the real growth and pressing need was for urban work, particularly with the urban poor. The needs of the rural poor seemed to be forgotten. National initiatives based on things such as the rediscovery of urban poverty and subsequent War on Poverty also tended to shift the profession's focus away from rural practice (Locke, 2009). As social work schools educated the next waves of professionals, urban models of social work, not rural ones, were the core of practice.

A revival of rural social work began in the late 1960s and continued through the 1970s (Davenport & Davenport, 1984). Several factors contributed to this revival, including increased federal recognition that the size of the rural population was increasing in number, despite the declining percentage of the population that was rural. Appropriately responding to this wave of national interest, rural social work was viewed with renewed interest by the social work profession and education.

The renaissance in the 1970s of modern rural social work is attributed to a workshop presented at the 1969 annual program meeting of the Council on Social Work Education (CSWE, 1969) in Cleveland, Ohio (Ginsberg, 2011a; Locke, 2009; National Rural Social Work Caucus, n.d.). This presentation, "Education for Social Work in Rural Settings," was described as an "Examination of education for practice in small, economically viable communities as well as socio-economically depressed areas in order to identify the implications for social work education" (CSWE, 1969, p. 17). The meeting and presentation stimulated renewed interest in rural social work and later led to meetings of social work educators and the National Association of Social Workers (NASW) around rural issues and rural practice (Ginsberg, 1993a, 1993b, 2011a). As awareness of rural social work grew, a task force of the Southern Regional Education Board (1976) published a set of educational assumptions for rural social work, specifying the content needed for effective practice.

Two subsequent events in 1976 led to the continued development of rural social work as it exists today. One of these was the creation of the National Rural Social Work Caucus, formed in 1976 at an institute for social work practitioners and educators hosted by the University of Tennessee (Ginsberg, 2011a; Hickman, 2014; Locke, 2009). The caucus was, and continues to be, a loosely organized group of professionals from across the United States and other countries who focus on rural social work and human services. The caucus discusses current issues, ideas, and innovations at its annual institutes. Today the National Rural Social Work Caucus remains the principal specialty group for rural social work, and through its institutes much literature on rural social work has been developed.

The second key event of 1976 was the publication of Ginsberg's *Social Work in Rural Communities: A Book of Readings*. This collection of readings about rural social work was the first book-length publication in the field in many years, and it presented much of the then-current thinking on practice and education. Before this book, information on rural social work had been scattered, hard to find, and sometimes dated. *Social Work in Rural Communities* was influential in developing and maintaining an interest in rural work and education. Though long out of print, the book has been republished several times in new editions, often with new readings (see Ginsberg, 2011b).

Ongoing activities of the National Rural Social Work Caucus also have generated a professional rural social work journal (Hickman, 2014; Locke, 2009). *Human Service in the Rural Environment* initially began as a newsletter in the late 1970s; then it grew to be a professional journal in the 1980s and was published into the early 1990s when the institution that hosted publication withdrew support. The journal published practice and scholarly articles, research, and photo essays on rural social welfare, and it was an important resource for rural social welfare. The caucus also has engaged in advocacy efforts to have presentations about rural social work in the CSWE annual meeting program and a rural policy statement approved by the NASW (National Rural Social Work Caucus, n.d.). The CSWE did begin to include rural sessions in its program, and in 1977 the NASW Delegate Assembly adopted a policy statement on rural social work (Davenport & Davenport, 1984) that is an informational piece for social work and encourages advocacy on policy issues affecting rural people and communities.

CONTINUED GROWTH: THE 1980S AND 1990S

The revitalization of rural practice that began in the 1970s continued and grew in the 1980s and 1990s. Several new books and articles in professional journals provided rich new sources of information for rural social workers (Ginsberg, 1993b). An edited book of readings by Johnson (1980) presented information about rural social work history, practice, education, and specific problems and services. Farley, Griffiths, Skidmore, and Thackeray (1982) authored a book on rural social work practice, the first comprehensive coverage of the topic in almost fifty years. Martinez-Brawley (1980a, 1981) published two books on the history of rural social work and its origins. These works continued a theme from early years, suggesting that rural social work was primarily work in small towns and rural areas. The rural journal *Human Services in the Rural Environment* continued to publish articles about rural practice in a journal format. With this expansion of literature, the contemporary body of information about rural issues and topics expanded considerably.

The National Rural Social Work Caucus has remained a relatively informal association of social workers and educators, with a grassroots organization. They remained active in the promotion of rural social work and rural policy. Each year, the caucus continued to hold its National Institute on Social Work and Human Services in the Rural Environment at different sites around the country to highlight the diversity of rural life. Many of the ideas presented at this institute found their way into print through either conference proceedings or articles in *Human Services in the Rural Environment.*

Professional interest in rural social work continued to be strong throughout the 1990s. The National Rural Social Work Caucus organized efforts to respond to proposed changes in the NASW Code of Ethics in the early 1990s. Members of the caucus argued that proposed language prohibiting dual (or multiple) relationships between a social worker and a client would prove difficult for many rural workers to follow (Miller, 1998). Through extensive discussions and organized effort, the caucus was able to influence a change in that section's language in the 1996 Code of Ethics to a broader wording that could also apply to rural social workers, permitting but not encouraging dual relationships while maintaining appropriate boundaries for clients in order to prevent harm if dual relationships were unavoidable.

In the 1990s several important publications appeared on rural social work. Among the more prominent of them are Martinez-Brawley's (1990) *Perspectives on the Small Community: Humanistic Views for Practitioners*; the second and third editions of Ginsberg's (1993b, 1998) *Social Work in Rural Communities*; and Carlton-LaNey, Edwards, and Reid's (1999) *Preserving and Strengthening Small Towns and Rural Communities.* Host institutions of the annual institute of the Rural Social Work Caucus published proceedings of its meetings. This filled a void created when the journal *Human Services in the Rural Environment* ceased publication in the early 1990s.

THE TWENTY-FIRST CENTURY

The first decade of the twenty-first century has seen significant developments in rural social work. The National Rural Social Work Caucus has remained an active advocacy group, and it is approaching the fortieth anniversary of its conference. The caucus has taken responsibility for monitoring and updating the NASW Rural Policy Statement. It is also recognized by the NASW as a constituency group, working to advance rural issues in the profession. The caucus has also served as a vehicle for professional development, and several members have gone on to become social work leaders (Locke, 2009). The rural track continues at CSWE meetings, and the CSWE recognizes the caucus as a partner organization.

Contemporary Rural Social Work emerged in 2009 as a journal devoted to rural social work, social policy, and professional education, helping fill the void of *Human Services in the Rural Environment.* In 2002, an initiative of the US Department of Health and Human Services established the Rural Assistance Center (2013) as a rural health and human services "information portal." The center continues to provide resources on rural grants, funding, programs, and research. New books addressing rural social work published during the early 2000s included Martinez-Brawley (2000), on small communities; Scales and Streeter (2004; see also Scales, Streeter, & Cooper, 2014), on assets and strengths of the rural community; Ginsberg (2005, 2011b) published new editions of his influential book with new material; and Lohmann and Lohmann (2005), on rural practice.

Despite all this progress in the field, social work education has not entirely caught up, and there is still a need to prepare rural social workers. The NASW (2009) policy statement on rural social work indicates that the profession needs to give more attention to the education of rural social workers, and the CSWE's (2011) statistics on social work education indicate that 33.1 percent of BSW programs and 18.3 percent of MSW programs are located in rural areas. But the CSWE (2011) does not collect information on whether any of the BSW programs offer rural content other than that of the generalist model or use rural field placements, and only ten of the MSW programs nationwide report having a concentration in rural social work. Thus the rural location of programs may not equate to the delivery of significant rural practice content.

RECONNECTING WITH THE PAST: RURAL SOCIAL WORK THEN AND NOW

For some people, history may be a dry exercise in what is already past, and we might reasonably ask, "Why spend so much time looking at it?" The answer to this is that the past has influenced where we are today, and it continues to do so. When we look at writings from the past, it is remarkable how much influence early views of rural social work still shape our perceptions and how many issues remain much the same. Thus, while rural communities, economies, and social conditions have changed over the years, the underlying conditions of rural life may not have changed so much.

To illustrate the fact that rural social work has not drifted too far from its origins, it is helpful to look at some commonly occurring themes in the rural literature. Here we'll look at professional isolation, generalist practice, use of strengths and assets, community involvement, and closeness of the community. When we look at these works, if we allow for changes in language and vocabulary over time, it is hard to avoid the similarities of the authors' views, some of whom wrote almost eight-five years apart, in different social and economic conditions, and with a fundamentally different social welfare system.

Professional Isolation

A common theme in the field of rural work is professional isolation: social workers who practice in rural communities tend to be isolated from other social workers. Rural service delivery occurs over a wide geographic area, with low concentrations of clients. In 1927 the rural practice literature noted "The average rural social worker is usually the only such person in her county. . . . She does not have the advantages of frequent conferences with other social workers, she has no supervisor with more training and experience than herself to go to for help and counsel" (Matthews, 1927/1980, p. 164). And this is from 2011: "Workers tend to be employed alone. . . . The resulting lack of supervision and isolation are sources of concern" (Ginsberg, 2011a, p. 8). Even though they are written many years apart, these statements share the view that rural social workers are more isolated that urban practitioners typically are, because they tend to work alone. Although over the intervening years of these statements the social welfare system changed, roads and vehicles improved, and technological innovations revolutionized communication, professional isolation, distance, travel, and limited communication remain important issues for rural social work.

Generalist Practice

Another theme in rural practice is the importance of using a generalist approach to social work, which includes practice with individuals, families, groups, organizations, and communities. The concept of the generalist rural social worker has existed for some time, though it is sometimes called by a different name. Generalist practice still remains the most widely accepted model of rural practice today. Matthews (1927/1980) described the rural social worker as a "general practitioner. . . . A worker in a large city [who works] as a small part of a large machine. A country worker is usually the whole machine herself" (p. 164). In 1933 Brown wrote, "So closely related are these two approaches that it is important that the rural social worker be trained in both community organization and social casework" (p. 29). In 2009, the NASW's policy statement on rural social work stated, "Most authors agree that generalist preparation is the best approach for rural practice" (p. 297). To this, Locke and Winship (2005) add, "A central idea about social work practice in rural areas namely that the social worker will, by the very nature of the rural context, be expected to practice out of a generalist model or orientation" (p. 3).

Use of Strengths and Assets

While there has been much written on what rural people and communities lack in terms of resources and services, rural social workers have long recognized that rural environments possess assets and strengths that can be used to address social problems. In 1933, Brown, writing about assessments, said, "Each person whom the social worker consults contributes his version of the existing problems and it is her tasks to assemble all this evidence and to use her special skill in discerning the heart of the trouble and the strengths and weaknesses of the people involved" (pp. 20–21). Even earlier, Bailey (1908) discussed assets available in rural communities:

> Every kind of organization that now exists in the open country, or can be readily extended to the open country, may be made the means of carrying the gospel of co-operation, companionship and better farm life to the persons who live on the land. The number of such organizations and associations is surprisingly large. . . . It is not so necessary to organize new groups as it is to fertilize and redirect the old ones. Rural institutions ought to be effective because they are for the most part natural expressions of indigenous needs, the outcome of the community's work. (p. 88)

Among the potentially available community resources that Bailey (1908) identified in the rural community were schools, churches, fraternal societies, men's and women's Christian associations, musical clubs, reading or literary associations, women's clubs, historical associations, and athletic associations.

Authors today have proposed using a strengths and assets approach as well. Scales and Streeter (2004) wrote, "We believe that practice models that keep us focused on the strengths, assets, and capacities of people are critical for social work practice in rural communities" (p. 4). Daley and Avant (2014) added:

> Then what we have is really a question of looking at whether the glass is half empty or half full. We can look at rural practice as occurring in a context where many important things like transportation, health care, formal services, and social service professionals are in short supply, or we can look at the positive adaptive behaviors that rural people use to develop informal resources to meet their needs. (p. 13)

Community Involvement

Rural social workers know that they are an integral part of the community, and this was one of the earliest points made about rural practice. According to Matthews (1927/1980), "The rural social worker must understand every working phase of her county" (p. 165), and "a small community or rural county is intensely personal in its makeup and attitudes" (p. 166). Brown (1933) devoted a considerable portion of her book on rural practice to macro practice. She highlights practice skills including knowing the community, working with the local social and political structure, and working with local institutions to generate support for social work.

More recent authors such as Ginsberg (2005) have indicated that rural social workers are often seen as outsiders, particularly if they are not originally from a community in which they are working. Daley and Pierce (2011) and Riebschleger (2007) have highlighted the importance of rural cultural competence and working within the norms of the community. Moreover, Ginsberg (2011a) noted, "Successful social workers in rural communities . . . must involve themselves with the people of the community, the leaders, the grass roots community members, local clergy, and local elected officials" (p. 12).

Closeness of the Community

Many have remarked on the closeness of the rural community in terms of people knowing one another and having multiple, overlapping relationships are common. Everyone is on view in a small community, and few people hide (Schott, 1980, p. 155). This was well known to early social workers. Brown (1922) wrote:

> In the country it is the social worker who is in that equivocal position. The city volunteer usually works in a district far from her own home and learns both method and facts regarding her case from the trained worker and in the case record, but in the country the same trained worker may find that the volunteer has been a neighbor of her client for thirty years and knows more about his family history and present situation than the average social worker could unearth about a city family in a month. (p. 286)

More recent writers, like Watkins (2004), have noted the mutuality and involvement of members of small communities. Fenby (1980) and Schott (1980) both have described rural practice as an environment in which social workers often have contact with clients and are highly visible. Strom-Gottfried (2005) illustrates the visibility of the social worker in these terms:

> "So," my neighbor said as we watched our sons' soccer game from the bleachers, "you were out to see Inez today. Is she going off the deep end today?" . . . Reaching into my toolbox of stock answers, I replied, "Sue, I'm sure you understand that confidentiality prohibits me from talking about my work—I can't even confirm that person is a client!" "Hah!" she snorted, "save it for the folks in Monticello. Up here everybody knows your business. I saw your car up at Inez's place when I was on my school bus run. Everyone knows she's had problems." (p. 141)

Although this is a fictionalized account, it rings true and accurately captures rural closeness and its effects on practice.

CONCLUSION

Interest in social work with rural communities developed in the 1910s. Initially, the country life movement expressed concerns about disparities in urban and rural life and wanted to develop rural communities into places that offered good incomes and healthy living conditions through modernization. The idea of the movement was to build on existing organizations in the community by involving churches, clubs, services, and fraternal organizations. The early emphasis in rural work was on community organization and development, but it soon became clear that there was a need for social casework as well. The YMCA, YWCA, and 4-H established branches in rural communities to provide a group work approach to moral and character development that benefited country towns and villages. The extension of home services by the American Red Cross during World War I brought a strong emphasis on social casework and work with families to rural communities.

By the 1920s rural social workers acknowledged that practice required adapting traditional urban social work skills and methods to work with people in rural areas. The 1930s brought a shift in services from a private to a publicly based model, and more services were extended to rural people. Josephine Brown (1933) penned the first book on rural practice methods for the profession, and many of her ideas still influence current thinking in the field. The US entry into World War II shifted focus away from rural areas and rural social work, and almost thirty years passed before the profession began to rediscover rural practice.

The 1970s experienced renewed interest in rural social work. In many respects, the rebirth of interest in the field involved a rediscovery of the ideas of previous generations. Although there have been peaks and valleys of interest since that time, rural social work has expanded and matured as more publications and organizations have contributed to a better understanding of the field.

In summary, as rural social work has been revived, the field has acquired more depth and breadth in terms of knowledge, literature, and advocacy efforts. These are reminders of what a small but committed group of organized social workers can do. The end result is that an important area of practice—which for all intents and purposes was ignored and abandoned—has rebounded to be stronger than it was before and is now flourishing.

REFERENCES

Abbott, G. (1980). Developing standards of rural child welfare. In E. E. Martinez-Brawley (Ed.), *Pioneer efforts in rural social welfare* (pp. 186–198). University Park, PA: Pennsylvania State University Press.

Atkinson, M. I. (1980). The rural community program of relief. In E. E. Martinez-Brawley (Ed.), *Pioneer efforts in rural social welfare* (pp. 228–237). University Park, PA: Pennsylvania State University Press.

Bailey, L. G. (1908). Rural development in relation to social welfare. In A. Johnson (Ed.), *Proceedings of the national conference on charities and corrections* (pp. 83–91). Fort Wayne, IN: Press of Fort Wayne Printing.

Brown, J. (1922). The use of volunteers in rural social work: In Dakota County, Minnesota. In *Proceedings of the National Conference on Social Work* (p. 286). Chicago, IL: University of Chicago Press.

Brown, J. C. (1933). *The rural community and social casework.* New York, NY: Family Welfare Association of America.

Brown, P. (1980). Our rural past: May 11, 1935, the New Deal lights up seven million farms. In H. W. Johnson (Ed.), *Rural human services: A book of readings* (pp. 140–142). Itasca, IL: Peacock.

Buxton, E. B. (1976). Delivering services in rural areas. In L. H. Ginsberg (Ed.), *Social work in rural communities: A book of readings* (pp. 29–38). New York, NY: Council on Social Work Education.

Carlton-LaNey, I. B., Edwards, R. L., & Reid P. N. (Eds.) (1999). *Preserving and strengthening small towns and rural communities.* Washington, DC: NASW Press.

Chambers, C. (1980). Myths of rural America. In H. W. Johnson (Ed.), *Rural human services: A book of readings* (pp. 172–173). Itasca, IL: Peacock.

Council on Social Work Education. (1969). Education for social work in rural settings. In *Annual Program Meeting* (p. 17). New York, NY: Author.

Council on Social Work Education. (2011). *2011 Annual statistics on social work education in the United States.* Retrieved from http://www.cswe.org/File.aspx?id = 62011.

Daley, M. R., & Avant, F. L. (2014). Down home social work: A strengths based model for professional practice. In T. L. Scales, S. Cooper, & C. L. Streeter (Eds.), *Rural social work: Building and sustaining community assets* (2nd ed., pp. 5–17). New York, NY: Wiley.

Daley, M. R., & Pierce, B. (2011). Educating for rural competence: Curriculum concepts, models and course content. In L. H. Ginsberg (Ed.), *Social work in rural* communities (5th ed., pp. 125–140). Alexandria, VA: Council on Social Work Education.

Davenport, J., & Davenport, J. A. (1984). Josephine Brown's classic book still guides rural social work. *Social Casework, 65*(7), 413–419.

Davis, W. C. (1998). *Three roads to the Alamo.* New York, NY: HarperCollins.

Donovan, J. (2008). *A terrible glory.* New York, NY: Back Bay Books.

Drew, D. C. (1922). The rural work of the Young Men's Christian Association. In *Proceedings of the National Conference of Social Work* (pp. 327–331). Chicago, IL: University of Chicago Press.

Egan, T. (2006). *The worst hard time.* New York, NY: Mariner Books.

Farley, O. W., Griffiths, K. A., Skidmore, R. A., & Thackeray, M. G. (1982). *Rural social work practice.* New York, NY: Free Press.

Fenby, B. L. (1980). Social work in a rural setting. In H. W. Johnson (Ed.), *Rural human services: A book of readings* (pp. 149–152). Itasca, IL: Peacock.

Galen, V., & Alexander D. (2011). Rural settlements: Rural social work at the forks of Troublesome Creek. In L. Ginsberg (Ed.), *Social work in rural communities* (5th ed., pp. 5–20). Alexandria, VA: Council on Social Work Education.

Gallagher, G. W. (2011). *The Union war.* Cambridge, MA: Harvard University Press.

Ginsberg, L. H. (1976). An overview of social work education for rural areas. In L. H. Ginsberg (Ed.), *Social work in rural communities: A book of readings* (pp. 1–12). New York, NY: Council on Social Work Education.

Ginsberg, L. H. (1993a). An overview of rural social work. In L. H. Ginsberg (Ed.), *Social work in rural communities* (2nd ed., pp. 2–17). Alexandria, VA: Council on Social Work Education.

Ginsberg, L. H. (1993b). Preface. In L. H. Ginsberg (Ed.), *Social work in rural communities* (2nd ed., pp. v–viii). Alexandria, VA: Council on Social Work Education.

Ginsberg, L. H. (Ed.) (1998). *Social work in rural communities* (3rd ed.). Alexandria, VA: Council on Social Work Education.

Ginsberg, L. H. (2005). The overall context of rural practice. In L. H. Ginsberg (Ed.), *Social work in rural communities* (4th ed., pp. 4–7). Alexandria, VA: Council on Social Work Education.

Ginsberg, L. (2011a). Introduction to basics of rural social work. In L. Ginsberg (Ed.), *Social work in rural communities* (5th ed., pp. 5–20). Alexandria, VA: Council on Social Work Education.

Ginsberg, L. (Ed.) (2011b). *Social work in rural communities* (5th ed.). Alexandria, VA: Council on Social Work Education.

Guinn, J. (2011). *The last gunfight.* New York, NY: Simon & Schuster.

Hickman, S. A. (2014). Rural is real: History of the National Rural Social Work Caucus and the NASW professional policy statement on rural social work. In T. L. Scales, C. L. Streeter, & H. S. Cooper (Eds.), *Rural social work: Building and sustaining community capacity* (2nd ed., pp. 19–28). Hoboken, NJ: Wiley.

Johnson, H. W. (Ed.) (1980). *Rural human services: A book of readings.* Itasca, IL: Peacock.

Johnston, R. E. (1980). Rural clubs for boys and girls. In E. E. Martinez-Brawley (Ed.), *Pioneer efforts in rural social welfare* (pp. 86–89). University Park, PA: Pennsylvania State University Press.

King, A. (1980). Home service and civilian charities. In E. E. Martinez-Brawley (Ed.), *Pioneer efforts in rural social welfare* (pp. 72–77). University Park, PA: Pennsylvania State University Press.

Lindeman, E. C. (1924). The relation between urban and rural social work. In *Proceedings of the National Conference on Social Work* (p. 39). Chicago, IL: University of Chicago Press.

Locke, B. L. (2009). The National Rural Social Work Caucus: 32 years of achievement. *Contemporary Rural Social Work, 1*, 1–7. Retrieved from http://journal.und.edu/crsw/issue/view/22.

Locke, B. L., & Winship, J. (2005). Social work in rural America. In N. Lohmann & R. A. Lohmann (Eds.), *Rural social work practice* (pp. 3–6). New York, NY: Columbia University Press.

Lohmann, N., & Lohmann, R. A. (Eds.) (2005). *Rural social work practice*. New York, NY: Columbia University Press.

Martinez-Brawley, E. E. (1980a). The country life movement. In E. E. Martinez-Brawley (Ed.), *Pioneer efforts in rural social welfare* (pp. 3–4). University Park, PA: Pennsylvania State University Press.

Martinez-Brawley, E. E. (Ed.) (1980b). *Pioneer efforts in rural social welfare*. University Park, PA: Pennsylvania State University Press.

Martinez-Brawley, E. E. (1981). *Seven decades of rural social work: From Country Life Commission to Rural Caucus*. New York, NY: Praeger.

Martinez-Brawley, E. E. (1990). *Perspectives on the small community humanistic views for practitioners*. Silver Spring, MD: NASW Press.

Martinez-Brawley, E. E. (2000). *Close to home: Human services in the small community*. Washington, DC: NASW Press.

Matthews, H. J. (1980). Special problems of rural social work. In E. E. Martinez-Brawley (Ed.), *Pioneer efforts in rural social welfare* (pp. 163–172). University Park, PA: Pennsylvania State University Press. (Originally published in 1927).

Middleton, F. C. (1919). Think together, work together, play together: Community clubs in Manitoba. In *Proceedings of the National Conference of Social Work* (pp. 556–561). Chicago, IL: Rogers & Hall.

Miller, P. J. (1998). Dual relationships and rural practice: A dilemma of practice and culture. In L. H. Ginsberg (Ed.), *Social work in rural communities* (3rd ed., pp. 55–62). Alexandria, VA: Council on Social Work Education.

National Archives. (n.d.). *The Freedmen's Bureau, 1865–1872*. Retrieved from http://www.archives.gov/research/african-americans/freedmens-bureau/.

National Association of Social Workers. (2009). Rural social work. In *Social work speaks: National Association of Social Workers policy statements* (8th ed., pp. 297–302). Washington, DC: Author.

National Rural Social Work Caucus. (n.d.). *The Rural Social Work Caucus 1976–1984: A history and descriptive analysis*. Retrieved from http://ruralsocialwork.org/history.cfm.

Persons, W. F. (1980). Home service in one rural county. In E. E. Martinez-Brawley (Ed.), *Pioneer efforts in rural social welfare* (pp. 66–71). University Park, PA: Pennsylvania State University Press.

Richmond, M. E. (1917). *Social diagnosis*. New York, NY: Russell Sage Foundation.

Riebschleger, J. (2007). Social workers' suggestions for effective rural practice. *Families in Society*, *88*(2), 203–213.

Rural Assistance Center. (2013). *About the Rural Assistance Center*. Retrieved from http://www.raconline.org/about/.

Sanderson, D. (1980). Trends and problems in rural social work. In E. E. Martinez-Brawley (Ed.), *Pioneer efforts in rural social welfare* (pp. 204–211). University Park, PA: Pennsylvania State University Press.

Scales, L. T., & Streeter, C. L. (2004). Asset building to sustain rural communities. In L. T. Scales & C. L. Streeter (Eds.), *Rural social work: Building and sustaining community assets* (pp. 1–6). Belmont, CA: Thomson/Brooks Cole.

Scales, T. L., Streeter, C. L., & Cooper, H. S. (Eds.). (2014). *Rural social work: Building and sustaining community capacity* (2nd ed.). Hoboken, NJ: Wiley.

Schecter, B. (2005). *The devil's own work*. New York, NY: Walker.

Schott, M. (1980). Casework: Rural. In H. W. Johnson (Ed.), *Rural human services: A book of readings* (pp. 153–158). Itasca, IL: Peacock.

Southern Regional Education Board. (1976). Educational assumptions for rural social work. In L. H. Ginsberg (Ed.), *Social work in rural communities: A book of readings* (pp. 40–45). New York, NY: Council on Social Work Education.

Strom-Gottfried, K. (2005). Ethical practice in rural environments. In L. H. Ginsberg (Ed.), *Social work in rural communities* (4th ed., pp. 141–155). Alexandria, VA: Council on Social Work Education.

Stuart, P. H. (2004). Social welfare and rural people: From the colonial era to the present. In T. L. Scales & C. L. Streeter (Eds.), *Rural social work: Building and sustaining community assets* (pp. 21–33). Belmont, CA: Thomson/Brooks Cole.

Swanson, M. (1980), The country life movement: An introduction. In E. E. Martinez-Brawley (Ed.), *Pioneer efforts in rural social welfare* (pp. 5–7). University Park, PA: Pennsylvania State University Press.

Twente, E. E. (1980). Social casework in rural communities. In *Proceedings of the National Conference on Social Work* (pp. 122–132). Chicago, IL: University of Chicago Press.

Urban Dictionary (n.d.). *Bought the farm.* Retrieved from http://www.urbandictionary.com/define.php?term=Bought%20The%20F arm.

Watkins, T. R. (2004). Natural helping networks: Assets for rural communities. In T. L. Scales & C. L. Streeter (Eds.), *Rural social work: Building and sustaining community assets* (pp. 65–76). Belmont, CA: Brooks Cole/Thomson.

Whitten, D. O. (2010). *Depression of 1893*. Retrieved from http://eh.net/encyclopedia/the-depression-of-1893/.

Winter, T. (2002). *Making men, making class: The YMCA and workingmen, 1877–1920*. Chicago, IL: University of Chicago Press.

Rural social work is culturally focused, creative, and adaptive: the quilt of the National Rural Social Work Caucus commemorates the tradition of past conferences.

7

CHAPTER SEVEN

A Model for Rural Social Work

RURALITY AND THE PRACTICE OF RURAL SOCIAL WORK

As HAS BEEN SUGGESTED in earlier chapters, rural social work requires some adaptation of the methods and skills that were primarily developed for urban practice. Rural social workers also have to employ a knowledge base specific to the rural context and the people who reside there. So the key concerns for rural social workers are adapting to rural practice, how rurality shapes practice, having an appropriate model of practice, and approaching practice from an asset or strengths perspective of the rural context. Discussions of some of the differences between rural and urban social work have led some people to speculate that perhaps a distinct model of practice is needed for the rural community, whereas others have maintained that practice models need only be adapted for rural work (Ginsberg, 2005a; York, Denton, & Moran, 1998). However, most contemporary writers suggest that social work skills and methods are adaptable enough to meet the needs of practice for small towns and rural areas.

There is also a general agreement in the profession that rurality influences practice. The two models most commonly proposed for rural practice are a community focus and the generalist approach. These models are not mutually exclusive, and the primary differences between them seem to be how heavily they weight the macro or community aspects of social work. Another consideration is the overall perspective for viewing the rural social environment. Should it be an asset- or strengths-based perspective, or should it be one that centers on addressing community deficits? This chapter examines these topics in more depth and presents a model that workers can employ in rural social work practice.

RURAL SOCIAL WORK: IS IT DIFFERENT FROM URBAN PRACTICE?

It does not take a long time or much experience for social workers in a rural community to learn that there are some differences between the professional work in that environment and what is usually experienced of them in a larger community or city. Whether it is the culture, residents' views, their personal relationships, fewer options for services, or distance and travel, it is often necessary for social workers to develop skills and strategies for adapting to the local conditions. Fitting good social work skills into a rural work environment requires enculturation (i.e., learning and using another culture), adaptability, and creativity, which social workers often have to learn on the job.

Yet a good foundation in social work is sufficient for rural practice, and social workers need only adjust professional models and methods of social work to fit the context (Ginsberg, 2011a). This has been understood for some time, as Josephine Brown (1933) wrote: "The social case worker in the rural community will find that, while the fundamental principles of case work are the same whether she works in city, town, village, or open country, there are certain modifications in method which may be advisable in making an adjustment to rural conditions" (p. 120). In other words, rural social work is just social work adapted to the smaller community setting.

Although rural social work practice in many respects is similar to social work practice in larger settings, it can be considered a distinct field of practice. Several authors have contended that professional work with people living in rural areas has an adequate number of unique characteristics to justify its being identified as a distinct field of practice (Carlton-LaNey, Edwards, & Reid, 1999b; Daley & Avant, 2004b; Daley & Pierce, 2011; Ginsberg, 2005a, 2011a; Johnson, 1980; Lohmann & Lohmann, 2005a; National Association of Social Workers, NASW, 2009, 2012b).

This point of view is not uncommon, as rural professionals in other fields also tend to view their work as different from that of their urban colleagues (Mellow, 2005). Rural practice tends to involve work with a minority and oppressed population, and as in work with any population, it requires learning about people's common values, beliefs, and behaviors (Daley & Avant, 2004b; Daley & Pierce, 2011). So, rural social work may be similar to other fields of practice, such as child welfare, mental health, and health-care-related social work, which share enough knowledge and skills for workers to incorporate in order to enhance their professional practice.

Recent years have seen an increase in social work education programs that address rural issues, especially at the undergraduate level (Daley & Pierce, 2011; Ginsberg, 2011a). Hopefully, these programs are able to contextualize rural content to the professional model in order to develop a greater pool of new social workers who have knowledge and skills for working in rural areas. The resurgence of interest in rural social work in the literature in the twenty-first century also has provided more resources for students and practitioners (Carlton-LaNey, Edwards, & Reid, 1999a; Ginsberg, 2005b, 2011b; Lohmann & Lohmann, 2005b, Martinez-Brawley, 2000; Scales & Streeter, 2004a).

GENERALIST SOCIAL WORK VERSUS COMMUNITY-BASED PRACTICE

The field of rural social work is somewhat divided as to the best practice methods. Some people suggest that rural work is primarily community practice that involves community development. Yet most current authors indicate that a generalist method that employs multiple methods to address individual, family, group, organizational, and community problems is best suited for rural social work. These are not highly conflicting viewpoints, as everyone realizes that rural social workers frequently have to deliver direct services to individuals and families, and that some community development is usually needed as well.

Some of the writers favoring a community-based approach include Jacobsen (1980), Martinez-Brawley (1993), White and Marks (1999), and

Belanger (2005). These authors all seem to guide social workers toward identifying both resources and infrastructure—including formal and informal services available—and enhancing that infrastructure for the benefit of the broader community. This helps provide a wider range of services, and it may help proactively avoid the development of social problems.

Since the late 1960s rural social work has looked increasingly to generalist practice as the preferred mode of intervention. Several authors have recommended the generalist method of practice as being most aptly matched to the needs of rural practice (Daley, 2010; Daley & Avant 1999, 2004a, 2004b; Daley & Pierce, 2011; Davenport & Davenport, 1998; Ginsberg, 1998, 2005a, 2005b, 2011a; Locke & Winship, 2005; Lohmann, 2005; NASW, 2012b; Riebschleger, 2007; Southern Regional Education Board, 1998; Waltman, 2011; York et al., 1998).

Generalist practice, based on social systems theory, uses five social systems and the interactions between those systems as the basis for understanding problems and developing strategies for empowering clients. The five social systems are individual, family, group, organization, and community (Kirst-Ashman & Hull, 2006). This is a broad model of social work that is very adaptable to many types of problems and situations and can employ multiple interventions based on specific problems presented. The method also is well suited for a rural community because it emphasizes a person-in-environment or an ecological systems perspective that views clients in terms of their interaction with the environment.

The method also includes a strengths perspective and a problem-solving method for social work (Association of Baccalaureate Social Work Program Directors, n.d.). Identifying individual and family strengths or community assets is essential to the helping process, as it also involves identifying and employing valuable resources that might otherwise be ignored if a social worker were to focus only on problems. This is important for rural practice, where too often the center of concern is on what is deficient or lacking in clients or communities. Examples of existing strengths or assets are a community spirit of cooperation or helping and the abilities of the church, neighbors, family members, or service organizations. Problem solving provides a framework for professional action, including engagement, assessment, planning, intervention, and termination. The problem-solving method is flexible enough to permit the use of multiple helping strategies for different kinds of problems. This is an important consideration for the varied demands placed on rural social workers. In some communities, the one-worker office can be expected to handle almost anything.

Generalist practice has the additional advantage of being applicable to work with rural people and communities in many settings. Not all rural people live in rural areas, and social workers frequently have to provide service to those clients. Rurality exists in two systems: the community and the individual (Schnore, 1966). As rural people can and do move out of their community, their rurality goes with them. As a result, even in urban areas, social workers can find themselves working with rural individuals, family groups, or whole communities, and they need rural knowledge and skills in order to do so (Daley & Avant, 2004b; NASW, 2009). But community-based models of rural work tend to assume that work with rural people occurs in the context of a sparsely populated geographic area—hence the discussion of *social work in rural areas* in much of the social work literature (Carlton-LaNey et al., 1999a; Ginsberg, 2005a, 2005b; Scales & Streeter, 2004b). Rural social work, though, occurs wherever rural people live, and a generalist practice is flexible enough to address this.

Indeed, most communities fall somewhere on an urban-rural continuum (Mellow, 2005). Today, rural communities are influenced to some degree by urban traditions, and urban communities are influenced by transplanted rural people. In part, better communication and transportation networks have helped produce this change. Gone are the days when most rural residents never left their county of residence; daily Internet and television also have influenced these changes. The extension of government services and branches of large corporations into rural communities has facilitated some degree of urban intrusion into rural communities. Similarly, rural culture appears in urban areas, with clothing stores selling western wear and restaurants like Cracker Barrel that feature a rural atmosphere and food. As a result, social workers may work with rural people almost anywhere, and the generalist method is broad enough to meet the needs of these clients.

RURAL STRENGTHS AND ASSETS

Rural social work arose out of basic concerns for the lives of people who lived in small towns and the countryside. Socially conscious people realized that the social, technological, and economic progress that had improved people's lives in cities in the early twentieth century had largely bypassed rural communities (Galen & Alexander, 2011). Invariably, rural communities were compared to cities in terms of what was not there and what the smaller communities needed, in order to "catch up." This was not an unreasonable assessment given the circumstances that existed at the time: many communities did not have electricity or reliable drinking water and sewage, education was sparse, and health care not widely available. Resources, when they existed, were often informal, with churches, family members, concerned neighbors, and citizens filling in where they were able.

In the early days, rural social workers and authors writing about rural social work tended to focus on what was needed and what was lacking in the rural community. This tradition has continued to today, and much rural literature contains either an implicit or explicit deficit perspective. Portrayals of rural people in the media have served to reinforce the stereotypical views that country people are lacking in education or job skills, are simple, use old-fashioned ways, and live in backward communities.

Yet some people who worked with rural people early on saw more than just need in rural communities; they looked at the strengths of rural communities. Bailey (1908) noted the large number of organizations in existence to improve people's lives, and Brown (1933) pointed out the importance of using client strengths in working with rural clients and their families.

But it was the emergence of the strengths perspective in modern social work, facilitated by the work of Dennis Saleebey (2006) and others, that helped social work professionals focus more clearly on the importance of this view of practice. Saleebey (2006) emphasized the importance of using both strengths and assets as an essential part of social work practice:

> The person or family in front of you and the community around you possess assets, resources, wisdom, and knowledge that, at the outset you probably know nothing about. First *and* foremost,

> the strengths perspective is about discerning those resources, and respecting them and the potential they may have for reversing misfortune, countering illness, easing pain, and reaching goals. (p. 16)

So this perspective involves looking beyond the limitations of clients and communities to identify what is positive and what is already working. These strengths or assets can then be engaged to become an important part of empowering clients or communities to develop solutions for the troubles they face.

While the strengths perspective has been known in social work for several years, the work of Scales and Streeter (2004b) has suggested the broad use of this perspective in rural social work particularly. Their anthology was the first to broadly address rural assets in social work. Daley and Avant (2004b), despite that much of their focus was on rural collective or community issues, extended the strengths concept to work with rural systems, including individuals and families.

The use of a strengths approach to rural practice continues to emerge as an important aspect of practice, because although communities may not be rich in formal resources, the greatest resources rural areas have are its people, whom should not be overlooked. Scales and Streeter (2004a) also have stressed the depth of spirit and the creative potential of rural people. Rural areas have a sense of community and strong family connections (Carlton-LaNey et al., 1999b). Rural people tend to be resilient and can be self-reliant. All of these are important potential strengths for rural social workers to draw in, and if used creatively, they can be very effective. Social workers who ignore such strengths while lamenting the lack of services are unlikely to achieve optimal results.

RURAL RELATIONSHIPS AND SOCIAL WORK PRACTICE

Rural human relationships are typically characterized as close and personal (Daley & Pierce, 2011; Ginsberg, 1998; NASW, 2012b). As a result, rural people tend to be more comfortable dealing and interacting with people whom they know or with whom they are familiar, and they tend to distrust those they consider either outsiders or strangers (Ginsberg,

2011a; NASW 2012b). Often their relationships are face-to-face (Ginsberg, 2005a). Thus, rural people may prefer banking where they know the teller or a bank officer and are able to walk into the lobby, as opposed to dealing with electronic banking or a phone menu, particularly one that routes them to an overseas call center. Even when dealing with pharmacists at a big-box store, they are more likely to have some personal connection than they would in a larger city.

These types of human relationships in rural areas are usually classified as characteristic of a *Gemeinschaft* community. Sociologists developed the theoretical concepts of *Gemeinschaft* and *Gesellschaft* to describe and explain differences in the types of interaction between people in rural and urban communities. The categories "*Gemeinschaft*" and "*Gesellschaft*" help us classify all kinds of transactions that occur in a community, be they social, political, or economic.

Of course, social workers tend to be most concerned about social relationships, both functional and problematic ones. But political and economic relationships can be relevant as well. And *Gemeinschaft* and *Gesellschaft* help social workers understand people and communities in terms of their interactions with the systems of their community (Collins, 1988). This can be very important for social workers, particularly those using a generalist approach.

The *Gemeinschaft* community is generally associated with small towns, villages, and rural areas. *Gemeinschaft* relationships are characterized as personal, lasting, and based on who a person is in terms of family and social relationships, character traits, and the person's social standing in the community. A person is less likely to be perceived in terms of the formal position or job he or she holds and more likely to be seen in terms of whom he or she knows, whom he or she is related to, and where he or she is from. In a *Gemeinschaft* community people tend to have much in common, and social institutions like church and family are very important, because they are key to maintaining and educating people about the values, traditions, and social customs of the community. According to Martinez-Brawley (2000), who employs a *Gemeinschaft-Gesellschaft* framework in discussing rural communities, small towns and rural communities tend to have a traditional authority or power structure, whereas urban communities use a more rational and formal approach.

The concept of the *Gesellschaft* community is more apt to apply to urban communities. In urban communities social and especially commercial relationships occur more frequently with persons whom an individual does not know well, and such relationships are often formal—so much so that they may be conducted through written or contractual means. People are more anonymous and less liable to know one another personally or even know much about other people. *Gesellschaft* communities are more likely to transact social or economic business based on a person's formal position or qualifications. For example, in the city clients may be more willing to accept a social worker on the basis of academic or professional credentials, or a valid agency identification badge, whereas rural clients may want to know about these things but place more emphasis on what they know about a person's character, connections, and reputation. Since people do not know one another as well as in *Gemeinschaft* communities, business and services tend to be more cautiously pursued, perhaps at arm's length.

Several authors recommend the use of the *Gemeinschaft* and *Gesellschaft* framework for rural social workers in understanding people's interactions (Burkemper, 2005; Daley & Pierce, 2011; Ginsberg, 2011a, 2011b; Martinez-Brawley, 2000). The idea of *Gemeinschaft* is clearly very helpful in understanding social relationships in a rural community, but *Gesellschaft* may also be helpful—effectively few real communities are entirely personal in their interactions (Daley & Avant, 2014). The ideas of *Gemeinschaft* and *Gesellschaft* can help us understand the types of interactions between people and community systems, and identify the congruence of clients' behavior with community norms.

Understanding *Gemeinschaft* is important for rural social workers because it reflects precisely the type of values discussed in chapter 2: importance of family, place, friendship, personal relationships, and connection to the land. It is easy to forget that these things are expected in a rural community, especially when many modern expectations have crept in from urban life and tend to be reinforced by education, the media, and imposition from outside sources. In many respects, the individual drive to succeed, individualistic purpose-driven activity, egoism, and impersonal interaction that are typically found in *Gesellschaft* communities can cause friction when they are transferred to the rural community (Appelrouth &

Edles, 2007). *Gemeinschaft* and *Gesellschaft* are also ways to categorize the nature of social relationships and exchanges between persons and systems. Social exchange theory, developed in social psychology, helps explain why people's interactions occur the way they do. Social exchange theory is based on the idea that interpersonal and economic exchanges are the basic form of human interaction. These exchanges happen because people expect to benefit in some way. Strong relationships develop with people who are able to give the greatest benefit, or from whom potential benefits may ensue. Social exchange theory explains the links that people develop and affects the nature of social exchanges (Collins, 1988). *Gemeinschaft* and *Gesellschaft* are useful ways of explaining these exchanges (Daley, 2010).

The personalized exchanges that occur in a rural community are a way of adapting to an environment in which resources may not be easily accessible and formal social welfare services not readily available (Daley & Avant, 1999; Ginsberg, 1998; NASW, 2009). Under these circumstances, one's relatives, neighbors, and friends are a more reliable source of help than social welfare services. And the community tends to have a view of helping its own. Understanding how exchanges in the community work is important for social workers because informal networks may extend beyond friends, family, and the clergy to the barber, beautician, or owner of the local store.

A hypothetical example can help illustrate these exchanges in a rural community. Fredonia is a rural community of about twenty-five thousand people in Will Scott County, which covers about a thousand square miles, with a total countywide population of fifty thousand. Fredonia is the largest town in the county, it is the county seat, and it serves as a regional center for services and health care. Fredonia's county hospital serves indigent and low-income patients. The county hospital identified a potential unmet need when staff noticed that a large number of residents from the north end of the county were coming to the hospital for basic health care. The northern part of the county, about forty miles from the hospital, had very limited health care. To save on costs, the hospital wanted to avoid providing basic health care in its emergency room. It also wanted to reach out to this population in the county. As a result, the hospital decided to establish a rural health clinic in the northern part of the county, about thirty-five miles from the hospital, in Garfield, a town of a thousand people. Once the clinic opened, few people used it even though it was more convenient for them. The hospital found that residents did not trust outsiders from the larger city of Fredonia coming into their community, and they were wary of the professionals sent to staff the clinic. Garfield residents were suspicious of some of the doctors and nurses of Asian descent who staffed the rural clinic. Some Garfield residents suspected that they would get better care in Fredonia. The clinic closed because of low usage, and people continued to go to Fredonia's emergency room for basic health care. The hospital realized that it should have worked more closely with the small town where the clinic was established to gain acceptance from the community, which would have yielded better overall results. This is a lesson in service delivery from which rural social workers can learn.

A MODEL FOR RURAL SOCIAL WORK

Rural communities are diverse in terms of people, economy, social and cultural traditions, and proximity to other communities. As a practical matter, no two rural communities are exactly alike, even though there may be several common elements, and this speaks to the complexity of working with rural people and communities. For social workers to respond appropriately, stereotypes of a "simple life" in the country must fall by the wayside. Social problems in rural areas can vary widely, and they tend to be heavily influenced by the specific characteristics of the community in which people live. Rural social workers need a flexible approach to meet the challenges of practice with rural communities.

The NASW's (2006) policy statement on rural social work indicates that social workers are in an excellent position to help rural people enhance their lives and support their families. Clearly, though, there is no single intervention that best meets the needs of every situation that rural social workers will confront. But generalist practice is flexible enough to allow for multiple interventions in the social systems that affect people's lives. It works well with the diverse demands of the one-worker office and in addressing needs from the individual level to the community.

The problem-solving method is an important element of generalist practice that provides a framework for professional social work. The stages of problem solving are engagement, assessment, intervention, and evaluation (Compton, Galaway, & Cournoyer, 2005). These stages include establishing a relationship with a client, collecting and analyzing information about the presenting problem, deciding on a course of action, implementing the intervention, evaluating the results of the intervention, and then terminating the relationship. A person-in-environment perspective is also part of the generalist method; this perspective is based on the idea that a person's behavior results from interactions with surrounding social systems. For example, a person may be influenced by an organization if he or she has to travel long distances or arrive at arbitrary appointment times without consideration of the reliability of transportation or work schedules.

To understand the interactions between social systems that are basic to the generalist perspective, it is also critical to incorporate a rural perspective on the social exchanges that constitute those interactions. Analyzing social interactions becomes a critical part of establishing a relationship, collecting information, making assessments, developing plans, and implementing interventions. The concepts of *Gemeinschaft* and *Gesellschaft* are very useful concepts for understanding rural communities and the social interactions within them. Otherwise, it is all too easy to see rural people as strongly clinging to old ways of doing things, or insisting on personal relationships, as resistant or out of date, when they are really adhering to community norms. Understanding and responding appropriately can help to enhance professional practice.

DOWN-HOME MODEL OF SOCIAL WORK

Considering what has been discussed to this point, I suggest a multifaceted model of practice that incorporates elements of community, generalist practice, and a strengths perspective. The model of rural social work presented here is the down-home model, proposed by Daley and Avant (2004b, 2014). The down-home model of social work is a modified type of the generalist method that incorporates the elements of generalist practice, social exchange, and a strengths perspective. The generalist method adapted here includes the use of multiple social systems, a person-in-environment perspective, and problem solving. It views social problems that occur in the context of a wider community. This approach to practice takes into account the effects of a rural community on a person's behavior. It also permits the use of direct interventions with individuals and families, and community interventions where contextual factors in the community, such as the exclusion of undocumented immigrants from services, play an important role in producing social problems.

The term *generalist practice* as used in the model should be construed broadly; it includes both generalist and advanced generalist methods. Both are based on a systems framework, but generalist practice is foundation-level practice, and advanced generalist practice involves the application of advanced social work (e.g., clinical mental health skills) within a generalist framework (Daley & Avant, 2004a). Clearly, both are needed, as rural communities are in need of specialized and basic services.

The strengths perspective, while an integral part of the generalist method, receives greater emphasis in the down-home model to counterbalance a tendency to look only at deficits. Analysis of social exchange is also important for understanding problems and working better with people in the community. The concepts of *Gemeinschaft* and *Gesellschaft* are incorporated into the down-home model of social work as a way of analyzing social exchanges, emphasizing the effects of community norms on individual and collective behavior, and helping to design appropriate interventions.

Figures 1 and 2 illustrate the down-home social work model. Figure 1 represents the key elements of generalist and advanced generalist practice. Social systems, problem solving, and the person-in-environment perspective are all part of this model. Figure 2 depicts the down-home model described in the preceding paragraphs and adds additional detail, by showing how components of generalist practice, social exchange, and the strengths perspective all contribute to the down-home model of rural social work practice.

It should also be understood that rural social work, as in any other field of practice, always occurs within the context of social work ethics. Social workers' Code of Ethics (NASW, 2012a) represents a set of common expectations about how social workers interact with clients, colleagues, employing organizations, the profession itself, and society.

FIGURE 1
Key Elements of Generalist Practice

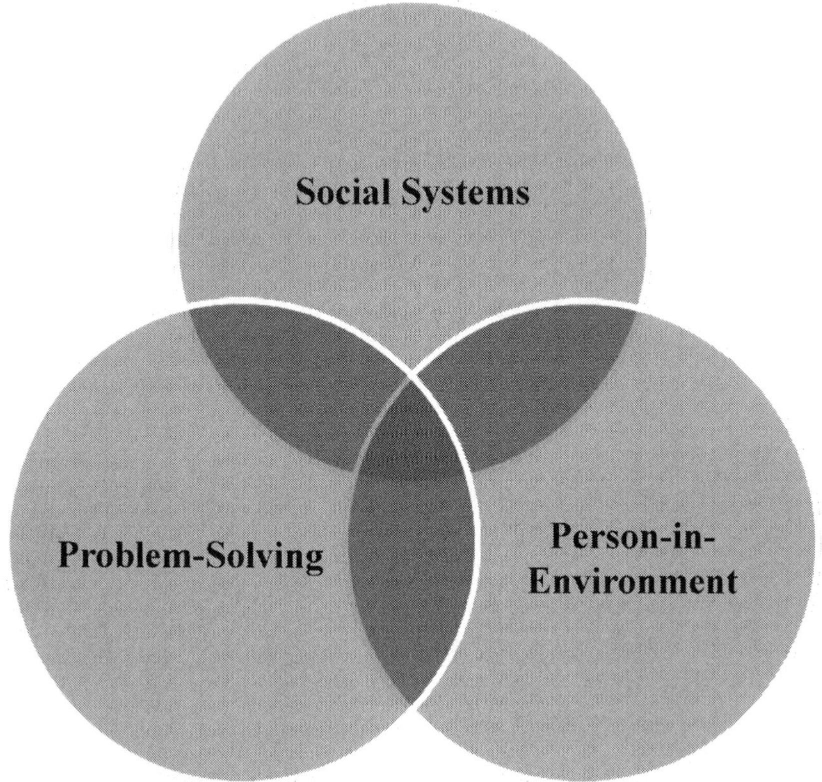

Social work ethics, then, influence how social workers can apply the down-home model in working with clients and communities. As in other aspects of rural social work, the ethics of social work, such as dual or multiple relationships between a worker and clients, may need to be adapted to the smaller community. The how and why of such adaptations are the subject of chapter 8.

APPLYING THE DOWN-HOME MODEL

Practice models are simply tools to use for getting something done in social work. They are only as useful as professionals' ability to apply

FIGURE 2
Down-Home Model for Rural Social Work Practice

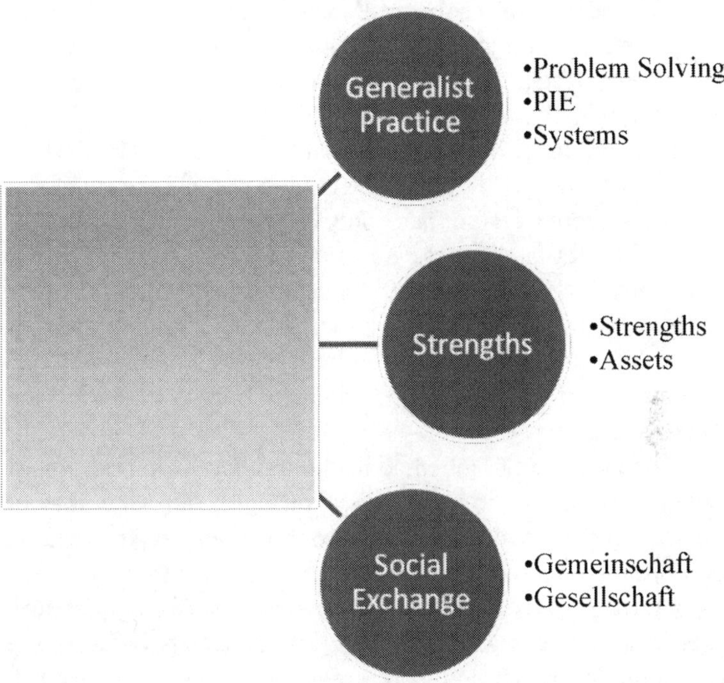

them to the task at hand in specific situations. The down-home model of social work is both complex and general, and its use may or may not be intuitive for social workers. A case example of a rural family in need of assistance can help illustrate potential applications of the down-home model to rural practice. Consider the following scenario:

> The Jacobs family lives in a seventy-year-old frame house four miles outside of the town of Easton. Easton itself, with a population of 567, is roughly 250 miles from a metropolitan area and 75 miles from the town of River City, which has a population of 28,000. The roads from Easton to both River City and the metropolitan area have two lanes and pass through several small towns. Travel times from Easton are an hour and a half to River City and four and a half hours to the metropolitan area. Easton has a

county social service office in the town hall, but it is staffed only one day per week by a social worker from River City.

The Jacobs family consists of Peter, forty-six, an independent logger; his wife, Hilda, forty-two, who works part-time at a store in Easton that sells food, gas, and fishing and hunting equipment, and that houses the local mechanic; Frieda, fifteen years old and in ninth grade; and Jonny, thirteen years old and in seventh grade. Peter and Hilda both have a high school education, and Frieda and Jonny attend the county consolidated high school.

The Jacobs family lives on a narrow dirt road one mile off the road into Easton. They own three vehicles: a 2002 pickup truck with an extended cab, a 1979 pickup, and a log truck used for work. Each day Hilda must drive both children one mile out to the main road to catch the bus, and she waits with them if the weather is bad.

The Jacobs family inherited the house they live in from Peter's grandmother, and so they own it outright, but a number of repairs need to be made, including to the well pump, the furnace, and the insulation. Hilda makes enough money from her part-time work to cover the family's basic expenses. The logging business has been depressed over the past two years because of a downturn in the housing market, and Peter makes less than half of what he used to hauling logs. Other local employment options are limited for Peter, as the lumber mill, which previously was the largest employer in Easton, has cut back to operating only three days per week. Peter is also experiencing severe back pain from years of driving a log truck over rough roads and the hard labor associated with his job.

When one of the Jacobses needs medical care, the family usually has to drive to River City. Their 2002 pickup is the only vehicle they have that is reliable enough to make a trip of that distance, as the log truck is too cumbersome on the narrow and winding roads.

With rising fuel costs and winter approaching, Hilda has come to Easton's county social services office to ask for help. She explains that their water pump is on its last legs, that Peter needs medical care for his back, and that she is not sure how they can afford to heat the house this winter if Peter is unable to work. She is somewhat embarrassed to ask for help because her family has never been on "welfare" before.

Approaching this case from the person-in-environment perspective, the social worker could identify several internal and external forces affecting this family. Also, the social worker should consider the effects of all five social systems on the family, such as individual systems like Peter Jacobs's health and need for medical care. Family issues include the children needing transportation to and from school if Hilda and Peter travel for Peter to receive medical treatment. There are also community forces like the availability of formal services and the economic climate in the area, both of which contribute to the family's need for income. The family's community involvement may also be relevant—they might be members of one of the two churches in town, or perhaps they have extended family members or friends who reside in the area and may be able to help.

From a strengths perspective, we know that the family has been self-sufficient and wants to make it on their own if they can. Information about their social exchanges with community members can reveal their involvement in local churches or groups, which may serve as a strength and provide a source of help. Social exchanges between the family and other social systems in terms of the small-town ethos, or *Gemeinschaft*, can be most helpful in building successful interventions. Analyzing social exchanges with the family and community can be important for preventing structural barriers to the family receiving assistance. For example, if the family has a strong sense of self-reliance, they might view receiving outside help as a sign of weakness. Thus, the social worker may need to come to an agreement with the family about the types of help they are willing to accept. Moreover, because the social worker in this case lives in River City, he or she must be sensitive to the fact that the family may view the social worker as an outsider. Bringing services in from another community to repair the pump and fix the insulation may meet with some resistance, and the social worker should first evaluate how the family and community would perceive that. The family might also resist traveling to River City or even the metropolitan area to receive health care from an unknown resource. This hypothetical case illustrates just a few examples of using the generalist method, social exchange, and strengths and assets from the down-home model for rural practice.

CONCLUSION

Ever since social workers began to work with rural people and communities they have recognized that the traditional models of practice that they had learned did not entirely fit for the clients with whom they worked, the social problems they addressed, and the social environment in which they practiced. Increasingly, professionals came to believe in adapting to the needs of the rural community. The field of rural social work developed around practice that was successfully adapted to rural work and a specialized body of knowledge that could be used to work effectively with clients and small communities.

Generalist social work emerged as the commonly accepted model of practice for work with rural clients and communities. Social workers using the generalist method are well suited to practice in small communities because there tend to be few workers there to respond to the needs of a wide area, and workers often need to address many kinds of problems and issues. Methods such as generalist practice employ multiple skills and interventions in response to the varied needs of rural areas. Thus, to serve a broad community, social workers who are flexible and provide broad-based basic services are essential.

Rural people also need to work with social workers who can deliver specialized services, as professionals with specialized skills are often in short supply in rural areas. Advanced generalist practice offers a method for delivering specialized services within a broad-based, adaptable framework for practitioners. The emergence of more advanced generalist educational programs in recent years is an encouraging sign for rural work, as more social workers are more likely today to have specialized skills but practice with a generalist orientation.

Generalist and advanced generalist methods of practice are based on social systems theory and incorporate work with individuals, families, groups, organizations, and communities into the helping process. This method also uses an overall person-in-environment perspective that assesses and responds to the interactions between people and the social systems that affect their behavior and social condition. Typically, generalist practice incorporates a strengths perspective that identifies and works with clients' positive coping strategies and abilities and the assets present in a small community. Problem solving also provides a framework that is fitted to the specific presenting problems and can help organize efforts for positive change.

The down-home model of rural social work practice presented in this chapter adapts the generalist method and theoretical perspectives from social exchange and strengths to the needs of rural work. It combines the multisystem generalist model of practice with a person-in-environment perspective, as well as problem solving. The down-home model also reinforces the strengths perspective to counter a prevailing tendency to view rural communities as rife with deficits. Another component of the down-home model is its focus on analyzing social exchanges as a means of understanding and working with the interactions between people and systems in the rural environment. The concepts of *Gemeinschaft* and *Gesellschaft* are useful in understanding the nature of social exchange, because they offer a framework for identifying behaviors associated with rural and urban communities. Since relationships are important to members of a rural community, the assessment of these relationships and work with them becomes particularly important for guiding practice.

The down-home model can be applied to other settings, but it is particularly relevant to rural practice. The fact is that social workers in virtually any setting may need some understanding of rural people and a framework for working with them. Much rural social work occurs in geographic communities that by some definition are rural, because rural people do move to larger cities. These rural urbanites retain their culture to some degree, which affects their behavior. Often, they re-form rural social communities or neighborhoods in the urban setting. When urban social workers come into contact with rural urbanites, they will need some understanding of rural culture to work with them successfully.

The concepts and model presented in this chapter may be helpful in providing a starting point for enterprising social workers who are looking to work with rural people and in rural areas. Rural people are an important subgroup of the population, and as helping professionals, social workers should do their best to empower them.

REFERENCES

Appelrouth, S., & Edles, L. D. (2007). *Sociological theory in the contemporary era.* Thousand Oaks, CA: Pine Forge Press.

Association of Baccalaureate Social Work Program Directors. (n.d.). *Definitions: Generalist practice.* Retrieved from http://www.bpdonline.org/bpd_prod/BPDWCMWEB/Resources/Definitions/BPDWCMWEB/Resources/Definitions.aspx?hkey = 3e3a936d-fe8a-4bd9-8d41-45fdf190bc68.

Bailey, L. G. (1908). Rural development in relation to social welfare. In A. Johnson (Ed.), *Proceedings of the National Conference on Charities and Corrections* (pp. 83–91). Fort Wayne, IN: Press of Fort Wayne Printing.

Belanger, K. (2005). In search of a theory to guide rural practice: The case for social capital. In L. H. Ginsberg (Ed.), *Social work in rural communities* (4th ed., pp. 4–7). Alexandria, VA: Council on Social Work Education.

Brown, J. (1933). *The rural community and social casework.* New York, NY: Family Welfare Association of America.

Burkemper, E. M. (2005). Ethical mental health social work practice in the small community. In L. H. Ginsberg (Ed.), *Social work in rural communities* (4th ed., pp. 175–188). Alexandria, VA: Council on Social Work Education.

Carlton-LaNey, I. B., Edwards, R. L., & Reid, P. N. (Eds.) (1999a). *Preserving and strengthening small towns and rural communities.* Washington, DC: NASW Press.

Carlton-LaNey, I. B., Edwards, R. L., & Reid, P. N. (1999b). Small towns and rural communities: From romantic notions to harsh realities. In I. B. Carlton-LaNey, R. L. Edwards, & P. N. Reid (Eds.), *Preserving and strengthening small towns and rural communities* (pp. 5–12). Washington, DC: NASW Press.

Collins, R. (1988). *Theoretical sociology.* Washington, DC: Harcourt Brace Jovanovich.

Compton, B. R., Galaway, B., & Cournoyer, B. R. (2005). *Social work process.* Belmont, CA: Thompson-Brooks Cole.

Daley, M. R. (2010). A conceptual model for rural social work. *Contemporary Rural Social Work,* 2. Retrieved from http://und.edu/contemporary-rural-social-work-journal/2010/index.cfm.

Daley, M. R., & Avant, F. (1999). Attracting and retaining professionals for social work practice in rural areas: An example from East Texas.

In I. B. Carlton-La Ney, R. L. Edwards, & P. N. Reid (Eds.), *Preserving and strengthening small towns and rural communities* (pp. 335–345). Washington, DC: NASW Press.

Daley, M. R., & Avant, F. (2004a). Advanced generalist for rural practice. In A. Roy & F. Vecchiola (Eds.), *Advanced generalist practice: Models, readings, and essays* (pp. 37–57). Peosta, IA: Bowers.

Daley, M., & Avant, F. (2004b). Reconceptualizing the framework for practice. In T. L. Scales & C. L. Streeter (Eds.), *Rural social work: Building and sustaining community assets* (pp. 34–42). Belmont, CA: Thomson/Brooks Cole.

Daley, M. R., & Avant, F. L. (2014). Down home social work: A strengths based model for professional practice. In T. L. Scales, C. L. Streeter, & H. S. Cooper (Eds.), *Rural social work: Building and sustaining community capacity* (2nd ed., pp. 5–17). Hoboken, NJ: Wiley.

Daley, M. R., & Pierce, B. (2011). Educating for rural competence: Curriculum concepts, models and course content. In L. Ginsberg (Ed.), *Social work in rural communities* (5th ed., pp. 125–140). Alexandria, VA: Council on Social Work Education.

Davenport, J., III, & Davenport, J. A. (1998). Rural communities in transition. In L. H. Ginsberg (Ed.), *Social work in rural communities* (3rd ed., pp. 39–54). Alexandria, VA: Council on Social Work Education.

Galen, V., & Alexander D. (2011). Rural settlements: Rural social work at the forks of Troublesome Creek. In L. Ginsberg (Ed.), *Social work in rural communities* (5th ed., pp. 5–20). Alexandria, VA: Council on Social Work Education.

Ginsberg, L. H. (1998). Introduction: An overview of rural social work. In L. H. Ginsberg (Ed.), *Social work in rural communities* (3rd ed., pp. 3–22). Alexandria, VA: Council on Social Work Education.

Ginsberg, L. H. (2005a). The overall context of rural practice. In L. H. Ginsberg (Ed.), *Social work in rural communities* (4th ed., pp. 4–7). Alexandria, VA: Council on Social Work Education.

Ginsberg, L. H. (2005b). *Social work in rural communities* (4th ed.). Alexandria, VA: Council on Social Work Education.

Ginsberg, L. (2011a). Introduction to basics of rural social work. In L. Ginsberg (Ed.), *Social work in rural communities* (5th ed., pp. 5–20). Alexandria, VA: Council on Social Work Education.

Ginsberg, L. (Ed.) (2011b). *Social work in rural communities* (5th ed.). Alexandria, VA: Council on Social Work Education.

Jacobsen, G. M. (1980). Rural communities and community development. In H. W. Johnson (Ed.), *Rural human services: A book of readings* (pp. 196–202). Itasca, IL: Peacock.

Johnson, L. C. (1980). Human service delivery patterns in nonmetropolitan communities. In H. W. Johnson (Ed.), *Rural human services: A book of readings* (pp. 65–74). Itasca, IL: Peacock.

Kirst-Ashman, K. K., & Hull, G. H. (2006). *Understanding generalist practice* (4th ed.). Belmont, CA: Thompson Brooks/Cole.

Locke, B. L., & Winship, J. (2005). Social work in rural America. In N. Lohmann & R. A. Lohmann (Eds.), *Rural social work practice* (pp. 3–6). New York, NY: Columbia University Press.

Lohmann, N. (2005). Social work education for rural practice. In N. Lohmann & R. A. Lohmann (Eds.), *Rural social work practice* (pp. 293–311). New York, NY: Columbia University Press.

Lohmann, N., & Lohmann, R. A. (2005a). Introduction. In N. Lohmann & R. A. Lohmann (Eds.), *Rural social work practice* (pp. 3–24). New York, NY: Columbia University Press.

Lohmann, N., & Lohmann, R. A. (Eds.). (2005b). *Rural social work practice.* New York, NY: Columbia University Press.

Martinez-Brawley, E. E. (1993). Community oriented rural practice. In L. H. Ginsberg (Ed.), *Social work in rural communities* (2nd ed., pp. 67–81). Alexandria, VA: Council on Social Work Education.

Martinez-Brawley, E. E. (2000). *Close to home: Human services in the small community.* Washington, DC: NASW Press.

Mellow, M. (2005). The work of rural professionals: Doing the gemeinschaft-gesellschaft gavotte. *Rural Sociology, 70*(1), 50–69.

National Association of Social Workers. (2006). Rural social work policy statement. In *Social work speaks: National Association of Social Workers policy statements* (7th ed., pp. 321–326). Washington, DC: NASW Press.

National Association of Social Workers. (2009). Rural social work. *Social work speaks: National Association of Social Workers policy statements* (8th ed., pp. 297–302). Washington, DC: NASW Press.

National Association of Social Workers. (2012a). Code of ethics of the National Association of Social Workers. In *Social work speaks:*

National Association of Social Workers policy statements (9th ed., pp. 375–391). Washington, DC: NASW Press.

National Association of Social Workers. (2012b). Rural social work. In *Social work speaks: National Association of Social Workers policy statements* (9th ed., pp. 296–300). Washington, DC: NASW Press.

Riebschleger, J. (2007). Social workers' suggestions for effective rural practice. *Families in Society*, *88*(2), 203–213.

Saleebey, D. (2006). Introduction: Power in the people. In D. Saleebey (Ed.), *The strengths perspective in social work practice* (4th ed., pp. 1–24). Boston, MA: Allyn & Bacon.

Scales, L. T., & Streeter, C. L (2004a). Asset building to sustain rural communities. In L. T. Scales & C. L. Streeter (Eds.), *Rural social work: Building and sustaining community assets* (pp. 1–6). Belmont, CA: Brooks Cole/Thomson.

Scales, L. T., & Streeter, C. L. (Eds.) (2004b). *Rural social work: Building and sustaining community assets*. Belmont, CA: Brooks Cole/ Thomson.

Schnore, L. F. (1966). The rural-urban variable: An urbanite's perspective. *Rural Sociology*, *31*(2), 131–143.

Southern Regional Education Board. (1998). Educational assumptions for rural social work. In L. H. Ginsberg (Ed.), *Social work in rural communities* (3rd ed., pp. 23–26). Alexandria, VA: Council on Social Work Education.

Waltman, G. H. (2011). Reflections on rural social work. *Families in Society*, *92*(2), 236–239.

White, C., & Marks, K. (1999). A strengths-based approach to rural sustainable development. In I. B. Carlton-LaNey, R. L. Edwards, & P. N. Reid (Eds.), *Preserving and strengthening small towns and rural communities* (pp. 27–42). Washington, DC: NASW Press.

York, R. O., Denton, R. T., & Moran, J. R. (1998). Rural and urban social work practice: Is there a difference? In L. H. Ginsberg (Ed.), *Social work in rural communities* (3rd ed., pp. 83–97). Alexandria, VA: Council on Social Work Education.

Small town barber and beauty shops are places where a great deal of information and gossip are exchanged informally. This kind of discussion can pose potential risks to confidentiality.

CHAPTER EIGHT

Ethical Rural Practice

UNDOUBTEDLY ONE of the most frequently discussed aspects of rural social work is how the professional Code of Ethics applies to practice. Much of the discussion focuses on how to adapt ethical principles to the close-knit context of a rural community. For a long time, rural social workers have understood the unique ethical questions they sometimes face. But in the past twenty years, this issue has received increased attention and has been explicated in greater detail.

The early 1990s were a time of intense dialogue in social work about the interface of rural social work and the National Association of Social Workers' (NASW, 2012) professional Code of Ethics. During that period the NASW was in the process of making comprehensive revisions to the code. In 1993 NASW adopted a modified version of the code that included standards on nonsexual dual relationships, which created a great deal of controversy among rural social workers (Miller, 1998). Rural social workers were concerned because the new principles effectively prohibited dual relationships between social workers and clients. Many rural practitioners, particularly those in smaller communities, believed that it would be almost impossible to avoid all types of dual relationships, and that doing so would make rural social work incredibly difficult. The provision on dual relationships heightened potential vulnerability to ethics violations for rural social workers, as they might be prohibited from patronizing stores or garages, attending churches, or even getting their hair cut if a client worked at the business—all the transactions might create a dual relationship. In smaller communities it might not even be feasible to avoid all dual relationships, especially if the provision is interpreted as extending to include dual relationships with family members of clients, as well.

These concerns generated a great deal of anxiety, and rural social workers organized and mobilized through the National Rural Social Work Caucus to make changes to the language of the dual relationship provision. These efforts were successful, and in 1996 the section on dual relationships in the Code of Ethics was modified to permit dual relationships if unavoidable and if clients were protected from harm. During the course of the discussion about dual relationships, other aspects of the Code of Ethics were also scrutinized, as was the need to adapt practice to the rural environment and how this might affect social work. Subsequently, informative articles and chapters discussing social work ethics in a rural environment appeared in the professional literature, creating a much richer understanding of how to practice ethically with rural people as a result.

THE RURAL FISHBOWL AS A CONTEXT FOR ETHICAL PRACTICE

In rural communities people tend to know a lot about one another. Because most of the residents' interactions with individuals, organizations, and communities are personal in nature, people learn quite a bit about the lives, behavior, and economic standing of other community members. Some of what rural people know about others is through direct observation or social interaction, and some they learn indirectly through informal communication, which travels through one's family, friends, or acquaintances. With fewer people, all of whom are easily recognized, what people say and do is more widely known in rural areas than it is in a larger city.

In other words, there are not as many secrets in small towns, and people are not as anonymous as they might be in a big city. In some ways this means that rural people are always subject to observation. This kind of environment has been referred to as living and working in a fishbowl (Daley & Doughty, 2006)—like it or not, more people know your business in a rural area. So in rural life others are more likely to know your relatives or friends, what you do for a living, where you went to school and whether you were a good student, your past successes and mistakes, what kind of car you drive, who visited your house last week, your community involvement, and who your friends are. Some things may not be common knowledge, but many things are.

This kind of knowledge facilitates the personal relationships that are so much a part of social and business interactions in small communities. This kind of knowledge and personal interaction are functional in a rural environment, yet for professional social workers, this kind of widespread knowledge can present some ethical challenges. Both workers and clients are already known by everyone, and social workers can be sure that others will take note of any interventions. As Schott (1980) observed, "Nobody hides in a small town," and "everyone knows who is on welfare" (p. 135). Social workers may also find that observations about their personal behavior creep into the community's evaluation of their professional abilities.

Knowledge of others in a small community can be an advantage, too, for social workers, because it is easier to get information about people, but the potential disadvantage is that confidentiality can be difficult to maintain under the best of circumstances. In addition, community members might view professional principles like confidentiality as rude or trying to hide something people already know. Dual relationships have already been mentioned, but people in rural communities often have so many areas of social intersection that maintaining an appropriate professional distance in a helping relationship is a delicate balance between rural norms for personal interactions and the need to clarify one's professional role.

Several potential ethical issues in rural social work have been identified in the literature. Many of these appear be directly related to the close-knit quality of rural life. The major ethical challenges that have been identified are the difficulty of maintaining confidentiality, the fact that specialized professional expertise is not available, the difficulty of getting supervision, the fact that social workers are well known in the community, and the difficulty of avoiding dual and multiple relationships (Burkemper, 2005; Daley & Avant 1999; Daley & Hickman, 2011; Ginsberg, 1998, 2005; Green, 2003; Gumpert & Black, 2005; Miller, 1998; NASW, 2006).

The remainder of this chapter examines these ethical issues for rural practice and provides some suggestions about how to strengthen one's practice.

SOCIAL WORK ETHICS AND ETHICAL DECISION MAKING

Ethical behavior is simply good practice, and guidelines contained in an ethical code give professionals general guidelines for their activities. Since social work ethics are meant to apply to all social workers in different types of jobs across a wide variety of settings, they are necessarily broad principles for action. They apply to rural and urban social workers, direct practitioners, community organizers, and agency supervisors. The application of an ethical code to professional practice is necessarily a complex enterprise given the specific context, general standards of professional practice, and degrees of judgment and prudence.

In the United States the most broadly accepted standard is the NASW's (2012) Code of Ethics; in Canada it is the Canadian Association of Social Workers' (CASW, n.d.) Code of Ethics. The NASW represents the greatest number of social workers in the United States, and agreeing to abide by its Code of Ethics is a requirement for membership (NASW, 2012, n.d.). The CASW is a national association for social workers in the provinces and territories of Canada. The codes of ethics of both the NASW and the CASW are very influential in shaping the profession's view of what constitutes ethical behavior, and the two codes share many principles.

In the United States the NASW (2012) Code of Ethics is the standard for teaching values and ethics in social work (Council on Social Work Education, 2012), and state licensing bodies often incorporate the NASW code directly into their codes of conduct. About 50 percent of states reference the Code of Ethics in laws or administrative codes governing social work behavior (Morgan & Carvino, 2006), and even more are based entirely on the NASW Code of Ethics.

There has been some discussion in recent years of whether the context of rural practice is sufficiently different to merit a separate code of ethics. There are indeed some sections of the US and Canadian social work codes of ethics that are more challenging for rural social workers, yet most people agree that the existing codes can handle rural-specific issues, and that there is thus little need for a separate ethical code for rural social work (Boisen & Bosh, 2005; Daley & Doughty, 2006). As in any other practice setting, sound judgment and a working knowledge of ethical principles should be enough for workers to adapt and provide strong practice in their work with rural people.

Knowledge of a code of ethics is not enough, though, for rural social workers. Social work practice is a complex endeavor, and ethical decisions are often not clear cut. Models of ethical decision making help social workers evaluate relevant conditions in terms of the ethical code and develop a prudent course of action (Strom-Gottfried, 2007). There are several such models available, and it is wise for social workers to adopt one, since often knowledge of the code is not at issue, but application of that knowledge to real-life situations.

The model of ethical decision making presented here is that developed by Strom-Gottfried (2007); it includes six questions for social workers to consider in guiding ethical practice and covers the major considerations in approaching practice from an ethical perspective:

- Who will be helpful?
- What are my choices?
- When have I faced a similar dilemma?
- Where do ethical and clinical guidelines lead me?
- Why am I selecting a particular course of action?
- How should I enact my decision?

Many ethical choices have few completely clear or positive alternatives, and there may be a risk of creating some harm no matter which alternative a social worker selects. Since so many ethical considerations in rural practice center on either harm to clients or potential harm to clients, it is prudent to use the concept of least harm as a decision-making rule (Dolgoff, Loewenberg, & Harrington, 2005), particularly when making the most difficult decisions. Choosing a path of least harm refers to the process of selecting a path of intervention that has the least potential for negative consequences for the client while also trying to maximize the benefits of an array of services. For example, in a rural community some elderly

clients may live in substandard housing with few supports. Clearly there are benefits to encouraging them to move to a better living arrangement, but there may also be negative consequences, such as reducing clients' feelings of independence and severing ties with a place that could have significant meaning. Social workers may have to evaluate the benefits and harms of this approach with developing ways to improve existing housing, which also may have both benefits and negative consequences. Each of several courses of action may have disadvantages. All things being equal, it is best for social workers to opt for the choice that the client agrees with, and that has the greatest likelihood of a positive result and the least likelihood of negative consequences.

DUAL RELATIONSHIPS

Some of the earliest discussion about ethical rural practice was specifically about dealing with the dual relationships of social workers and clients (Miller, 1998). Because rural communities tend to be small, and because people have personal connections with many others in the community, it is often hard for social workers to avoid having nonprofessional relationships with clients and their families. If social workers develop both professional and nonprofessional relationships with clients, it may constitute a conflict of interest. Because of the nature of professional helping relationships and the potential vulnerability of clients, it is necessary for social workers to maintain clear professional boundaries to reduce the possibility of harm to clients. A potential for harm arises because there is a risk of the client either being exploited by or misinterpreting the nature of the relationship with the social worker.

Ethical standards on dual relationships and conflicts of interest with clients are covered in section 1.06 of the 2012 NASW Code of Ethics. The CASW's (n.d.) Code of Ethics addresses dual relationships in its values 3 and 4, which speak to placing the needs of others above self-interest in a professional capacity and to maintaining professional boundaries.

Dual relationships consist of social worker–client associations that are nonprofessional in nature and have the potential for conflicting interests to arise that may influence a social worker to act out of self-interest or in some other manner that is not in the client's best interests. Examples of dual relationships include social, family, or business relationships with a client, and in all nonprofessional relationships between worker and client there is potential for harm (Galbreath, 2005; Strom-Gottfried, 2000). Potentially, even accepting gifts from clients or bartering with them runs the risk of being viewed as a type of dual relationship and can be considered poor practice (Strom-Gottfried, 2000). Section 1.13(b) of the NASW (2012) Code of Ethics addresses accepting gifts or bartering with clients. Ethical issues arising from dual relationships and similar issues fall under a broad category of social worker behavior called boundary violations, which reflect lack of clarity in the relationship between social workers and clients (Strom-Gottfried, 2000). Boundary violations occur when social workers use poor professional judgment in terms of maintaining appropriate limits on professional and nonprofessional relationships. Responsible ethical behavior puts full responsibility on social workers to manage any dual relationship in a way that prevents harm to clients (NASW, 2012). An important point is that blurring the distinction between a professional and a nonprofessional relationship (e.g., a friendship) potentially puts clients at risk of exploitation or harm, and it can be risky practice. For example, clients who view their relationship with a social worker as that of being mutual friends might easily feel that their trust is violated if the social worker moves to terminate their professional relationship. So, keeping the professional nature of a helping relationship distinct from a personal one is important for ethical practice.

In rural communities there are fewer businesses, schools, churches, and social and recreational activities, and so there is a greater potential for social workers to interface with clients in a nonprofessional way. If a social worker has extended family in the community, and so does the client, then the potential for a dual relationship, even if inadvertent, is even more likely. In reality, this would mean that social workers in rural areas would have to travel many miles to repair their car, hire landscaping service, go shopping, or get a haircut. These types of things might be simply considered an inconvenience, but often they are impractical.

Fortunately for rural practice, neither the NASW nor the CASW Code of Ethics completely prohibits dual relationships. On occasions when dual relationships are unavoidable, the NASW (2012) code suggests that "social workers should take steps to protect clients and are responsible for setting clear, appropriate, and culturally sensitive boundaries" (p. 381). The emphasis is on social workers identifying the dual relationship and appropriately managing it through good judgment. The best practice for rural social workers, then, is to avoid dual relationships when possible and take great care to manage them when they are unavoidable.

There is little doubt that the dual relationship is the most frequently and comprehensively discussed ethical issue in rural social work (Bodor, 2005; Boisen & Bosch, 2005, 2011; Burkemper, 2005; Daley & Doughty, 2006; Galambos, Watt, Anderson, & Danis, 2005; Galbreath, 2005; Green, 2003; Gumpert & Black, 2005; Miller, 1998; Strom-Gottfried, 2005; Watkins, 2004). That the profession should be concerned with dual relationships in rural areas is entirely appropriate, as such relationships are potentially very problematic, and managing them requires a great deal of skill. For example, when Daley and Doughty (2006) examined ethical violations reported to one state licensing agency, they noted that in rural areas, boundary violations were the second most common type of ethical complaint, with such violations alleged in almost 20 percent of ethics complaints filed. Slightly more than half, 52 percent, of the rural boundary violations reported were for nonsexual dual relationships. However, an interesting finding of their research was that the reported percentage of boundary violations for rural social workers was somewhat lower than for urban social workers. This suggests that rural social workers might have found ways to more successfully manage or even avoid dual relationships.

In some circumstances avoiding dual relationships may be more problematic than trying to manage them, especially in a small community (Reamer, 1998). Rural communities frequently view impersonality or professional distance as rude (Martinez-Brawley, 2000). If dual relationships are not always avoidable in smaller communities, an important consideration for a social worker is how to manage them. For example, for a social function like a dinner or family reunion, or a community function like a church supper or baseball fund-raiser, purposely excluding clients, or members of clients' families, could easily be seen as a snub and could generate ill will. People might perceive that the social worker in such cases is trying to put on airs. Such behavior, though perhaps prudent or desirable from a professional point of view, might create the impression that a social worker feels superior to community members or self-important, or does not really understand or belong in the community. This can ultimately affect how people respond to the social worker.

Of course, there might even be subtler issues. For example, a social worker and his or her client might both have a child who is involved in the one sports team in the community. Does the social worker need to remove his or her child from sports to avoid a dual relationship? Or another example is this: if a community has one car and truck repair shop, which is where the social worker's client works, where does the social worker go for repairs? When these kinds of issues arise, it is wise for rural social workers to view them through an ethical lens.

One of the first considerations is evaluating the potential for a dual relationship, the options in managing it, and the potential for harm to the client. The possibility for harm should be evaluated from various perspectives: client, social worker, colleagues, supervisors, and community. A second consideration is whether there is a reasonable way to avoid the relationship. Referring the client to another social worker or service can be an answer if this is a viable option, but if the next social worker is thirty miles away, this probably is not a good choice.

If dual relationships and potential conflicts of interest are unavoidable, as they often are in rural work, then the social worker should consider how to manage the relationship and protect the client. It is important to assess the potential for harm, and all options available may involve some degree of risk. But the greater the potential harm, the stronger the safeguards should be. In selecting from among alternatives, more questions from the model of ethical decision making need to be addressed, including the following:

- whether the course of action taken is based on a risk assessment, is culturally sensitive, is based on client preference, and is reasonable
- whether a similar situation has been faced before
- where the guidelines of good practice suggest that the social worker go

In the end, a professional relationship should not appear suspicious to others, and considering all of these dimensions will help avoid that. What is important is that the social worker neither gives or receives—or is perceived as giving or receiving—any special treatment as part of the relationship.

Other thorny ethical issues for rural social worker are barter and gifts. These can be seen as a type of boundary violation in a professional relationship that may create conflicts of interest and/or exploitation. Barter is addressed in section 1.13 of the 2012 NASW Code of Ethics. Gifts could be considered extra compensation that may influence a social worker's actions. But in many rural communities barter and gifts are common and accepted, and often gifts are offered as an expression of goodwill, with no expectation of the recipient benefiting. Barter and gifts are basic and important forms of social interaction and exchange in rural life. Common examples of this include offering someone jelly, produce, or homemade food. Rejecting such offers can be seen as rude, and social workers have to consider weighing the relative harm that might occur to a client. The difficulty with barter and gifts is that it is often difficult to establish a fair market value for such things, and accepting gifts might be viewed as accepting additional compensation for services that will unduly influence professional judgment. In general, accepting a few ears of corn as a gesture of goodwill is probably fine, but accepting a handmade quilt worth hundreds of dollars is another matter entirely. Of course, it depends on the circumstances of each situation. Consider the following case example:

> Amanda is a BSW social worker employed for about four months as a county juvenile probation officer in the town of Freemont. Freemont is a town of 16,500 residents that serves as a regional center for Madison County, a rural county with a population of 43,200. One of Amanda's probationers is Fernando, a twelve-year-old Hispanic boy who has been in trouble for repeated truancy. Fernando's father, Juan, works for a local automotive repair shop and his mother, Lupe, works in housekeeping at a local motel. Lupe also sells her popular homemade tamales, for eight dollars a dozen, to make extra income. Both parents speak English but not very well, and they are at a disadvantage in dealing with the school and court systems. Amanda is working to assess what would help the family improve Fernando's school attendance and to identify any other needs that may be present.

> Amanda and Fernando's family both attend the same church, but they usually attend different services, as one is offered in Spanish. Amanda also patronizes the same auto shop where Juan works, as it is the best in town, and Amanda's son plays with Fernando on the same team in the youth soccer league. In an expression of gratitude for her helping the family, Lupe offers Amanda a gift of a dozen fresh tamales, and Fernando says that he will work on Amanda's car for no charge.

What is Amanda to do? A frank discussion with the clients about their nonprofessional relationship in the context of professional helping is in order. First, they need to reach some agreement as to how they will handle chance meetings at church. Do they act as if they do not know each other so that others do not discover that the family is a client, or do they approach it as any other chance public meeting and agree not to discuss business there? What about car repairs? If she does that, will it affect how Juan's employer views his work? Or should she just have the work done and pay for it as any other customer would? Should she accept the tamales as a gift, or should she pay for them? Is $8 worth of goods enough for anyone to expect that Amanda will offer the clients preferential treatment or that it will exploit the client?

CONFIDENTIALITY

All social workers are aware of the need to maintain confidentiality about client information they receive in the course of the professional relationship. Confidentiality is important in encouraging clients to trust social workers and in enhancing the engagement process (Barsky, 2010). Since a strong worker-client relationship is the foundation of professional helping, confidentiality is important to the helping process as well. When clients know that a social worker has integrity and will not disclose sensitive information, it is likely to help empower clients. Confidentiality is covered in section 1.07 of the 2012 NASW Code of Ethics, and it is a complex concept requiring in-depth knowledge and sophistication in professional judgment.

Rural communities present real challenges in maintaining client confidentiality, as the very fabric of the rural community often works against anything being kept entirely confidential for very long. The analogy of life in the fishbowl is entirely appropriate for rural areas, because so much is known to the public. At some level, people's family stories, their own history, and their behavior are likely to be known widely, and so most people are not anonymous faces in the crowd. Individuals and their cars are readily recognized, and their relationships and transactions in the community business known (Carlton-LaNey, Edwards, & Reid, 1999). In rural communities it is common for people to have close relationships and frequent exchanges with, and even know the habits of, other community members. As a result, it is difficult to hide information, especially social, business, and personal problems. These are the kinds of issues that rural people tend to notice and discuss. They might not necessarily be busybodies, but often people talk because there is a general sense of concern about community members and people may want to help. Given that confidential information is often already widely known before social workers ever become involved, personal matters such as marital problems, financial issues, a death in the family, or someone dealing with an alcohol or drug problem (Ginsberg, 1998) may already be part of the community's conversation.

It is really not surprising in this type of environment that client confidentiality has been identified as a potential ethical issue (Burkemper, 2005; Daley & Doughty, 2006; Daley & Pierce, 2011; Galambos et al., 2005; Green, 2003; Gumpert & Black, 2005; Strom-Gottfried, 2005). This concern is not unique to social work, as it has also been raised in regard to rural psychologists (Helbok, Marinelli, & Walls, 2006). Adequately addressing the complex elements of confidentiality outlined in section 1.07 of the 2012 NASW Code of Ethics requires very sophisticated practice judgments, and the fishbowl rural life adds another element to that complexity.

There are four things for rural social workers to consider as possible threats to client confidentiality. The first is common knowledge. The reasons for which clients seek help are likely already known in much of the community. The "horse is out of the barn," so to speak, and people know about or can guess as to clients' problems and what they are doing about them. Indeed, people might use any knowledge they have to probe clients or social workers for more information. This might give the appearance of a social worker having breached confidentiality, when in fact this is not true. One solution is for workers to discuss this with clients at an early stage of the engagement process.

The second consideration is that eyes are everywhere. Rural people recognize community members in all sorts of settings. They might see people traveling from place to place, or observe their cars parked on a street. They might notice who visits the client's house and the frequency of any visits. People can then assess what they know, place a social worker and client together, and make assumptions about what is going on. These observations may or may not be accurate, but they might give the appearance of a breach of confidentiality. This is best addressed early in the relationship and should take into consideration how, where, and under what circumstances the worker should conduct meetings. This kind of decision is usually best made with clients' input.

The third consideration is the family factor. A client's family is an important source of support in a rural community, but the family can also be a source of information about the client to others in the community. If the client discusses something with a family member, or if a social worker collects information from a family member, that information is sometimes communicated to others through casual conversation, which may appear to be a breach of confidentiality. Family members are not held to the same standard of confidentiality as social workers are, and some prudence in discussions with family members about possible effects on the client of such conversations is advisable.

The fourth thing for social workers to consider is that "other agencies know this already." Community-based agencies are often a small circle and part of the close-knit rural community. Clients who have multiple issues and have sought help previously are probably known to more than one agency. Perhaps a client has not visited a particular agency, but a close family member has, and so that agency has preexisting knowledge of the client. Social workers and agencies should handle confidential client information appropriately, but all agency workers are not social workers. Other staff might not practice confidentiality in the same ways as social workers and disclose what they know to others. It is important for rural social workers to identify what other agencies know already, particularly if a client has worked with other agencies before. This will help create awareness about what client information is already known. Discussions with the client to cover what other agencies know can also be helpful in clarifying how the social worker will use confidential information and the circumstances under which it might be disclosed.

Evidence seems to suggest that rural social workers generally find ways to manage client confidentiality effectively. A study of ethical complaints against social workers found that reports of confidentiality violations were similar for both rural and urban workers, both at only 10 percent (Daley & Doughty, 2006). Several strategies for managing confidentiality in rural practice have been proposed. Both Burkemper (2005) and Strom-Gottfried (2005) support the idea of using informed consent as an effective tool to decrease the risk of confidentiality violations in rural practice. Clearly developed understandings among both clients and family members about confidentiality and how to manage sensitive information help reduce social workers' risk of violating ethics (Strom-Gottfried, 2005). Involving community agencies in an appropriate way can also help clarify what kind of client information may be general knowledge, thus guiding efforts to keep additional sensitive information from public knowledge (Gumpert & Black, 2005). Consider the following scenario:

> Lars is a forty-five-year-old man with a history of treatment for bipolar disorder. He has had periods in which the disorder is controlled well, and during those times he is usually employed and lives independently. But when his disorder is not well controlled, Lars self-medicates by drinking excessively, and his behavior toward others becomes loud and offensive. He has often lost his job during these periods and has had to move in with his brother. His behavior is well known to the community, a town of 4,600 people, and he is known locally as "Looney Lars." Recently, Lars has begun to drink heavily, and two days ago was seen recklessly shooting his shotgun late at night in front of his brother's house. The neighbors called the local sheriff, but since Lars's brother lived outside of town, where it was legal for him to shoot his gun, they only warned Lars and took away his ammunition. Lars's brother has had it and says Lars cannot live at his house any more, and he made a referral to local mental health services.

There are several confidentiality issues that this scenario could raise for a social worker. Given Lars's history of troublesome behavior, the community already knows about at least some of his situation. People in such a small town might even know that Lars has a mental illness and has been treated for it in the past. Lars's brother might feel that he has to discuss the situation with friends and neighbors to explain his own actions. It is also likely that some people will know when Lars goes to the mental health services center for screening and treatment. So the kind of confidentiality one might expect in a large city is nonexistent.

The social worker may need to be explicit in discussion with Lars that people in town already know some information about him (and perhaps considerable information) and explore his comfort level with ongoing treatment in a way that protects as much of his confidentiality as possible. The social worker may need Lars's informed consent to get records about his past treatments. The social worker also needs to collect information to make informed choices about all the questions raised in the ethical decision-making model. Lars and/or his brother and past service providers could be helpful in providing information.

COMPETENCY AND ADEQUACY OF PRACTICE

One of the most perplexing ethical dilemmas that rural social workers face may be requests for help in areas where they do not have a strong professional background. No social worker is equally skilled in every arena of practice, but in most instances social workers very capably help clients to the best of their ability. Yet there still may be areas where clients need help and a social worker appears to lack the appropriate background to respond. Social worker competence is addressed in sections 1.04(a)–(c), 4.01(a)–c(c), and 4.06 of the 2012 NASW Code of Ethics. The sections speak to representation and provision of services only within boundaries of training, education, and supervision; remaining proficient and accepting responsibility on the basis of competence; practice within recognized knowledge; and accurately presenting professional qualifications.

In many states BSW-level and some MSW-level practice without close supervision is subject to licensing restrictions and may be prohibited. This is generally the case for clinical services. In a small community social workers may be asked to assist clients with a mental health issue, for example. However, a dilemma arises when a social worker lacks the professional background or credentials to provide that service, even if he or she is still the best-qualified person to deal with the situation. What is the social worker to do—ignore the call for help? Then the ethical conflict becomes that of professional competency versus the need to serve the client. This problem is more acute in rural areas because there are fewer workers and resources, and sometimes fewer social workers with advanced skills. If an appropriate professional and/or service are otherwise available, then a good referral is the solution. But in a rural area, a social worker who lacks ideal professional credentials may be the best of limited options.

The match, or lack thereof, between rural worker competency and clients' need has been identified either as poor practice and/or social work incompetence in the professional literature on ethics (Burkemper, 2005; Croxton, Jayaratne, & Mattison, 2002; Daley & Doughty 2006; Strom-Gottfried, 2005). "Poor practice" describes social workers whose skills do not appear to measure up to the expected level of professional standards required for a particular service. This type of situation is also referred to as a matter of professional competency. In essence, this is referring to significantly substandard performance by a social worker, as a result of inadequate preparation or background. An example is being asked to diagnose a mental illness or provide treatment services without an appropriate license, or failure to use professional supervision appropriately. A less-than-ideal social work practice that still falls within professional norms is not desirable, but it may not be an ethical violation per se.

Occasions do arise when rural social workers are asked to cross over generally accepted practice standards in the name of helping clients. This type of request is usually because people in the community know, respect, and trust the social worker. Community members might be unaware of professional standards, or they might not particularly care and instead want a problem solved or what is best for a client. But it is incumbent on social workers to be responsible for recognizing appropriate professional standards for service and supervision and to act accordingly.

For rural social workers, poor practice is an area of some ethical risk. Daley and Doughty (2006) found that poor practice is the area of greatest difference between rural and urban social workers in terms of reported ethics violations. They found a higher percentage of poor practice complaints for rural than for urban social workers. With 27 percent of reports for rural social workers being for poor practice, it was the most frequently reported violation (Daley & Doughty, 2006). In a study of social work ethics violations reported to the NASW, Strom-Gottfried (2000) also found a high percentage of reports for poor practice, 38 percent, although she did not differentiate between rural and urban practice settings. In that study the most common form of poor practice was use of inappropriate treatment methods, which may indicate either inadequate preparation or poor professional judgment.

Poor practice is an especially challenging area for rural social workers because they tend to be somewhat autonomous in their practice, have broad responsibilities, and face challenges in working with distant supervisors and colleagues. Continuing education is also more difficult for them (Burkemper, 2005; Croxton et al., 2002; Ginsberg, 1998). In addition, rural communities have high percentages of BSW social workers and low percentages of MSW social workers with advanced and specialized training (Daley & Avant, 1999). Consequently, rural social workers are more likely to be in situations that require advanced practice skills and/or for which they might not be adequately prepared. Compounding the situation, appropriate supervision may not be readily available (Daley & Doughty, 2006). The ethical dilemma rural social workers face under such conditions is whether to provide the service they can or provide no service at all (Croxton et al., 2002).

Under these circumstances, what can rural social workers do to practice ethically? Social workers can meet the challenges of distance, isolation, and available resources through careful advanced planning. Some of the following suggestions may prove useful in that regard.

Know Your Limitations

Social workers should take a good inventory of their professional preparation and try to understand its limitations as well as the requirements of any professional license they hold. For example, generalist practice is a good background for rural social work and in many practice situations.

But it is not necessarily an ideal background for providing clinical services to people with terminal illness, for example, and members of their families. Advanced education, continuing education, and relevant work experience under supervision may help workers develop skills to a point at which they meet accepted professional standards for this area of practice. It might not be easy, and it will take some work, but if specific skills are in demand in the community, then it would be wise for social workers to develop them.

Strong Professional Networks

It is also wise for social workers to develop supervisory and consultative arrangements with professional colleagues to assist them in evaluating situations and developing plans for dealing with those situations effectively. This may take some extra work and travel if there are few social workers in the community, but the time will be well spent. Other social workers can be excellent partners in talking through problems, solutions, and decisions. Other social workers also can provide an additional perspective and help avoid any lurking ethical pitfalls. In fact, consulting with supervisors and colleagues is typically viewed as an effective way to show reasonable planning efforts with a client and strengthen practice (Strom-Gottfried, 2005). Arrangements with colleagues also provide social workers with the potential for valuable professional learning and growth, both of which help reduce the ethical risk of practicing beyond one's expertise.

Learn about Available Resources

Resources are a basic part of any social worker's tool kit because accessing services and resources to meet client needs is an important part of effective service delivery. Learning about resources has added significance in a rural community because there may not be as many resources from which to choose, and resources might be spread over a wide area, especially specialized services. Larger rural clinics and mental health centers that deliver a wider array of specialized services might be regional centers, not in the immediate area. Learning about available resources will take some time and outreach, as social workers will have to make contacts with key people in other agencies so that referrals go more smoothly when needed.

Use of the ethical decision-making model and assessment of potential for harm to a client are useful in determining how social workers should engage in appropriate practice. Rural workers should not feel like a lone wolf—they should ask for help when needed. Consider the following case scenario:

> Jane is a social worker with an MSW, licensed at the graduate social work level, and she has two years of experience. Earlier in the year she accepted a "Social Worker II" position in the Garfield County satellite clinic of the Holyfield Regional Mental Health Center, located in Arthur City. The satellite clinic is in Guiteau, a town of 9,200 people that is seventy-five miles from Arthur City. Jane is the only social worker, and the clinic is also staffed by a mental health nurse, two caseworkers, a secretary, and a mental health aide. A woman named Ruby is brought to the clinic by a local constable who picked her up for "erratic behavior." According to the constable, Ruby has been seen walking the streets frequently, enters businesses with no apparent purpose, asks strange questions of people she does not know, is often seen talking to and answering herself, and sometimes has a dirty and unkempt appearance. Ruby's husband comes to the clinic as well and wants her committed for treatment in Guiteau. Ruby and her husband both want her to leave the community, and they have neither the funds nor the transportation to make regular trips to Arthur City. The constable is not comfortable dealing with Ruby anymore, as he has already made several trips to their house. Jane feels pressure to act without delay.

In exploring her options in this case, Jane would need to assess the urgency of Ruby's current situation and existing options for a mental health screening, as well as develop potential options. Jane may be able to provide some counseling services, but by law she needs to be under supervision to do so, and just how she would get the appropriate supervision would have to be explored.

PERSONAL AND PROFESSIONAL IDENTITY

The closeness of a rural community can create potential ethical challenges for social workers regarding separation of personal and professional life. Sections 4.03 and 1.06 of the 2012 NASW Code of Ethics ("Private Conduct and Conflicts of Interest") indicate that social workers are expected to keep separate their personal and professional roles. In many circumstances, that is easy enough because social workers work in one environment and live in another. But in rural areas, there is much less separation between the personal and the professional world. Just as the community's eyes are on the client, they are on the social worker, and there is not the personal anonymity that one might find in a larger city.

Rural people tend to view others in personal terms—who they are related to, who knows them, and what is known about them. In a rural setting there is much less concern for a person's formal position of social worker, and perhaps for their professional accomplishments. The rural focus on the personal versus the professional can create professional concerns for social workers because it often blurs the personal-professional role. So when social workers return home from work to the community, others might still view them as a social worker. Similarly, when social workers go to work, they may not be viewed as professionals, but as, for example, the niece or nephew of the woman who lives down the street. Rural residents frequently do not distinguish personal and professional.

This lack of distinction can create some tension for rural social workers who are trying to create and maintain a personal and professional self while also trying to gain acceptance in the community (Strom-Gottfried, 2005). On the one hand is the need to maintain professional distance, and on the other hand is the need to be accepted by the community. As a practical matter, rural social workers have to adapt to community norms of personal relationships (Ginsberg, 1998; Martinez-Brawley, 2000). If there is too much professional distance, social workers will not be accepted, as small communities often expect that professionals be known personally first in order to fit in. Formal professional credentials and positions tend to be a secondary consideration and are not as blindly accepted as they are in urban practice. Being viewed as too formal or distant is likely to reduce clients' and the community's desire to cooperate.

Ethical issues can arise in one of two ways. First, community members might observe the social worker's behavior or lifestyle, and if it does not conform to norms, then it might affect the social worker's reputation. Second, any personal disclosure made to clients in the course of service delivery could be interpreted as weakness and information spread to the community. For example, in working with a client who has a drinking problem, to build rapport, a social worker might disclose that the issue is something with which he or she struggled personally. However, the client might misinterpret this as a display of weakness, and then spread the information through the community grapevine, thus diminishing the general opinion of the social worker. Or, a social worker might be working with a family on money management, yet observations of the social worker's own shopping and spending habits could leave the impression that his or her skills in that area are questionable.

The fishbowl environment of a rural community means that any personal disclosure has the potential of being a double edged-sword for social workers, and so they should make such disclosures with caution. Revealing too much or the wrong kind of information might risk that information's spread to the whole community, because while client information may be confidential, information about the social worker may not—besides, people are likely to think it makes good gossip. This kind of talk occurs everywhere, but the rural community tends to have smaller social networks with overlapping connections, and so any information, especially negative information, can find its way into all kinds of relationships.

When social workers are not open enough with clients or the community, it can raise issues of either competence (section 4.01 of the 2012 NASW Code of Ethics) or misrepresentation (section 4.06). But when social workers disclose too much about themselves, it can raise questions of private versus professional conduct (section 4.03) and/or affect the level of competence (section 4.01). Balancing these concerns is a delicate act given the nature of a rural community.

When community members and/or clients see social workers as different from the norm, or as having personal issues of their own, they might question their ability to either understand needs or provide help. If social workers themselves seek help for personal or family needs or show a personal weakness, these things too can become known in a small community (Green, 2003). If social workers are aware of this, they might be reluctant to seek the help they need in the interests of maintaining their professional reputation. The result of this might be a conflict with the ethical provision in section 4.05(b) of the 2012 NASW Code of Ethics, which states that social workers should get help when problems or difficulties interfere with their performance and judgment (see also Strom-Gottfried, 2005). Social workers are ethically responsible for identifying when their personal problems interfere with the performance of their professional duties by seeking assistance to ameliorate those problems. In rural life some of these ethical choices are difficult.

The point is not just that the lack of anonymity leads to potential challenges for social workers, but that they have awareness of this so that they can avoid difficulties. Once again, the question is how to manage these challenges in the rural community. There is no substitute for prudence, self-awareness, and good professional judgment in dealing with these challenges. In this respect, using the ethical decision-making model, assessing the potential for harm, and drawing on professional networks can be helpful to social workers in thinking through what is appropriate and what is not. If a social worker is uncomfortable in having all aspects of his or her personal life on view, then he or she might need to work in other communities where they are not known. When a social worker requires specific types of services to address personal issues, and it is important for the community not to be aware of them, then seeking help outside the community is an appropriate action. Consider the following example:

> Bill is a twenty-seven-year-old social worker who began his career in Iowa. Soon after finishing school, taking a job, and moving to a new community in Iowa, Bill and his wife began to have marital problems. Within six months they divorced. Bill began taking prescription medications to help him cope with the breakup of his marriage. He eventually realized that he was abusing the medication and that it was affecting his work, and so he sought help. Bill's treatment was successful, and Bill decided to take a new job and move to a new area. He accepted a job as a social worker in the Division of Family Services in a different state, in the town of Honeysuckle. Honeysuckle is a town of 26,300 people that serves three rural counties. After working there for six months Bill has

learned that many of the families he works with have substance abuse issues with alcohol, marijuana, and methamphetamine. Bill is a bit of an outsider and some folks in Honeysuckle call him "that Yankee." Bill understands that some sharing of his experiences may help him work better with the Honeysuckle population, but he is cautious because it is a small community. He also wants to continue follow-up services for his own substance abuse issues. The mental health center in Honeysuckle has a group that meets every two weeks and he is considering enrolling, but he is also thinking about driving the hour and a half to the city of Jackson to get services.

In this case Bill will have to consider the merits of convenience in using follow-up services in Honeysuckle, as it will certainly save him time, energy, and expense over commuting to Jackson for services. However, in receiving services locally, he may encounter some clients or their friends or relatives who could be using the same group. Such group meetings would certainly create uncomfortable and possibly ethically compromising relationships. Use of the local group could also mean that Bill's past substance abuse issues could become known in the community and would be the subject of some speculation about his past and perhaps his competence. Even parking his car near where the group is offered could be a way that the local community finds out about his past. Bill will have to carefully weigh these issues, as well as any self-disclosure about his past substance abuse issues.

RELATIONSHIPS WITH COLLEAGUES

While the most extensive discussion of social work ethics has centered on the worker-client relationship, all social work practice occurs in a broader context, many times in an agency context. Social workers routinely interact with colleagues, supervisors, support staff, and others in the agency and community. Expectations for professional conduct extend beyond the client to include other professionals and coworkers who interact with the social worker in the course of doing business. Relationships with colleagues and supervisors are important to getting the job done, and these relationships may be at least as common as those with clients. The NASW

Code of Ethics addresses the profession's expectations for the social worker in relationships with colleagues and supervisors in sections 2, 3, and 4.

Being able to work collaboratively with colleagues and supervisors is a significant part of social work because these people can ultimately affect a social worker's ability to help clients. When friction or bad relationships develop between professionals, clients and the public can suffer as a result. Clients might be exploited to resolve differences between colleagues, and valuable time and energy are lost in disputes that could otherwise go toward providing service. Angry or hurt colleagues can thwart the best efforts of any social worker. In any event, the quality of service can suffer.

A rural community provides a context in which developing and maintaining good professional relationships with one's peers is essential. Yet while most agree that a rural community has complex, multiple, and overlapping relationships between social workers and clients, few extend the discussion to the effects on collegial relationships as Daley and Hickman (2011) do. The close personal relationships common in smaller towns also extend to limited professional and service communities, and contact with service providers is often frequent, personal, and close. The close relationships are necessary for the rural community to work well (Martinez-Brawley, 2000), but close professional or personal relationships can create potential for significant ethical conflict if they go bad. It is important for social workers to treat other colleagues and supervisors appropriately.

Because of the size and informality of a rural community, social workers are likely to have multiple overlapping relationships with colleagues. The close relationships that rural social workers have with community members might even compromise their ability to develop a trusting and open relationship with their supervisors (Green, 2003). For example, a worker and supervisor may have an intricate network of friends, relatives, and colleagues. Concern about the subject of discussions outside the office getting back to a worker or supervisor could affect the openness of any discussions they have. The nature of social relationships in a town can also affect professional interactions. For example, say a social worker supervises a worker who is related to the president of the local bank. This undoubtedly affects the supervisory relationship to some degree, as any conflicts or disagreements in the community could easily carry over into the office, personal grudges may move into the professional arena, and vice versa. For example, if the supervisor gets into a disagreement with someone in the community who turns out to be a close friend or relative of the worker, any ill feelings generated may be channeled through that worker back into the workplace. In situations of this kind, it might matter who knows whom, how, what old favors are owed, and what feuds still exist.

Sections 2 and 3 of the NASW's (2012) Code of Ethics cover social workers' ethical relationships with colleagues and supervisors. In these sections the Code of Ethics defines what is expected in these types of interactions. Although the Code of Ethics is not specific about what to do and what not to do, it generally prescribes that honesty, respect, and fairness characterize relationships. Social workers' sound professional judgment in following these principles is the key to ethical practice.

Another specific ethical challenge that rural social workers face is the issue of unwarranted negative criticism of colleagues (section 2.01(b); NASW, 2012). In offices everywhere there is a tendency to gossip or talk at the water cooler. This is not exclusively a rural phenomenon, and social workers are certainly not exempt from it. Besides being time consuming, though, discussing others in the work environment can be disruptive, especially when office talk takes on a critical tone. Ginsberg (2001) advises against making any criticism, accusation, or tattling because most people resent this. Openly criticizing the competency and skill of another professional in his or her absence may be especially troublesome. In a rural community there is less anonymity and social distance between people, and it is more likely that information about that criticism gets back to people through other sources, such as friends, family, and church contacts, either directly or indirectly. Something said while shopping or over dinner might be easily overheard by someone else, which could create professional conflict that may erupt with clients, in the office, or even in a public arena. And these kinds of conflicts may have long-lasting repercussions.

Under these circumstances rural social workers should be very careful about how they discuss their colleagues. More personal conversations, such as about how a colleague dresses or where he or she was last night, belong somewhere besides the workplace, or at the very least behind closed doors. If there truly is an issue with a colleague, the Code of Ethics suggests that a social worker discuss the matter with his or her colleague directly, which shows appropriate professional respect and can lead to a resolution. If the issue is a misinterpretation or misunderstanding, then it can be resolved without undue conflict or hard feelings. If there is no resolution, only after careful thought should the social worker have a discussion with a supervisor. Consider the following case example:

> Erin is a social worker employed by the Northeastern Tri-County Agency on Aging. She is responsible for supervising the In-Home Case Management Program, and she occasionally provides direct services. Erin is well experienced, is licensed, and is well respected by her peers. Four months ago the agency director hired a new staff member, Betty, with a background in counseling to oversee the intake program. For the past two months Erin has noticed, among other things, that Betty has been condescending to her and to members of the case management team; that Betty is frequently not available to her staff, so they have been coming to Erin for advice; and that Betty has been openly critical of the case management team for not referring most clients for counseling. Erin has discovered that Betty has little experience with the elderly, as her work experience has been primarily in play therapy with children. But Erin also understands that she should approach this situation cautiously because Betty's sister is a prominent lawyer and her brother is an influential minister in town. There is clearly friction between Erin and Betty that could extend into other areas, especially since Erin is dating a lawyer and is a member of the church where Betty's brother is the minister.

In this case, Erin would need more detailed information to suggest a specific solution to her problem, but some of the possible implications of conflict between colleagues are apparent.

ETHICAL RURAL PRACTICE

Among rural social workers there is consensus that the rural environment poses its own ethical risks for practitioners, which are important to manage (Daley & Doughty, 2006; Daley & Hickman, 2011; Daley & Pierce,

2011; Galbreath, 2005; Ginsberg, 2005; Martinez-Brawley, 2000; NASW, 2006). Many of these risks appear tied to the close, personal nature of relationships, the fishbowl environment, and multiple overlapping relationships that are more likely to occur in a rural community (Boisen & Bosh, 2005). Although much of this chapter has focused on the potential risks faced by rural social workers, it is important to consider general strategies for managing these risks to promote good ethical practice.

Most social workers in rural settings manage ethical hurdles quite well and appear to have found ways to adapt practice to rural environments (Daley & Doughty, 2006). There is no single approach to use in doing this, but skilled social workers will find ways to naturally adapt to a rural community. Some practical suggestions drawn from the ethics literature for promoting ethical practice may prove helpful for adapting ethical practice to rural settings. Many suggestions are not unique to rural work but represent sound practice strategies overall. Of course, sound professional judgment and assessment of the risk of harm in using these tools is essential. The following sections cover the steps social workers should take in using these tools and creating an approach.

Identify Potential Ethical Issues and Conflicts

Every social worker must assess the cases and situations with which he or she deals, and part of that assessment should include an analysis of ethical problems that may arise. Potential ethical issues must first be identified to be effectively addressed, lest they become actual problems (Burkemper, 2005; Reamer, 2006). A prerequisite for a social worker's ethical assessment is a good working knowledge of the relevant code of ethics (Gumpert & Black, 2005). An ethical code and its principles can always be used as a reference when specific situations or questions arise. Through experience in applying the code to real-life situations, social workers learn the complexities of how the code works and can then incorporate patterns of ethical behavior into practice. In screening situations for ethical issues, social workers should use a standard of reasonable prudence. If they have any doubt about whether something is an ethical issue, then it bears a deeper look, and perhaps discussions with colleagues or supervisors. Use of an ethical decision-making model is also very helpful.

Seek Consultation from Colleagues or Supervisors

Professional colleagues and supervisors are an important resource for assessing risks and suggesting strategies for managing ethical risk (Boisen & Bosch, 2005; Daley & Doughty, 2006; Dolgoff et al., 2005; Galbreath, 2005; Reamer, 2006; Strom-Gottfried, 2005). Consultation demonstrates that the social worker has been reasonable in making attempts to practice within an ethical framework. The importance of supervision and consultation cannot be overstated; they provide an independent assessment and another perspective, and they draw on the experience and practice skills of others. Because rural social workers face more challenges in accessing supervisors and colleagues, they should spend extra time and effort in building strong connections with others (Burkemper, 2005; Daley & Doughty, 2006; Galbreath, 2005; Ginsberg, 1998, 2005).

Use Informed Consent

The multiple relationships that often exist in the rural community can be a source of confusion for clients, family members, and community members when engaging with a professional social worker. The expectation that relationships develop on a personal, rather than impersonal, basis is another potential source of confusion. These expectations sometimes make it difficult for clients to interpret the social worker's role appropriately. Is a social worker a professional, neighbor, church member, or something else? Under these circumstances, professional boundaries can become fuzzy, and a potential for ethical problems arises. Use of informed consent to clarify the respective roles of client and social worker is a good way to avoid any misunderstandings that could lead to ethical problems (Burkemper, 2005; Galambos et al. 2005; Gumpert & Black, 2005; NASW, 2012; Strom-Gottfried, 2005). Discussions about informed consent are also an effective way to introduce and clarify confidentiality, and to explain its limitations and how information will be used, as well as circumstances in which disclosure may be made. During these discussions some attention should be given to the visibility of individuals in a rural community and the informal networks of communication, in order to prepare clients for the possibility that people surmise things that have not been disclosed.

Documentation

In any ethical practice the responsibility for ensuring that professional boundaries are maintained and appropriate practice standards met falls squarely on the shoulders of the social worker (Boisen & Bosh, 2005; Galbreath, 2005). It is on the rare occasion when disputes between client and worker arise that the extent to which the social worker actually did something is called into question. Social workers are well served by keeping good records of their work, which is also sound professional practice. Documentation may even protect social workers from charges of malfeasance, misfeasance, or nonfeasance (Reamer, 2006). In other words, good documentation may provide protection in the case of complaints about professional actions that are harmful or illegal, professional work improperly done, or failure to do required work. Accurate and detailed contemporaneous records can show professional decisions, practice methods used, and discussions and disclosures with clients, and it can reduce reliance on memory of what may have happened in the past. Documentation can also contain information on the use of supervision or consultation.

CONCLUSION

Rural communities present social workers with a unique social structure and cultural conventions that require the adapting of methods for ethical practice. Rural people are close, interconnected, and interact on a personal basis. The fishbowl environment of small towns also puts much of people's lives, past, and behavior in the public domain.

Social work with rural people needs to be especially sensitive to situations that might entail dual relationships, bartering and gifts, threats to confidentiality, competency to practice, personal and professional identity, and relationships with colleagues. Despite heightened ethical risks in these areas, rural practitioners can manage such risks with sound professional judgment. Important considerations for sound ethical practice include the use of an ethical decision-making model, assessment of potential harm, collaborative work with clients, the seeking out of consultation and supervision, use of informed consent, and documentation.

The best approach to address potential ethical issues in rural practice is nearly always to avoid them if practicable, but this might not be an option on every occasion. When ethical concerns arise, it is the social worker's responsibility to protect clients, the community, and the profession by setting clear and appropriate boundaries (NASW, 2012). This can be done only on the basis of a good understanding of the professional code of ethics, the rural community, and rural social work (Boisen & Bosch, 2005; Burkemper, 2005; Daley & Avant, 2004; Daley & Hickman, 2011; Ginsberg, 2005; Gumpert & Black, 2005; Martinez-Brawley, 2000).

Assessing client, family, and community in terms of interventions and codes of ethics is a complex endeavor requiring critical thinking and good judgment. It is commendable that so many rural social workers learn to do this and to do it well. The ongoing discussions of rural social work and the NASW Code of Ethics around dual relationships have been productive in that they have led to a broader consideration of rural concerns in the past few years. The subsequent emergence of literature highlighting rural challenges to confidentiality, personal and professional identity, competency of practice, and relationships with colleagues is a positive sign that more thought is being devoted to adapting social work to rural communities. But, then, rural social workers may have been moving ahead of the literature all along, as practitioners have been ethically delivering services to smaller communities for some time.

REFERENCES

Barsky, A. E. (2010). *Ethics and values in social work.* New York, NY: Oxford University Press.

Bodor, R. C. (2005). Nonsexual dual and multiple relationships: When urban worldviews define rural reality. In B. Locke & V. Majewski (Eds.), *Finding our voices, having our say: Meeting the challenges of rural communities* (pp. 104–119). Morgantown, WV: West Virginia Division of Social Work.

Boisen, L. S., & Bosh, L.A. (2005). Dual relationships and rural social work: Is there a rural code? In L. H. Ginsberg (Ed.), *Social work in rural communities* (4th ed., pp. 189–203). Alexandria, VA: Council on Social Work Education.

Boisen, L. S., & Bosh, L.A. (2011). Dual relationships in rural areas. In L. H. Ginsberg (Ed.), *Social work in rural communities* (5th ed., pp. 111–123). Alexandria, VA: Council on Social Work Education.

Burkemper, E. M. (2005). Ethical mental health social work practice in the small community. In L. H. Ginsberg (Ed.), *Social work in rural communities* (4th ed., pp. 175–188). Alexandria, VA: Council on Social Work Education.

Canadian Association of Social Workers. (n.d.) *CASW code of ethics.* Retrieved from http://www.casw-acts.ca/en/what-social-work/casw-code-ethics.

Carlton-LaNey, I. B., Edwards, R. L., & Reid, P. N. (1999). Small towns and rural communities: From romantic notions to harsh realities. In I. B. Carlton-LaNey, R. L. Edwards, & P. N. Reid (Eds.), *Preserving and strengthening small towns and rural communities* (pp. 5–12). Washington, DC: NASW Press.

Council on Social Work Education. (2012). *Educational policy and accreditation standards.* Retrieved from http://www.cswe.org/File.aspx?id=41861.

Croxton, T. A., Jayaratne, S., & Mattison, D. (2002). Social work practice behaviors and beliefs: Rural-urban differences. *Advances in Social Work, 3*, 117–132.

Daley, M. R., & Avant, F. L. (1999). Attracting and retaining professionals for social work practice in rural areas: An example from East Texas. In I. B. Carlton-LaNey, R. L. Edwards, & P. N. Reid (Eds.), *Preserving and strengthening small towns and rural communities* (pp. 335–345). Washington, DC: NASW Press.

Daley, M. R., & Avant, F. L. (2004). Rural social work: Reconceptualizing the framework for practice. In T. L. Scales & C. L. Streeter (Eds.), *Rural social work: Building and sustaining community assets* (pp. 34–42). Belmont, CA: Thompson Brooks/Cole.

Daley, M. R., & Doughty, M. O. (2006). Ethics complaints in social work practice: A rural-urban comparison. *Journal of Social Work Values and Ethics, 3*. Retrieved from http://www.jswvearchives.com/content/view/28/44/.

Daley, M. R., & Hickman, S. (2011). Dual relations and beyond: Understanding and addressing ethical challenges for rural social work. *Journal of Social Work Values and Ethics, 8*, 1. Retrieved from http://www.socialworker.com/jswve/spr11/spr11daleyhickman.pdf.

Daley, M. R., & Pierce, B. (2011). Educating for rural competence: Curriculum concepts, models and course content. In L. Ginsberg (Ed.),

Social work in rural communities (5th ed., pp. 125–140). Alexandria, VA: Council on Social Work Education.

Dolgoff, R., Loewenberg, F. M., & Harrington, D. (2005). *Ethical decisions for social work practice* (7th ed.). Belmont, CA: Thompson Brooks/Cole.

Galambos, C., Watt, J. W., Anderson, K., & Danis, F. (2005). Ethics forum: Rural social work practice: Maintaining confidentiality in the face of dual relationships. *Journal of Social Work Values and Ethics, 2*. Retrieved from http://www.socialworker.com/jswve/content/blog category/11/37/.

Galbreath, W. B. (2005). Dual relationships in rural communities. In N. Lohmann & R. A. Lohmann (Eds.), *Rural social work practice* (pp. 105–123). New York, NY: Columbia University Press.

Ginsberg, L. H. (1998). Introduction: An overview of rural social work. In L. H. Ginsberg (Ed.), *Social work in rural communities* (3rd ed., pp. 12–13). Alexandria, VA: Council on Social Work Education.

Ginsberg, L. H. (2001). *Careers in social work* (2nd ed.). Boston, MA: Allyn & Bacon.

Ginsberg, L. H. (2005). The overall context of rural practice. In L. H. Ginsberg (Ed.), *Social work in rural communities* (4th ed., pp. 1–14). Alexandria, VA: Council on Social Work Education.

Green, R. (2003). Social work in rural areas: A personal and professional challenge. *Australian Social Work, 56*(3), 209–219.

Gumpert, J., & Black, P. N. (2005). Walking the tightrope between cultural competence and ethical practice: The dilemma of the rural practitioner. In L. H. Ginsberg (Ed.), *Social work in rural communities* (4th ed., pp. 157–174). Alexandria, VA: Council on Social Work Education.

Helbok, C. M., Marinelli, R. P., & Walls, R. T. (2006). National survey of ethical practices across rural and urban continuum. *Professional Psychology: Research and Practice, 37*(1), 36–44.

Martinez-Brawley, E. (2000). *Close to home: Human services in the small community*. Washington, DC: NASW Press.

Miller, P. J. (1998). Dual relationships and rural practice: A dilemma of practice and culture. In L. H. Ginsberg (Ed.), *Social work in rural communities* (3rd ed., pp. 55–62). Alexandria, VA: Council on Social Work Education.

Morgan, S., & Carvino, L. (2006). States that reference the NASW code of ethics in statute or regulation. In D. Hobdy, A. Murray, & S. Morgan (Eds.), *Social Work Ethics Summit* (pp. 1–6). Washington, DC: National Association of Social Workers.

National Association of Social Workers. (2006). Rural social work. In *Social work speaks: National Association of Social Workers policy statements* (7th ed., pp. 321–326). Washington, DC: NASW Press.

National Association of Social Workers. (2012). Code of ethics of the National Association of Social Workers. In *Social work speaks: National Association of Social Workers policy statements* (9th ed., pp. 375–391). Washington, DC: NASW Press.

National Association of Social Workers. (n.d.). *About NASW.* Retrieved from http://www.socialworkers.org/nasw/default.asp.

Reamer, F. G. (1998). *Ethical standards in social work: A critical review of the NASW code of ethics*. Washington, DC: NASW Press.

Reamer, F. G. (2006). *Social work values and ethics* (3rd ed.). New York, NY: Columbia University Press.

Schott, M. (1980). Casework: Rural. In H. W. Johnson (Ed.), *Rural human services: A book of readings* (pp. 135–158). Itasca, IL: Peacock.

Strom-Gottfried, K. (2000). Ensuring ethical practice: An examination of NASW Code violations, 1986–97. *Social Work, 45*(3), 251–261.

Strom-Gottfried, K. (2005). Ethical practice in rural environments. In L. H. Ginsberg (Ed.), *Social work in rural communities* (4th ed., pp. 141–155). Alexandria, VA: Council on Social Work Education.

Strom-Gottfried, K. (2007). *Straight talk about ethics*. Chicago, IL: Lyceum Books.

Watkins, T. R. (2004). Natural helping networks. In T. L. Scales & C. L. Streeter (Eds.), *Rural social work: Building and sustaining community assets* (pp. 65–76). Belmont, CA: Thomson/Brooks Cole.

Rural social workers are often housed in offices that offer multiple services and staff from a variety of professional backgrounds.

CHAPTER NINE

Rural Social Work Practice

THE RURAL CONTEXT for practice certainly requires adaptation of practice skills and approaches to the circumstances of a smaller community. Indeed, there is a lot to learn about working with a rural community and rural clients, and making these adaptations requires some flexibility. Pulling all the pieces together in a meaningful way, and one that works, requires a great deal of critical thinking. For those who are already somewhat familiar with rural life, ideas on how to apply this information effectively may have begun to take shape, but those who are new to rural life might still have several questions about how all this fits together and works.

The purpose of this chapter is to outline some practical implications of rural life so that readers can actually do social work with rural communities. The chapter uses the down-home practice framework presented earlier and examines application of the model using specific examples. So this chapter is hands-on and applied, as opposed to strictly theoretical. Perhaps, though, in this chapter the nuts and bolts of rural social work will become apparent.

THE PERSON-IN-ENVIRONMENT PERSPECTIVE

The concept of person-in-environment is essential to modern social work (Gambrill, 1997). The principle is that social workers view people in constant interaction with their environment (Compton, Galaway, & Cournoyer, 2005; Gambrill, 1997; Johnson & Yanca, 2001; Kirst-Ashman &

Hull, 2006). Interactions with the environment include both physical conditions and the social systems around people in a dynamic way. The person-in-environment perspective is based on the idea that personal issues and needs do not arise solely from either the individual or the environment, but from the interaction between the two, and problems that arise represent a mismatch between people and their broader environment.

A person-in-environment perspective is a fundamental component of the generalist model of social work. In the generalist model a person is seen as in continuous interaction with five social systems: individual, family, group, organization, and community. A person's behavior is seen as the result of interactions with those systems and not entirely a product of free will or inner motivations and drives.

As an example of the person-in-environment perspective, consider a child who attends school, and so is influenced by the personal, family, peer group, and organizational systems. The child comes to school with his or her own personality, motivations, wants, and desires. While at school the organization enforces norms of behavior that the student may not want to observe, such as sitting silently, taking notes, refraining from text messaging, and not talking during class. Both school norms and influences from parents to behave at school produce different actions from the child than he or she might normally choose. But if the student wants to be popular with a peer group, there might be some pressure to talk or act inappropriately in class that overrides the influences of family and organization. Then the student talks too much, does not pay attention, and is otherwise disruptive in the classroom. When this happens there is a mismatch between the person and the environment, a problem develops, and the student gets in trouble.

Social systems influence people's behavior, and in rural communities people tend to interact on a personal basis. Communities are close knit, and social workers and clients tend to be enmeshed in community systems. Even agencies and businesses are influenced by the people with whom they deal. For example, a mental health center is likely to know the client, the client's family, and most of the agencies with which the client has interacted. Past problems, and even family members' problems, are not secret, and that prior knowledge may influence how the client will be treated.

Another way of saying this is that in a rural community everyone and everything tends to be connected in some way. Of course, social interactions are dynamic, and relationships between people may change over time. Many clients experience problems because they do not fit well with the community expectations. They may also come into conflict with other people or organizations. In a rural community unpleasant interactions rarely stay between the two parties for long, as many other people soon know about them. When a client or family engages in behavior that angers people, grudges develop, information is spread, and the client may have trouble getting help as a result.

For rural social workers, it is vital to understand a client's social relationships. Some relationships lead to problems, some to solutions, and some to dead ends. But it is important to know what they are to effectively assess problems and implement change strategies. Old wounds and grudges may influence not only what kinds of problems a client experiences, but the ability to get services. Blindly stepping into an old argument, even if in the best interests of the client, runs the risk of it appearing that the social worker is taking sides. Animosity toward the social worker might develop, which in turn might affect the client, anything the social worker does, and even other clients. As with many rural relationships, social workers need to handle them sensitively. The person-in-environment perspective gives social workers a framework for assessing rural relationships.

THE STRENGTHS PERSPECTIVE

Social workers, by the nature of what they do professionally, work with problems of one kind or another and attempt to improve clients' social conditions, address barriers, and improve clients' psychosocial functioning. When one spends day after day working with problems that clients and communities present, there is a tendency to see clients as a big collection of problems. But clients cope and overcome obstacles, often against overwhelming odds. Client strengths and community assets are an important part of empowerment.

Rural communities have many positive attributes or assets that make life there worthwhile to residents. However, many portrayals of small-town social welfare primarily speak to problems and a lack of services.

For example, a small town might not have a mental health center or food-stamp office. All in all, the focus on a lack of services is unappealing for social workers in rural communities. Indeed, some rural areas do have higher-than-average poverty, less low-income housing, and higher rates of diseases such as obesity and diabetes. There are also areas where access to services or availability of specialized services is challenging. But to exclusively focus on these issues to the exclusion of highlighting rural assets such as natural helping networks, churches, and a community spirit of helping others is unfair and inaccurate. Instead of focusing on services and resources that a small community does not have, it is more productive to explore the ways in which the community deals with social problems.

The strengths perspective is an approach to social work that provides a counterbalance to a narrow focus on problems and need, and that is integral to the generalist method (Association of Baccalaureate Social Work Program Directors, n.d.; Saleebey, 2006). As Rapp (1998) points out, an exclusive focus on determining the source of a problem tends to skew social workers' perception toward only examining problems. The result is often a focus on individual pathology to the exclusion of environmental factors. With individuals and families, strengths occur while addressing problems, and in community work, positive attributes that can be mobilized are called assets (Saleebey, 2006; Scales & Streeter, 2004). Use of strengths in rural practice is particularly appropriate because of the importance of community and environmental factors in the development of problems. Strengths and assets are also important factors in devising strategies to empower people to meet their needs.

A strengths approach allows social workers to look beyond the pathology of the problem to use what is available to help resolve that problem. This helps avoid a narrow view of only what is wrong and reminds us to look for what is right. In a rural community there are many strengths and assets. For example, with rural people individual strengths could include things like relationships with others, optimism, and incredible resilience. Rural community assets include informal helping networks, willingness to help others, church, local organizations, and family. Using strengths and assets helps identify positive coping skills and capacities to empower people to use them as building blocks for resolving problems.

The idea is that individuals, families, and communities all have positive elements, no matter what kinds of problems they experience.

As an example, consider a family whose primary source of income is Temporary Assistance for Needy Families (TANF), a federal program that provides cash to families with dependent children. In virtually all communities this means that a family is poor—"on welfare," "on the dole," "down and out." These all convey the idea of failure, at least economically. A common supposition is that if the family members receiving TANF had skills or motivation, they would go to work to reduce their dependency on public support. But what kinds of strengths might this family have? Well, being able to manage a tight budget under difficult circumstances, being creative enough to find entertainment and recreation at little or no cost, and patching together enough assistance from other sources to stretch a dollar very thin are skills not everyone has. All these things require problem solving and strength, yet these things are not easy for everyone.

Rural social work benefits a great deal from the use of a strengths perspective for practice. The fact that many rural areas are not rich in formal services can distract social workers from looking for what *is* there. Society often portrays rural communities as backward or deficient, and this depiction also colors our view of rural people. Starting from this perspective, it is easy to assume that rural areas and the people who live there are a collection of problems, one without much redeeming value. Rural people are aware that some dismiss them as poorly educated or out of touch with the times, and they resent those views, a not-so-subtle form of discrimination that rural people return in kind with their view of city folk. People in rural areas may have less education than people in cities, but that does not mean that rural people lack intelligence. Consider this: rural people might not know much about subways, but then most city dwellers don't know much about milking a goat. Which is more important? Well, it depends on where you live.

There are often resources available in rural areas, though they may not be formal ones—urban biases presuppose that we should look for them in that form. But informal resources or assets can work as well as, if not better than, formal services. However, informal services will not be found if workers do not look for them.

GENERALIST PRACTICE AND SOCIAL SYSTEMS

Rural social workers have long discussed the value of a generalist approach to practice because the very nature of the work argues against overspecialization (Daley & Avant, 2004; Ginsberg, 2005; Gumpert & Saltman, 1998; Gumpert, Saltman, & Sauer-Jones, 2000; Schott, 1980). Even books on rural practice written before the generalist model was in widespread use recommended something similar to a generalist approach (Brown, 1933; Farley, Griffiths, Skidmore, & Thackeray, 1982).

As a practical matter, the structure and resources of a rural community dictate a broad-based approach to meet the needs of members. With few professional social workers in an area and an array of social problems that need services, it is often necessary for workers to step in where needed. Sometimes this means clinical intervention, but it can also mean case management, advocacy, resource development, or any other approach that might be needed. Workers and clients are enmeshed in the community, there are fewer alternatives for service, and it makes sense for social workers to work across systems. The use of a generalist approach for practice is borne out by information obtained from rural social workers, most of whom reported using multiple methods (Gumpert & Saltman, 1998; Gumpert et al., 2000).

Of course, rural communities need specialists, too, and there has been a call for more of them to move to rural areas, but so far they have not arrived in sufficient numbers (Daley & Avant, 1999, 2004; NASW, 2009; Waltman, 2011). But a generalist framework is adaptable enough to permit workers with specialized skills to use those skills. According to Compton et al. (2005), generalists usually engage in case management and often coordinate specialists' work. But generalists can have specialized skills, too. For example, advanced generalists who are MSW-level social workers have specialized skills that they can employ under the systems-based generalist framework. In addition, many MSWs with specialized concentrations also learn to use the generalist framework in their first year of graduate school. It is unfortunate that many in the profession equate specialization with being advanced and, by implication, better than generalist. Social workers in rural communities need both generalist and advanced generalist skills, including specialized skills like mental health treatment and administration.

Generalist practice uses a systems framework and problem solving (Association of Baccalaureate Social Work Program Directors, n.d.). The systems-based approach works well with rural communities because people are close to each other, their families, organizations, and the community itself. For example, in the individual system, rural people are close to friends, neighbors, and acquaintances. The family system is particularly important since rural people tend to value family for social interaction, support, and connections with others. Organizational systems are significant in rural life, as schools, feed stores, civic clubs, and churches take on functions that transcend their established purpose, and they serve as sources of help, support, and social interaction. The community system is a point of identification, sanction, and reward.

Social connections in a rural community are complex, constant, and overlapping. The exchanges between systems affect people's behavior in both subtle and obvious ways. Because social exchange in a rural community is so personal and so much a part of people's lives, it is critical to explore and understand the connections and exchanges to better assess why people act the way they do and to find ways to help them. Consider the following case scenario:

> Bobbi Jo Wilson is a divorced mother of two children, a two-year-old girl and a four-year-old boy. She lives in Throckmorton, Oklahoma, a town of four thousand. Bobbi Jo works as a waitress at a local truck stop four days a week. She brings home $240 per week and supplements her income with food stamps. She took the job six months ago when her divorce became final. She had to get a job quickly when her ex left, and she had a limited work history after high school. For transportation she drives a 1992 pickup. She rents a two-bedroom mobile home that needs repairs but is the best she can afford, since there is no local low-income housing in town. Bobbi Jo's parents provide day care for her children while she is at work, and she does receive some support in other ways from her parents and members of her church. Bobbi Jo recently learned that her son has developed a heart problem beyond the ability of the local doctor to treat, and the closest medical facility is in Cherokee, fifty miles away. She is depressed about her ability to get her son adequate treatment and about how badly her life has turned out.

Bobbi Jo's ex-husband is a roughneck for an oil company and travels a great deal. Despite earning a decent income, he does not provide child support. He has a drinking problem, and occasionally he shows up at her home drunk, demanding to see the children and often berating her loudly. The neighbors have called to complain about the noise to the police at least three times, saying you could "hear them fighting in the next county." The police come by and ask her ex-husband to leave. Bobbi Jo has been unable to get much help collecting child support and is afraid to call law enforcement herself because her ex's older brother is the county's chief deputy. She believes that her ex is spreading rumors that she is promiscuous and supplementing her income through prostitution. The rumors, though untrue, have caused some of her friends in town to stop talking to her and have made other employers reluctant to hire her. In addition to medical treatment for her son, in Cherokee there are also better employment options and a community college, where she might be able to get financial aid. But her pickup truck is not reliable enough to get there, she would have to take off work and lose income, and she does not want to move from her family or the community where she has lived all her life.

As is typical with many rural clients, there are several systems at work in this case example. At the individual level are issues with depression and the inability to access resources for her child's health care. There is also her underemployment, which affects the adequacy of her housing and the reliability of her transportation. Bobbi Jo's strengths are that she has completed high school, she appears to be taking good care of her children, and she is supporting the family as well as she can under the circumstances. At the group level, people she knows have ostracized her because of unfounded rumors over which she has no control, which may also be contributing to her depression and ability to get better employment. One of Bobbi Jo's strengths is that she is close to her family, who provides some support. At the organizational level, the medical services she needs, as well as education and better employment opportunities, are not available for fifty miles. Her difficulty asking for help from law enforcement falls in the organizational level as well. All these things obviously affect Bobbi Jo's ability to get the services that she needs. Her relationship with her church is a strength, and the church may be able to offer her some additional help. At the community level, Bobbi Jo appears to be attached to the community where she grew up. There are some family, social, and organizational supports there that she wants to keep. On the down side, the community is small enough that it does not offer all the services she needs, and some of the services that do exist don't work well for her.

It would be easy for a social worker to just target Bobbi Jo's individual-level problems by arranging transportation to medical care for her son and referring her to a local mental health or counseling center for her depression. But that would not address some of the other issues that underlie her present difficulty. Even if counseling or medical transportation were arranged, Bobbi Jo might still have to take off work, thus losing income. She might not even want to go to a mental health or counseling center for fear that people would see her, making the rumors even worse. There might be broader issues gleaned from this case related to how the community addresses child support enforcement and harassment of women. Or there might be a need to work out routine transportation to her son's medical treatment, as other members of the community might need health services in Cherokee too.

The point is that in a rural community several social systems often are at play in influencing problems and designing solutions. A well-designed intervention for the best outcome would involve a multisystem approach. Working with Bobbi Jo through a problem-solving approach or crisis intervention where appropriate may help relieve some of her stress. Focusing on the problems she considers most important and partializing problems for resolution may help her see that her situation can improve. In the absence of wraparound services, the social worker might need to design a customized set of services to address the complexity of issues confronting Bobbi Jo.

Obviously, the health of Bobbi Jo's child is a primary concern. Connecting the family to appropriate treatment and transportation is a priority. Mobilizing any existing transportation services, involving Bobbi Jo's parents or church, would be desirable. Perhaps a combination of all these things could address the transportation issue. Bobbi Jo's work and housing situation may also need to be addressed, since someone will need to be with her son while he is receiving treatment. Perhaps negotiating with her employer or helping her find financial assistance during the treatment period would help. Seeking child support and legal restraint from harassment by her ex may be in order, but that would have to be pursued with finesse, given her ex's connection to law enforcement. Seeking alternatives to housing may also be in order, but as long as current housing is adequate, this may be a lower priority. If some of the problems confronting Bobbi Jo are common in the community, then the social worker may need to engage in some advocacy to help develop solutions. This is, of course, the heart of generalist practice, to view problems as they come without predetermined perceptions and solutions. Given the complexity of relationships in rural communities, adhering rigidly to one approach may not be very effective.

PROBLEM SOLVING

The problem-solving method is the organizing principle for social work activities in generalist practice (Association of Baccalaureate Social Work Program Directors, n.d.; Compton et al., 2005; Gambrill, 1997; Johnson & Yanca, 2001; Kirst-Ashman & Hull, 2006). Problem solving consists of a set of structured activities by social workers to first identify problems and issues, and then take action to solve them (Compton et al., 2005). Various authors have identified the steps of the problem-solving method in several ways, but generally the steps contain the same elements:

- engaging clients in the professional helping process
- exploring the presenting problem and developing a tentative strategy for work with the client
- collecting data, assessing information, forming goals, and developing a service plan
- implementing the service plan
- evaluating intervention efforts and terminating the professional relationship (Compton et al., 2005)

The problem-solving process is general enough in design to be adaptable to most any type of practice, which is good for rural work. With this process, each client, problem, or issue can be engaged with an open view to let the situation determine the intervention. Thus, the work is not clinical or community work, child welfare or mental health work, but problem-solving social work that addresses all relevant systems. In other words, the professional is a social worker ready to deal with the needs of the people through good basic social work. This used to be called social casework, and many rural practitioners understood this to include both direct practice and community organization.

Problem solving by generalist social workers is flexible enough to allow for referral to specialists when needed. Of course, referrals to specialists may be hampered by availability and access to services. Many rural communities do not have specialists (Daley & Avant, 1999), and special arrangements often have to be made to engage such services.

Rural work often requires the adaptation of practice models and skills to adapt to the context of practice. Examining the phases of the problem-solving process and suggestions for adapting the process is helpful for illustrating how adaptations can be made.

Phase 1: Engaging Clients in the Professional Helping Process

Engaging clients and systems is one of the more challenging aspects of rural social work. The concept of *Gemeinschaft* indicates that most social interactions in a rural community are personal and often informal. Yet social workers come into contact with people with a formal position and operating from a practice model that discourages personal relationships in favor of impersonal professional relationships. Another complication arises if social workers are not originally from the community, because rural people often do not trust outsiders. It might not be any easier if social workers are from the community, because people relate to how they know a worker, not necessarily the formal position the social worker holds. Social workers have to achieve some degree of personal connection with clients while maintaining appropriate professional boundaries and protecting clients from potential harm.

Social workers who are not from the community have to establish some legitimacy with clients, or clients will keep them at arm's length. Degrees, professional licenses, and certifications go only so far, and most rural people don't want to hear much about them or are not impressed by them. In other words, formal qualifications might get social workers in the door, but they are usually not enough for workers to gain acceptance, because rural people care more about who the worker is. Using a formal approach might be like "spittin' in the wind," so to speak. Direct discussion and negotiation with clients about the nature of the relationship is often helpful.

Perhaps social workers who have grown up in a rural community have some credibility that provides a basis for building relationships. Being born or raised in a rural setting gives social workers some understanding of rural life and culture that helps them connect with rural people. But if social workers are not from the community where they practice, relationship building will still be more complicated. Even though a social worker may have grown up a few hours away, he or she might still be considered an outsider, as in many communities being born there is the firm criterion for belonging. Essentially, that social worker still has to earn community trust. One way to establish membership is through residence, but that may take five or ten years of living in the community. Rural concepts of time often differ from urban ones, and long-term residence can establish that one "belongs" in the town (Ginsberg, 1998). I have seen examples of people who lived in small towns for fifteen or twenty years and still hear, "You're new here, aren't you?" or "You're not from around here, are you?"

Through learning the likes, dislikes, and ways of the community, social workers show a desire to fit in with people and their ways, and this is a gateway to being accepted. Learning the local culture requires close observation of people, customs, and behavior. But many aspects of rural life may remain a bit of a mystery if their purpose is not immediately apparent. For example, in several small communities the first day of hunting season is a holiday and much normal activity is suspended. Many activities may be rescheduled to avoid conflicts, and students may even skip school. To outsiders this may appear odd, but attempting to challenge the tradition would likely produce conflict. Social workers' earnest attempts to engage community members and learn about the significance of things like "opening season" or church nights can prove beneficial for working with clients and for fitting in with the community.

It is often necessary to form friendships with people in the community who can, in effect, serve as guides to the local culture. Engaging in these relationships can be more beneficial than just instruction. Developing local relationships entails extensive social interaction, through which local people might come to decide that a social worker "will do" or will be all right. Once the social worker is deemed to be OK, local people often informally spread the word through the community gossip, and friends can be used as references in forming new relationships. Once you know someone in town who vouches for you, it is much easier to gain broader acceptance.

Social workers born or raised in the community may often take for granted the norms, values, and culture because they are accustomed to those things. In this case, it may be best to step back, think critically, and evaluate key elements of the culture for adapting practice approaches. One of the most challenging things for social workers who are from their practice community is that people already know them. But typically they are known for something other than being a social worker—moving beyond this is essential. For example, the worker may be "Mrs. Davis's boy," "someone I went to high school with," "a member of our church," or "my neighbor down the street." This much is fine, but it can easily create barriers in trying to act in a social work role. Frankly, it is a bit of a stretch for some to translate Mrs. Davis's boy or the neighbor girl who sold Girl Scout cookies into the idea of a professional who will help them. This is a starting point for the relationship, but frank and open discussion with clients is helpful to move forward with a professional helping process. Clearly, rural people recognize that the person in front of them is an adult and no longer the ten-year-old down the street. Discussing the past may be a good way to begin so that the topic can later change to providing professional services.

In building relationships, social workers should be aware that many rural people are reluctant to ask for or accept outside help. The strong cultural value of self-reliance makes it difficult to admit that one has not been able to overcome obstacles in his or her life, and asking for help is a tacit admission that the person has not been able to "take care of business," so to speak. Visibility in the community also works against potential clients asking for or using services because it will be known in the community. As a consequence, sensitivity to clients' and potential clients' beliefs about going to an agency instead of family or the church is important for social workers in helping to build a good working relationship.

So just how do rural social workers go about the business of establishing a professional relationship with people? It starts with breaking the ice. Rural people want to know essentially who the social worker is and that he or she knows something about them. A good way to engage people in conversations is by discussing something in which they are interested. Good all-purpose topics include the weather, local sports teams, or things in which a person shows an apparent interest. The weather is often a topic of conversation in rural communities, and many communities have local high school or college teams in which people show much interest. Finding a topic in which people are interested may be a little more difficult, but if social workers visit a home, for example, they may see cues to topics that might stimulate conversation. For example, Do they have a garden or raise livestock? Does someone in the family hunt or fish? What kinds of pictures are on the walls? Is there any indication that someone quilts, makes lace, is artistic, or crafts? Do they have older items like churns for butter or beaters for cleaning rugs? Any of these can be conversation starters, and demonstrating even some basic knowledge of a subject can help people warm up to taking care of business.

The community may also have social conventions about when in a conversation it is appropriate to address the professional matter at hand. Of course, social workers need to identify themselves initially—and doing so is appropriate in most settings. But when to come around to why a social worker is there and what needs to be done is often culturally determined. In the rural South, it is considered rude to introduce business matters too quickly, as social conventions of conversation and hospitality must be met first. This is also true of Native American cultures and in other parts of the country, too. In some places one should wait until the person introduces the idea of discussing what the social worker is there to do. Handling matters in this way may seem to some an interminable waste of time, yet failure to follow the time and social conventions screams that one is an outsider. Of course, if there is urgency in the social worker's visit, as in the investigation of child abuse or initiation of needed health care, some apologies may have to be made for brushing past social convention to address critical matters. In contrast, in areas like the Midwest, all this preliminary chatter may appear like the idea that the social worker cannot come to the point. Social workers must learn the conventions in the region in which they practice.

Individuals and family members are not the only ones with whom social workers form relationships—they also engage organizational and community systems. Forming working relationships with organizations and communities also involves interacting with people who are in positions to influence at least some of what the system does. In a rural community this may be a key minister, store owner, public official, or someone who because of his or her personal attributes has established a position of influence. In forming local relationships, social workers must be genuine and trustworthy because everyone in a small community is under observation, and not much is a secret. Doing the wrong thing can damage relationships that may take a long time to rebuild. Should a social worker "do someone dirt," or treat a person badly, it will become widely known.

In a sense, building relationships with people is the same whether they are clients, ministers, or community leaders as a connection and credibility must be established. But in forming community and organizational relationships, the social worker engages people who have established some sense of status or social standing. This may be because of their family connections, holding a key position, or achievement of legitimacy based on their skills and accomplishments. Some people with whom one works will be peers in the social welfare system.

People who hold these positions of formal and informal authority likely expect some degree of deference to their position, if not to them personally. Social workers will need to approach them appropriately and learn about their range of influence and social connections. It is also important to remember that the social worker's position may not convey the same status and respect in a rural area that it does in a city. Rural people value a sense of hard work and initiative, and to some people, the social welfare agency that a social worker represents may embody a way to promote dependency and idleness (Pittman-Munke, 2008). Whether one disagrees with that perception or not, it still represents an obstacle the worker has to overcome in building relationships at the macro level.

Infringing on a person's area of responsibility or violating a person's sense of propriety can result in hostility. Once triggered, hostility can be a hard thing to overcome, and people can thwart a lot of efforts either passively or informally. In a rural area this can be a serious problem because the pond is smaller, there are fewer alternatives to pursue, and the reverberations of one's actions may be felt more strongly. If possible, it is best to get off on the right foot with key decision makers and peers and to maintain good relationships. Conflict strategies may work in the short run but be harmful in the long run: one might win the battle but lose the war, so to speak. Rural communities are small places, and folks have long memories.

Phase 2: Exploring the Presenting Problem and Developing a Tentative Strategy

Identifying the presenting problem is an initial phase of work with clients or community that typically begins while forming a relationship. Arriving at a problem statement is a basic part of the problem-solving process, and developing an idea of the presenting problem is a step toward achieving that. The purpose of a presenting problem is to determine why help is needed and how the social worker may be of assistance. Usually the presenting problem is defined by the client who comes for service or by the person who made the referral (Pincus & Minihan, 1973). Getting to the presenting problem requires collecting basic information about the request for help to achieve clarity about the problem(s). The challenge for rural workers is gaining acceptance and trust from clients so that they will discuss their needs openly. Engaging clients as partners in the empowerment process is critical, and if social workers are not perceived as genuine, clients may never fully engage, and so a good picture of the presenting problem may not emerge.

It is important for social workers to recognize the conflicts facing many rural clients who seek out help from a social worker. Clients may be struggling with some of their own values, such as the idea that seeking outside help is a form of weakness and something to be discouraged. Indeed, this may add to the burden of the difficult circumstances that bring a client to seek out the social worker in the first place. Moreover, some of the solutions a social worker may suggest to address problems may conflict with clients' deeply and strongly held beliefs and values.

Even in helping a social worker may present a client with difficult decisions. However, knowledge of local and rural culture can help social workers anticipate some of these issues and make the change process for clients easier.

For most rural communities, contact with and use of social welfare services is a source of social stigma (Farley et al., 1982; Schott, 1980). Rural people are self-reliant and often scorn the use of formal services, especially ones that originate from outside the community. Publicly funded services are sometimes targets for this disdain, as they are often associated loosely with "welfare." Since it is hard to hide what one is doing from others in rural areas, clients are less likely to reach out to social workers and may show some hesitancy or resistance to sharing information. So reaching out to a social welfare agency or a social worker is a big thing that rural people do not take lightly and often do reluctantly. This is not ideal, because they might withhold important information, and a distorted view of the presenting problem may emerge. Until either the client or people in the community learn to trust a social worker and agency, it is unlikely that clients will be too open.

Once identified, the presenting problem is a starting point for the empowerment process. But before the social worker can move forward, more basic information related to the problem must be collected. A reason for this is that clients may not be able to clearly express their problems and needs. Through the relationship, the social worker can help the client to clarify what he or she considers the presenting problem. This is done so that client and worker can begin to negotiate some tentative goals. At this phase, the urgency of the request for help may indicate some type of action to prevent harm, even if limited information is available.

In a small community, social workers may already have some background information with which to work. People in a small community know other people, and the group of people who receives services is likely even smaller, and clients may be known by reputation. Many times workers may know about a client or have worked with a client's family member. There could also be community gossip about the client or his or her family members. Some of this information may be helpful, but social workers have to be careful to evaluate the quality of the information. It is wise to take things "with a grain of salt" because secondhand information or gossip is often not the most reliable information one can receive.

Social workers should be aware that they are part of the community gossip system (Ginsberg, 2005), which may affect how clients view them. Just as information flows in a community about clients, information about workers travels as well. Unless the worker is new, the community will already have some information about the worker's likes and dislikes, where the worker shops, and his or her successes and failures with clients. One should not forget that clients have a communication network as well, and a client may already have information about the social worker. Depending on what that information is, it can be a help or a hindrance.

Social workers use their interviewing and listening skills to elicit information and explore the client's view of the problem through the lens of the client's experience, which includes a client's rural environment. The purpose of data collection at this point is to clarify the presenting problem and develop a focus and tentative goals to discuss with the client. This helps the social worker decide whether the presenting problem falls within the range of services with which a worker can assist, deliver directly, or be addressed through referral. To do this, sometimes additional sources of information must be used. Family members, friends, and documentary records may contribute more data to the formation of tentative goals. These data may be needed because not all presenting problems are what they seem at first. For one, not all clients perceive the situation they are facing accurately. Their focus may be too narrow, they may be avoiding thinking about something painful, or their perceptions may have become distorted. Even people who report for the client might not identify the presenting problem accurately. People might not know or understand the situation, they might make moral judgments, and others might "have an ax to grind."

As tentative goals for services emerge, the social worker discusses them with the client to get input. This helps ensure that worker and client are on the same page about the problem and where the services should be going. It also helps get initial buy-in from the client on working together. Once a presenting problem and tentative goals have been identified, the social worker might move to collect more information to further assess the conditions related to the problem(s). Consider the following example:

> Wanda Jane is a twenty-six-year-old woman who lives alone and does cleaning work for a local store. At times she has been known

> to wander the streets signing or talking to herself. This is mildly disturbing to local community members and she is known in town as "Crazy Wanda." But she has never been seen at the mental health center. Last night the police picked her up downtown while she was singing and looking into store windows. This morning she was referred to the local mental health center for screening. In talking to Wanda Jane it is clear she does not understand why she was picked up, sent to the mental health center, or needs any services. Subsequent contacts with family members indicate that Wanda Jane periodically either quits taking or cannot afford medicine prescribed by the family doctor that makes her "not so crazy."

In this case, the social worker's tentative goals might be to get permission to discuss her medical condition with her doctor, to explore sources for lowering her medication costs, and to refer her to a case manager to check on her taking medication. All of these could be discussed with the client.

Phase 3: Collecting Data, Assessing Information, Forming Goals, and Developing a Service Plan

A generalist assessment consists of collecting data, evaluating that information (often called assessment), and developing a service plan. With the presenting problem as a starting point, social workers collect data that relate to the issue at hand, including strengths, problems, and needs. The point of collecting data is to get more information about the problem, but collected data may or may not be in a useful format. Data are most useful when problem-related data are analyzed, evaluated, and placed in context. Through analysis, social workers can identify systems affecting the client and dynamics between systems, and they can develop possible explanations for the causes of a problem.

Assessment is a part of problem solving that attempts to determine what is wrong and what is right about a particular issue confronting a client. To be able to help, a social worker needs a clear idea of the problem to be addressed (Farley et al., 1982). To move forward without this kind of information is akin to a physician prescribing a treatment without knowing the underlying condition. In some cases the treatment might work, in some it might not, and in others it may do more harm than good.

What is called for is a planned approach based on the underlying issues. Generalist assessment moves social workers in that direction.

One of the challenges social workers face in the assessment process is rural people's caution in dealing with formal systems and people they do not know well, and this may inhibit the flow of information needed to do an assessment. This caution should not be underestimated, because it has a strong influence on behavior. People talk about caution in sayings like "Don't squat with your spurs on," "Don't cut down your shade trees," "Don't fish in troubled waters," and "Don't go throwing manure up hill—it'll roll back down in your face." Building trust with clients can overcome this, but it may take time.

Another challenge in the assessment process is confidentiality (Farley et al., 1982). Social workers usually have to collect data from more than one source, and given the open eyes of the community, some of this will undoubtedly be seen by others. Clients may be reluctant to come in for fear of being seen talking to a social worker and then that knowledge getting out: What are they there for? What's up with them? Why do they need help? Guess who I saw at the counseling center? All these speculations make for juicy community gossip that can be embarrassing for clients. But people in a community also observe contacts with relatives, neighbors, schools, clinics, and social welfare agencies, and as the saying goes, "Sometimes the walls have ears." Once a social worker starts to reach out for information, confidentiality can be a significant challenge (Burkemper, 2005; Daley & Doughty, 2006; Daley & Hickman, 2011; Galambos, Watt, Anderson, & Danis, 2005; Gumpert & Black, 2005; Strom-Gottfried, 2005). Clients are often aware of this, and it is good practice to discuss concerns about confidentiality openly. Often clients can provide guidance about their comfort level with being observed and may even suggest ways to make the helping process less visible to the community.

While some people may be reluctant to reveal information about themselves, they might not be so hesitant to talk about others, particularly if they know something interesting—one can "draw more flies with honey than vinegar." People casting out tidbits of information about other people may actually be fishing for more information about them. In any event, community gossip requires a lot of collateral support to find out whether rumors are valid, unreliable, or malicious.

Analysis of the data received requires evaluating, organizing, and interpreting the information, and doing so from a rural perspective. Evaluation of information takes into account the source of information, data quality, and whether information comes from a source with a particular agenda. With these considerations, social workers can weight and organize data to interpret system interactions, as not all information is of the same quality. This helps develop an understanding of the source of the problem.

Once information has been received and evaluated, rural culture has to be weighed in interpreting the information. Failure to do so can lead to an inaccurate assessment of the situation. For example, a family that lives in old housing or a mobile home may be reluctant to move to better housing. From an urban perspective this could be interpreted as a lack of motivation, cooperation, or resistance. But what is it about their current home? Is the place an old family home to which they are attached? Homes are often symbols of independence, and ownership of property can convey social status. But what if there are other good affordable options? Are they concerned they will be identified as a welfare family "on the dole"? Will better housing move them out of the community? These are important considerations to rural people. Attachments to family homes are strong, as are ties to the community, and there may not be good options for better housing. Moving to public housing may symbolize a loss of status and independence. Without a background in rural culture, a social worker might misinterpret these kinds of concerns as resistance.

On the basis of an assessment of the situation, a comprehensive service plan is developed. A service plan identifies what will be done, who will carry out the activities, the time frame(s) for interventions, the activities needed, and the desired outcomes. Much rural practice involves finding, developing, and accessing resources for clients, and often social workers do case management. In this regard, the service plan should take into account the services the client needs and should identify what is needed but not immediately available (Farley et al., 1982). Where possible, the plan should make use of the natural assets of the rural community, like willingness to help neighbors, natural helping resources, churches, and community groups. In using these assets, social workers may have to actually influence their involvement, in effect doing specific resource development. If frequently needed services are not available when plans are developed, a social worker may be in a unique position to identify an unmet community need and spearhead advocacy to address the need systematically. Once the service plan has been developed to address problem(s) in the broader environment, and the client and worker have agreed to it, the process of intervention can begin.

Phase 4: Implementing the Service Plan

Rural practice is generalist, frequently complex, necessitates an extraordinary range of skills, and requires flexibility. The nature of rural work involves clients whose problems are multifaceted and an environment in which available resources may be scant. Rural interventions can include direct practice, referral, resource modeling, mobilization and development, client advocacy, group work, and community organization (Farley et al., 1982). Virtually any social worker looking at this list would agree that rural practice can require rural practitioners to intervene with all social systems. Rural social work and many of the activities it involves generally corresponds to the practice of case management wherein workers deliver direct and indirect services as well as coordinating services (Frankel & Gelman, 2004). A good bit of rural social work is case management, and much of the work centers on accessing and coordinating resources. But rural workers deliver a variety of direct services to address client needs as well.

Social workers provide some specialized services within their area of expertise and training for rural communities. Some work in clinical work, substance abuse treatment, mental health, and crisis intervention, to name a few. But there are clearly not enough specialists to go around. Some areas are lucky just to have one social worker for several counties. The odds are against a social worker's specialized expertise matching the range of service needs of everyone in the worker's service region. Even where there is a good match between worker specialty and community needs, there are usually many requests for the social worker's skills for other types of problems as well.

Virtually all rural social workers engage in macro work at some point. Brown (1933) was clear about this in her groundbreaking book on rural social work, and most subsequent writings on the subject have served to underline this point. Rural social workers are in too prominent a position, and the use and development of resources is too critical to the helping process, for them to do a credible job if they address only micro systems. Some macro work just goes with the territory.

There are many macro-level challenges that rural social workers confront. Pittman-Munke (2008) indicated that administrators in rural agencies face a number of difficulties, including the amount of time workers must spend traveling to visit clients, which means less time for service delivery; resistance to the use of new technology; difficulty retaining professional staff; and a lack of client confidentiality about activities and clients. Workers may also experience difficulty in working with community leaders and boards because of misperceptions about the nature and purpose of services. For example, I once worked with a community-based board that provided funding for services. The board was adamantly opposed to funding the services of a shelter for battered women because many of its members were convinced that the shelter's activities were focused on splitting up intact families. It took considerable education and persuasion to get them to shift their point of view enough to begin funding the shelter.

The advent of social work licensing and regulation has placed restraints on the kinds of services that social workers can deliver, and these are especially restrictive in regard to specialized clinical services. Despite a need in the community and the availability of limited numbers of professional social workers, most states restrict clinical work, especially unsupervised clinical work. Even though there may be a legitimate need and a licensed clinical worker does not work anywhere near the community, a social worker who may be available to help cannot deliver services. This is a significant problem for many rural areas because there tend to be fewer social workers with advanced levels of practice (Daley & Avant, 1999). About the best that a local social worker can do is sometimes to make a referral. These kinds of situations put rural social workers in the difficult situation of either deciding to risk providing services that violate the provision of their license and risk losing it or referring clients to distant services that they may be unable to access and so never get. To some degree, advances in twenty-first-century communications technology may help address this problem, but clients' views on virtual relationships and technological challenges still present some barriers to services.

Phase 5: Evaluating Intervention Efforts and Terminating the Professional Relationship

The closeness of rural communities may also affect the final stage of generalist practice, including evaluation and termination. Specifically, in addition to whatever kind of evaluative data on progress the social worker collects, there is likely to be some informal data provided by community members who observe clients. And for rural workers, many social work relationships never fully terminate, as it is not unusual to see former clients in the community even after services have been terminated (Fenby, 1980).

Social workers' efforts to formally evaluate their progress with clients certainly help with service effectiveness, as this allows workers to see objectively any progress a client is making and then adjust plans or interventions to better address needs. Folks in the community do talk, and clients who have demonstrated problems in the past have probably already been the subject of some kind of conversation. Once social workers become involved, there's new material for conversation, and observations become part of the grapevine. Rural social workers can expect to receive unsolicited information on a client from the grapevine. But social workers have to be aware of this, understand the possible unreliability of the information, and weigh it cautiously and carefully. There may be important nuggets of data in there that can be helpful. But professional work clearly cannot be guided by community gossip.

Evaluation of interventions serves another important function, and that is building a reputation for success for the worker and programs (Farley et al., 1982). Rural people are often skeptical of "the social worker" or "the agency," as many people have stereotypical ideas of what the worker and agency do. There are sometimes visions of social workers as child snatchers or people who whisk others off to the poor farm (the rural version of the poorhouse). Demonstration of effectiveness through evaluation helps build a reputation that dispels such myths. The resulting legitimacy may help better engage clients and extend the influence of the worker and agency in the community. Once the community comes to accept that a worker or agency helps people, it is easier for people to reach out for help, to find collaborative partners, and to have some standing in discussing the need for services.

CHARACTERISTICS OF RURAL SOCIAL WORKERS

What does it take to be a good rural social worker? Beyond the use of generalist or advanced generalist practice, there are other qualities that help rural social workers do a good job. The skills, qualities, and attributes needed for rural social work have emerged in the literature over the years. What the literature suggests is that rural practice requires creativity, flexibility, adaptability, and an ability to work autonomously. This is not to suggest that other fields of practice do not require these qualities, but these qualities are a significant advantage in working with rural communities.

First and foremost, to do rural work, social workers must enjoy living and working in a rural community and interacting with rural people. Social workers who do not really like small-town life or who look down on rural people will be spotted as malcontents or phonies—people will say they are "puttin' on the dog." Rural people do not have respect or tolerance for people who do not respect them. As the saying goes, "Don't wet on my leg and tell me it's raining."

Rural social workers must be flexible, creative, and resourceful in their work because of the structure of rural communities and their social welfare system (Daley & Pierce, 2011; Johnson, 1980; Riebschleger, 2007). While urban social workers more commonly look for available resources, rural workers may have fewer of them and have to look for alternatives. Dispersion of clients over a wider geographic area can create problems of access even when services are available. Few rural communities have much in the way of mass transit, and clients are dependent on personal cars and trucks to get where they need to go. Thus, transportation, or lack thereof, is a significant rural service issue. In some cases, rural people who need services might even be more highly concentrated than in larger cities, yet there might not be a good way to get them to services that do exist. For example, rural areas are known to experience high rates of poverty and unmet health-care needs (NASW, 2012), and rural social work frequently entails developing and creating services as much as it does finding resources.

The availability of informal helping networks, willingness of friends and neighbors to help, and a spirit of helping from local organizations is a major asset that workers can mobilize to help clients or the community. Since these are not usually thought of as traditional social welfare services, and they may not be immediately prepared to meet a client's needs, social workers would have to engage them, mobilize their help, and organize their efforts. This is basic community work and requires some degree of flexibility and creativity to carry out at the grassroots level. It takes seeing the problems and issues, identifying potentially available resources, and devising ways of helping, even if something has never been done this way before. Critical thinking, imagination in seeing the possibilities for help, and creativity and flexibility in developing assets are all required. If a specific service that might be needed is not available, then workers have to think about how to put one together. This is being creative, resourceful, and versatile. Good rural social workers may have all three of these characteristics.

The need for flexibility and versatility also lies in the wide ranging assignments given to some rural workers. Often rural social workers serve large geographic regions, and in some places the area is huge, with people and services spread pretty thinly. Consider, for example, a place like Brewster County, Texas. The county covers 6,169 square miles (Texas State Historical Association, n.d.) with a population of 9,481. Brewster County is bigger than the state of Connecticut, yet it has far fewer people. Many areas in the western and frontier US and Canada have similar low populations living across large areas.

Social workers assigned to one of these geographic areas may have to provide services to several scattered towns or even counties, requiring frequent travel from a home office. To provide regularity and predictability of services, workers might visit some communities on a regular schedule and operate out of more than one office. This is the modern social work equivalent of the old circuit-riding preacher. Still, the work requires knowledge of each community, the people in it, the services available regionally, and a lot of travel time. Certainly, each community can present different sets of issues and expectations, and rural social workers have to be prepared to respond to them all.

Self-motivation and an ability to work autonomously are valuable qualities for rural work, as rural social workers have to be independent and autonomous (Ginsberg, 2005; Riebschleger, 2007). This means they must decide what to do and when to do it. Rural practitioners might find that they are the only social worker for several counties and that there is only a small professional community. Even if there are a few workers in the same office, once a social worker goes on a home visit, he or she can be many miles from the office with unreliable cell phone service. Thus, social workers might have to act without backup or consultation about the situation. Colleagues may be out of the office too, off many miles in another direction, and it can be difficult to reach supervisors. In many respects, social workers can find themselves on their own, at least temporarily.

Even when in the office, there might be no professional colleagues there to look over one's work, provide support or advice, and assign duties. Workers will have to seek out supervision, consultation, professional support, and continuing education on their own initiative, as these supports are often not available locally. With the expansion of online and video options for continuing education, consultation, and supervision, there a number of options for remaining in the community and staying current that were not available even ten years ago.

One opportunity for professional development is the National Rural Social Work Caucus. This is a good resource and has held an annual national institute for more than thirty-five years, which is the major conference for rural social work. In typical rural fashion, the meetings are relatively informal, offer cutting-edge workshops, and encourage networking with other social workers and educators. It is somewhat of a family atmosphere that is open and welcoming of newcomers. The caucus also maintains a website and Listserv. Because the caucus often distributes information through an open but informal communication network, some say the organization exists only in rumor. The caucus also advocates on behalf of rural social work issues. Perhaps the best way to capture the philosophy and purpose of the National Rural Social Work Caucus is through the words of its theme song:

It's sort of like a rumor carried on the breeze,
Words like *change*, *community*, are drifting through the trees
The caucus don't have much structure, but it doesn't fade away,
Blooms like some perennial on those hot and humid days.

(Chorus)

A place of learning,
A place of solace,
Where folks don't put on airs
Easy to talk about what needs to be done
In the midst of those who care

As long as times, they get [or, "stay"] hard, then our work is never done
And as long as people feel at home when to these institutes they come
As long as we can laugh and sing, and let down our thinning hair
Then this traveling rural road show will pop up again somewhere

(Chorus)

And it's sort of like a rumor
Carried on the breeze. (Hickman, 2004, 2013; National Rural Social Work Caucus, n.d.; Winship & Hickman, 1992)

For additional information on rural social work, there are also online resources available at the Rural Assistance Center, the US Department of Agriculture, the Rural Policy and Research Institute, and other organizations, all of which provide current information about rural practice issues. However, it is difficult to find a good substitute for the professional relationships and networking that help sustain and reenergize professionals. If professional contacts are established, they can be maintained by phone, email, and occasional face-to-face visits. This may mean some time away from the community and clients, but the investment of time will be well worth it in the long run because social workers won't feel so isolated.

CONCLUSION

To be most effective, rural social work requires adapting traditional models of practice to the context and culture of the rural community. Since most models of professional practice were developed with an urban perspective, they contain elements that can be counterproductive when applied in rural areas. Most of the basic practice concepts work well with rural people, but some generally accepted aspects of social work practice, such as maintaining professional distance, can be considered rude in rural areas, where personalized relationships are the norm. Systems-based generalist and advanced generalist methods are best suited to rural work. In rural practice there are often few workers and low concentrations of people, and a social worker may be the only source of help, having to deal with a wide range of problems and issues. This argues against overspecialization, even though specialized services are often needed. Because rural communities are close knit, the community exerts a great deal of influence on both client and worker. Rural social workers are well served by using the person-in-environment perspective and employing strengths or assets in practice. Despite the extensive literature that suggests that rural communities lack basic services, many resources do exist in rural areas, and it is helpful for social workers to employ the many informal resources that do exist.

One of the more challenging tasks of rural practice is engaging clients in the helping process. Rural people tend to distrust people they do not know personally or who represent some formal organization. Social workers may have to demonstrate competency in rural culture to build a trusting relationship. Until that relationship is built, it will be difficult for them to get the kind of information they need to help empower clients.

Two other significant issues for rural social workers are the natural reluctance of rural people to use formal services and the difficulty in maintaining confidentiality. Rural people often avoid social welfare services for fear of being seen and stigmatized by others. The visibility of everyone in a small community also creates a risk of losing confidentiality in the helping process, which one might expect in a larger city. Once seen with a social worker or at an agency office, the natural assumption is that a person is a client. Dealing with this requires some degree of delicacy and finesse on the part of the social worker.

Knowledge of rural culture helps make assessments more accurate and can create service plans that best meet needs of individuals, families, and communities. Collecting information to evaluate the effects of interventions is helpful in improving the service plan, helping empower clients, and building credibility for workers and the agency in the community. Showing results of interventions can help the community develop trust in the worker and agency, which can be used as a basis for broader community and service development.

Rural work is best done by professionals who like living and working in smaller communities, and it is especially important that they like working with rural people. Rural social workers are more effective when autonomous, creative, flexible, and resourceful. In many cases rural social workers take after the Texas Ranger—"One riot, one ranger," or in this case, one county, one social worker. Sometimes rural practitioners need to be all things to all people. Not knowing what comes next or what need may arise, and with broad responsibility, rural social work rewards professionals who can respond to a variety of situations as they arise. Networking with other rural practitioners and supervisors can help workers not only renew their energy but also learn new ideas to incorporate into their work.

REFERENCES

Association of Baccalaureate Social Work Program Directors (n.d.). *Definitions: Generalist social work practice*. Retrieved from http://www.bpdonline.org/bpd_prod/BPDWCMWEB/Resources/Definitions/BPDWCMWEB/Resources/Definitions.aspx?hkey=3e3a936d-fe8a-4bd9-8d41-45fdf190bc68.

Brown, J. C. (1933). *The rural community and social casework.* New York, NY: Family Welfare Association of America.

Burkemper, E. M. (2005). Ethical mental health social work practice in the small community. In L. H. Ginsberg (Ed.), *Social work in rural communities* (4th ed., pp. 175–188). Alexandria, VA: Council on Social Work Education.

Compton, B. R., Galaway, B., & Cournoyer, B. R. (2005). *Social work process*. Belmont, CA: Thompson Brooks/Cole.

Daley, M. R., & Avant, F. (1999). Attracting and retaining professionals for social work practice in rural areas: An example from East Texas. In I. B. Carlton-LaNey, R. L. Edwards, & P. N. Reid (Eds.), *Preserving and strengthening small towns and rural communities* (pp. 335–345). Washington, DC: NASW Press.

Daley, M., & Avant, F. (2004). Reconceptualizing the framework for practice. In T. L. Scales & C. L. Streeter (Eds.), *Rural social work: Building and sustaining community assets* (pp. 34–42). Belmont, CA: Thomson.

Daley, M. R., & Doughty, M. O. (2006). Ethics complaints in social work practice: A rural-urban comparison. *Journal of Social Work Values and Ethics*, 3. Retrieved from http://www.socialworker.com/jswve/content/blogcategory/12/44/.

Daley, M. R., & Hickman, S. (2011). Dual relations and beyond: Understanding and addressing ethical challenges for rural social work. *Journal of Social Work Values and Ethics*, *8*, 1. Retrieved from http://www.socialworker.com/jswve/spr11/spr11daleyhickman.pdf.

Daley, M. R., & Pierce, B. (2011). Educating for rural competence: Curriculum concepts, models and course content. In L. Ginsberg (Ed.), *Social work in rural communities* (5th ed., pp. 125–140). Alexandria, VA: Council on Social Work Education.

Farley, O. W., Griffiths, K. A., Skidmore, R. A., & Thackeray, M. G. (1982). *Rural social work practice*. New York, NY: Free Press.

Fenby, B. L. (1980). Social work in a rural setting. In H. W. Johnson (Ed.), *Rural human services: A book of readings* (pp. 149–152). Itasca, IL: Peacock.

Frankel, A. J., & Gelman, S. R. (2004). *Case management* (2nd ed.). Chicago, IL: Lyceum Books.

Galambos, C., Watt, J. W., Anderson, K., & Danis, F. (2005). Ethics forum: Rural social work practice: Maintaining confidentiality in the face of dual relationships. *Journal of Social Work Values and Ethics*, 2. Retrieved from http://www.socialworker.com/jswve/content/blogcategory/11/37/.

Gambrill, E. (1997). *Social work practice: A critical thinker's guide*. New York, NY: Oxford University Press.

Ginsberg, L. H. (Ed.). (1998). Introduction: An overview of rural social work. In L. H. Ginsberg (Ed.), *Social work in rural communities* (3rd ed., pp. 2–17). Alexandria, VA: Council on Social Work Education.

Ginsberg, L. H. (2005). The overall context of rural practice. In L. H. Ginsberg (Ed.), *Social work in rural communities* (4th ed., pp. 4–7). Alexandria, VA: Council on Social Work Education.

Gumpert, J., & Black, P. N. (2005). Walking the tightrope between cultural competence and ethical practice: The dilemma of the rural practitioner. In L. H. Ginsberg (Ed.), *Social work in rural communities* (4th ed., pp. 157–174). Alexandria, VA: Council on Social Work Education.

Gumpert, J., & Saltman, J. E (1998). Social group work practice in rural areas: The practitioners speak. *Social Work with Groups, 21*(3), 19–34.

Gumpert, J., Saltman, J. E., & Sauer-Jones, D. (2000). Toward identifying the unique characteristics of social work practice in rural areas: From the voices of practitioners. *Journal of Baccalaureate Social Work, 6*(1), 19–35.

Hickman, S. A. (2004). Rural is real: Supporting professional practice through the rural social work caucus and the NASW professional policy statement for rural social work. In T. L. Scales & C. L. Streeter (Eds.), *Rural social work: Building and sustaining community assets* (pp. 43–50). Belmont, CA: Thompson/Brooks Cole.

Hickman, S. A. (2013). Rural is real: History of the national rural social work caucus and the NASW professional policy statement on rural social work. In T. L. Scales, C. L. Streeter, & H. S. Cooper (Eds.), *Rural social work: Building and sustaining community capacity* (2nd ed., pp. 19–28). Hoboken, NJ: Wiley.

Johnson, H. W. (1980). Working in the rural community. In H. W. Johnson (Ed.), *Rural human services: A book of readings* (pp. 143–148). Itasca, IL: Peacock.

Johnson, L. C., & Yanca, S. J. (2001). *Social work practice: A generalist approach.* Needham Heights, MA: Allyn & Bacon.

Kirst-Ashman, K. K., & Hull, G. H. (2006). *Understanding generalist practice.* Belmont, CA: Thompson Brooks/Cole.

National Association of Social Workers. (2009). Rural social work. In *Social work speaks: National Association of Social Workers policy statements* (8th ed., pp. 297–302). Washington, DC: NASW Press.

National Association of Social Workers. (2012). Rural social work. In *Social work speaks: National Association of Social Workers policy statements* (9th ed., pp. 296–301). Washington, DC: NASW Press.

National Rural Social Work Caucus. (n.d.). *Rural Caucus theme song.* Retrieved from http://www.ruralsocialwork.org/theme_song.cfm.

Pincus, A., & Minihan, A. (1973). *Social work practice: Model and method.* Itasca, IL: Peacock.

Pittman-Munke, P. (2008). The administration of social service agencies: The rural/small town challenge. In L. H. Ginsberg (Ed.), *Management and leadership in social work practice and education* (pp. 167–180). Alexandria, VA: Council on Social Work Education.

Rapp, C. A. (1998). *The strengths model.* New York, NY: Oxford University Press.

Riebschleger, J. (2007). Social workers' suggestions for effective rural practice. *Families in Society, 88*(2), 203–213.

Saleebey, D. (2006). Introduction: Power in the people. In D. Saleebey (Ed.), *The strengths perspective in social work practice* (4th ed., pp. 1–24). Boston, MA: Allyn & Bacon.

Scales, L. T., & Streeter, C. L. (2004). Asset building to sustain rural communities. In T. L. Scales & C. L. Streeter (Eds.), *Rural social work: Building and sustaining community assets* (pp. 1–6). Belmont, CA: Brooks/Cole Thomson.

Schott, M. (1980). Casework: Rural. In H. W. Johnson (Ed.), *Rural human services: A book of readings* (pp. 153–158). Itasca, IL: Peacock.

Strom-Gottfried, K. (2005). Ethical practice in rural environments. In L. H. Ginsberg (Ed.), *Social work in rural communities* (4th ed., pp. 141–155). Alexandria, VA: Council on Social Work Education.

Texas State Historical Association. (n.d.). *Brewster County.* Retrieved from http://www.tshaonline.org/handbook/online/articles/hcb14.

Waltman, G. H. (2011). Reflections on rural social work. *Families in Society, 92*(2), 236–239.

Winship, J., & Hickman, S. (1992). *Rural Social Work Caucus theme song (folk process).* Retrieved from http://blogs.millersville.edu/ruralconference2013/files/2013/07/RSWConferenceProgram2013.pdf.

Commercial fishing is an important source of employment in some rural areas, but faces increased competition from overseas markets. How to keep communities economically viable is an important concern for the future.

CHAPTER TEN

Challenges for the Future

RURAL COMMUNITIES are steeped in tradition and great importance is placed on the past, especially on families' lineage and accomplishments, the history and culture of a place, and the way things are done. These traditions provide stability and security, and lead people to resist change. Thus, it is not surprising that the colloquial phrase "if it ain't broke, don't fix it" appears to have its origins in the South long before it entered common use (Phrase Finder, 2013), and certainly it has the outward appearance of a rural point of view. So change comes slowly to rural areas, and innovations, fads, and fashion filter in over time. Change is frustratingly slow for some, sometimes encouraging outsiders to sometimes shake their heads in disbelief and encouraging some outward migration of young people to escape what seems to be the oppression of tradition.

Small towns and rural communities do transform over time; it is just the pace of change that tends to be slower than that of cities. Society indeed "builds a better mousetrap"; it just takes longer for a small community to get it. Old traditions remain. For example, women still quilt and pass those skills on through the generations but today, even in small towns, it is more common for most families to purchase quilts from a retailer. Butchering a hog for meat is still done, although increasingly people purchase ham and bacon at the grocery store. Milking a cow and churning butter is practiced, but it is less labor intensive to buy milk and butter produced by a commercial dairy.

Responding to change is nothing new for the country. In the early twentieth century innovations were things like electricity and running water; gasoline-powered cars, trucks, and tractors were rarities; and the quality of life that had changed for many in the cities was drawing the youth away. This is what spurred the country life movement of the early twentieth century to advocate change in order to retain the essence of rural life, which was viewed as one of the great strengths of the country (Swanson, 1980). The movement's efforts led, at least in part, to a transformation of rural life that benefited many people. But as is typical for small towns, change came slowly.

The transformation of rural America continues today, although for the most part, the pace of change is gradual. As a result, the small town of today is not the small town of 1900 or 1960, and overall, small-town life is qualitatively better than it was then. Almost everyone has electricity, with the benefits and convenience that it brings. Water may still come from wells, but it is pumped by a motor, not by hand, and is piped into houses. Health care, education, communication, roads, and transportation have improved. There is better access to information through the Internet, and broader choices for entertainment via cable television.

While many aspects of rural life have remained constant, the small towns of the twenty-first century are not the same as when Josephine Brown (1933) or when Leon Ginsberg (1976) wrote their groundbreaking books on rural social work. Today many of the social and cultural traditions of smaller communities would be still recognized by country people from the early part of the twentieth century. Family, traditions, church, connection to the land, and self-sufficiency are still crucial parts of community identity. But modern improvements in communication and transportation have added a cosmopolitan dimension to the traditions of the past. Rural life and educational levels have improved, although often not without a heavy dose of public support.

For rural people, life is complex and changing, which makes the traditional stereotypes of a rural community a real albatross for social workers who practice in the small town and countryside. The twenty-first-century challenges facing the rural community, the people who are part of it, and social workers are likely to be as different in a few years as current conditions are from those of the 1930s. To be ready for rural practice and practice of the future, we need to understand the community and people, how society is changing, and the ways in which the social work profession can respond to the needs of small towns and rural areas.

RURAL COMMUNITIES: PERCEPTION, REALITY, AND DEMANDS OF THE TWENTY-FIRST CENTURY

Rural communities have sometimes been called "Hidden America" (Moore, 2001), which reflects a general belief that they are not a part of society that people see, understand, or think about a great deal. This is in part because most people today live in cities, or at least on the outskirts of cities. Still, from time to time, urban residents do go to the country. They go for vacation and recreation, and they drive through the country on their way to another destination. When they do, they undoubtedly see and experience some of rural America. So if this is the case, why is rural America still hidden in the twenty-first century, and why do so many people look at it but not *see* it? Michael Harrington (1981) eloquently answered this question in his classic work on poverty, *The Other America*. As he wrote about the poor in Appalachia, Harrington (1981) observed:

> Beauty can be a mask for ugliness. That is what happens in the Appalachians. . . . It is not just the physical beauty that blinds the city man to the reality of these hills. The people are mountain folk. They are of old American stock, many of them Anglo-Saxon, and old traditions still survive among them. Seeing in them a romantic image of mountain life as independent, self-reliant, and athletic, a tourist could pass through these valleys and observe only quaintness. But not quite: for suddenly the mountain vista will reveal slashed, scarred hills and dirty little towns living under the shadow of decaying mining buildings. The irony is deep, for everything that turns the landscape into an idyll for the urban traveler conspires to hold people down. They suffer terribly at the hands of beauty. (pp. 42–43)

So in some ways, people see what they want to see. In the rural community outsiders often see the simpler, uncomplicated life of an idealized past, with views unspoiled by tall buildings, land devoid of the snarls and bustle of traffic, rich earth instead of acres of concrete, visible starry skies, the absence of crowds, and the presence of solitude. These are the things that people expect and want to see in the country. The unpleasant realities of poverty, run-down housing, ill health, bad roads, and decaying infrastructure are found easily enough in outsiders' own inner cities, and they come to the country to forget those things. Indeed, the needs of rural communities are easier and more pleasant to overlook.

The myth of the simple life in the country is as pervasive as it is appealing, and the myth is resilient despite evidence to the contrary. But this has been true for more than a century. Nineteenth-century social reformers encouraged the building of mental hospitals and child-care institutions in the country to take advantage of the healthy climate and the healing power of nature. Scouting programs were built at least in part on the presumed value of the wholesome environment of the outdoors and the self-reliance taught through coping with nature. For many people, a simpler life devoid of tight schedules, long lines, noisy traffic, and even cell phones is an ideal about which they yearn. These are beautiful thoughts, and in part true, but those who do not really know the country would do well to listen to the wisdom of author Doris Janzen Longacre: "The trouble with simple living is that, though it can be joyful, rich, and creative, it isn't simple." As Ginsberg (1976) correctly observed in his landmark book on rural social work, rural life is anything but simple. Indeed, amid beauty and peace there is hard work and struggle.

Even those who live or have lived in the country may have a limited view of rural life. They know the things with which they grew up, but sometimes they don't recognize them much, because those things are just part of the way things are. It takes some introspection to put rural life in context, and often experience with other communities, both rural and urban, helps highlight the unique features of small towns and rural life. There is an old, oft-repeated saying rural social workers use when talking about the communities in which they work: "When you've seen one rural community . . . you've seen one rural community" (Bertaina, 2011). The deeper meaning of this adage may not immediately sink in, but it is really a folksy acknowledgment of the rich diversity that characterizes rural communities across the country, and that often lies beneath the surface.

Rural communities come in all sizes: the county seat of forty thousand, the one-stoplight small town, the unincorporated area with a few buildings, and many more. Economies of country communities may be based on agriculture, small manufacturing, mining, timber, oil and gas extraction, hunting and fishing, tourism, and many other things. Today the people who live in rural communities increasingly reflect the diversity of our society, as an influx of new immigrants and migrants reaches new areas. The cultural traditions of country folk are about as varied as one can find anywhere. So when people see a rural community and begin to get a good idea of what the community and its people are like, they may develop an understanding of that community. But twenty miles down the road there might be a town of similar size but very different spirit and makeup. Hence judging all rural communities by a single example or stereotype is misleading because of the variety of rural society and life and the attributes of rural areas.

We tend to view small communities as desirable places to live, yet at the same time we also see them as devoid of many of the amenities and services that we often consider part of everyday life in the modern world. At the same time, oddly, we also consider that a virtue. As the rural sociologist Don Dillman (n.d.) once said, "Ironically, rural America has become viewed by a growing number of Americans as having a higher quality of life not because of what it has, but rather because of what it does not have!" However wistfully we might idealize the small community, few of us would permanently, and willingly, give up our smartphones, adequate health care, relatively higher incomes, and variety of consumer goods.

What kinds of issues might rural communities face as we move through the twenty-first century? One trend that affected rural life in the late twentieth century, and that affects it into the twenty-first, is globalization. The trend toward globalization in the economy is a process that has gone on for many years and promises to continue well into the future. Globalization has both positive and negative benefits for rural communities in North America. On the positive side, globalization has provided more markets for US agricultural produce, with about one-third of production now exported to overseas markets (Thompson, 2007). The export of agricultural goods accounts for approximately 25 percent of farm income, and additional income helps improve the economic state of rural agriculture and adds value to the land for many communities. As a result of globalization, rural people also can buy a greater variety of goods than ever before, and at reduced prices in many areas.

Despite the benefits provided through globalized trade and open markets, there are legitimate concerns for rural communities. The balance of trade in agricultural products has shrunk to about an even exchange, as the United States now imports much more produce from overseas (Thompson, 2007). So while large corporate agribusinesses may be profitable through sales and exports, independent medium-size and small farms can struggle to be profitable. This raises concerns about the loss of rural agricultural jobs to overseas labor forces. Farming families today earn most of their income from nonfarm sources (Thompson, 2007). This has provided more income stability for families than in the past, as people are no longer tied as closely to the ups and downs of the crop cycle. But this kind of change in lifestyle has been made possible by the location of manufacturing and service jobs within commuting distance of rural residents (Thompson, 2007). A major concern is that many rural manufacturing jobs have been lost because of increasing competition from product imports produced by lower-wage workers abroad (Economic Research Service, 2012)—such as the loss of jobs in the US textile market as factories closed and workers were laid off. According to Hamrick (2005), between 1994 and 2004 more than eight hundred thousand textile and apparel jobs were lost in the United States, and workers outside of metropolitan areas were disproportionately affected. Rural areas of the US Southeast were particularly hard hit as fabric and clothing production shifted overseas. "Globalization" in this sense hits people in the countryside hard, and they become resentful of overseas competition, whatever its possible benefits.

The traditional way US farm policy has attempted to encourage rural development also plays into the issue of globalization in ways that weaken small farms and rural communities. Most US support goes to the largest producers, which, coupled with increasing competition from low-wage overseas producers, encourages farm consolidation (Thompson, 2007). Consolidation, in turn, contributes to the loss of jobs in farming and rural economies.

Rural economies are not as robust as those of cities because they are not as diversified, and when the economy suffers, so does the infrastructure of the rural community. Unemployment and lower wages lead to lower sales and property values, which affects the tax revenue of the local government. Often having conservative views about taxation even in good times, small communities do not have much surplus for repairing buildings, providing police and fire protection, and offering social welfare services. So small communities, particularly those that are losing population, may face decaying infrastructure, empty buildings, and substandard housing. This is the case in many small communities with civic and commercial buildings that were constructed years ago, when the local economy was more prosperous. Such conditions affect the appearance of a community and may make them less desirable places to live, thus further reducing population and resources.

Rural values of self-reliance and self-help tend to make small communities less likely to fund social welfare services for those who may need them. The current societal trend of reducing funding for social services and entitlements may have a disproportionate effect on small towns. Most rural agencies that provide social services tend to be public, and public cost cutting can hit rural areas hard, as small communities often do not have private agencies to fill in the gaps (Ginsberg, 1976, 2011). And economic transfer payments from programs like Social Security provide a significant source of income for a portion of the people who reside in small towns. When those disappear, both local people and the economy suffer.

The real question is this: given these economic, political, and social factors, are rural communities in the throes of a slow death that will lead them to their demise by the end of the century? If rural communities do become a thing of the past, then our society will lose a large part of its character and history. But the fact is that, of necessity, rural areas have already begun to adapt to the changes of the late twentieth and early twenty-first centuries. Smaller communities are no longer as closely tied to agriculture as they once were. By 2004, between 85 and 95 percent of farm household income came from off-farm sources, and for smaller farming operations, agriculture was only a supplement to income (US Department of Agriculture, n.d.). Of concern to social workers is the important role of social welfare programs. Programs such as the Supplemental Nutrition Assistance Program (SNAP, or Food Stamps), Social Security, Supplemental Security Income, and publicly funded health-care services continue to remain important supplements to rural residents' income. Significant cuts in such programs might disproportionately affect small communities. However, as long as employment in the manufacturing and service sectors can remain viable within commuting distance from small towns, rural families will have the resources to provide income for their households.

There is hope for the future of rural communities, but the future will bring continued change in the economic base. A potential avenue of economic development lies in capturing niche markets that produce higher returns and operate in less competitive environments (VanWechel, Vachal, & Berwick, 2007). Examples of this include organic agriculture, the production of handmade quilts and tapestries, high-end or rustic furniture, and craft items. Agriculture may also examine the production of goods such as organic fruits and vegetables, milk, eggs, and meat. Some rural communities have already taken advantage of the natural beauty of their areas by developing tourism, and regions with an abundance of fish and wildlife might market themselves as desirable locations for hunters and fishermen.

Rural communities may also be able to tap into the current clean energy movement, which targets the development and use of biofuels, not fossil fuels. The development of local biofuel industries is a possible way to improve economic opportunity. Biofuels, such as ethanol used to fuel automobiles, are produced by fermenting corn, sugarcane, and even grass and trees, commodities typically found in the country. Additionally, biodiesel is made from vegetable oils and animal fats, and biogas is made from waste products. Wind power may also be an option for areas with space available to create wind farms. The US Department of Agriculture currently provides assistance and loans for rural areas that are attempting to build clean energy businesses (Rural Development, 2013).

Ultimately, to build an economy that will sustain and grow rural communities, some infrastructure development will be needed. One of the biggest infrastructure problems that rural communities face in the twenty-first century is the *digital divide* (National Association of Social Workers, NASW, 2012). The digital divide is inequality in access to modern communications, technology, and Internet. At present, rural communities are part of this inequality because they do not have the same level of access to electronic and technological resources that is available in the cities. Anyone who has driven off the interstate highways into the country knows that there are spots where cell phone reception is problematic. Commercial providers do not rush to provide cell towers and high-speed cable to smaller towns and rural areas because there are fewer customers and fewer profits to be made. But modern commerce increasingly moves on the information highway, and communities that lack good access will have difficulty attracting businesses and employers to locate in the area.

In the past rural communities often lacked access to cellular service, cable, and high-speed Internet altogether, but that is changing. According to a recent study in Minnesota, electronic technology is much more widely available than it was even a few years ago, yet disparity persists in the use of broadband in many homes (Center for Rural Policy and Development, 2012). Again, the major barrier to broadband availability appears to be its relatively high cost. Government intervention may be needed to spur the development of better accessibility to the Internet, as well as wireless and telecommunications, in rural areas. Waiting for businesses to make the move may not prove productive. After all, electricity did not reach many rural areas until government-sponsored help encouraged rural electrification. But the creation of a better digital infrastructure for smaller communities may help attract telecommuters who work elsewhere but live in the country, thereby enhancing the economy of rural areas. A better digital infrastructure may also attract different kinds of small business that make extensive use of digital resources and that find the available labor pool and facility costs appealing.

Small towns will need more than just good telecommunications access to attract business and manufacturing to the area. Of course, the primary attraction of locating a business in a rural community is the labor force. Rural people typically work hard, are productive, and tend to expect lower wages. Still, those things may not be enough. Services like health care, roads, and education likely need to be improved to attract outside interest. Sometimes local communities offer tax advantages to potential employers to sweeten the deal. This is a bit of a double-edged sword, because the community will receive less revenue while still having to improve infrastructure. So each small community should carefully consider offering incentives to businesses. External funds from state economic development entities may help offset costs, but rural communities will still have to be alert and creative in accessing these funds.

RURAL PEOPLE AND CHANGE FOR THE TWENTY-FIRST CENTURY

As Mark Twain is said to have remarked about small-town people, "Human nature cannot be studied in cities except at a disadvantage—a village is the place. There you can know your man inside and out—in a city you but know his crust; and his crust is usually a lie" (Anderson, Salano, & Stein, 1975). Much has changed since the early 1880s when Twain wrote that and much has not. In many ways rural people today are similar to what Twain described—sincere and straightforward. These traits have led outsiders to classify them as simple and unsophisticated, but nothing could be further from the truth. Country people do not hide behind pretenses. Pretense in a small town is easily detected because social relationships are too close, and phonies are quickly detected and kept at arm's length.

In the twenty-first century many traditional rural values hold strong. Churches and schools remain important institutions for social interaction, community identity, and support for members. Self-reliance and hard work are significant principles that motivate people in coping with everyday life, even when life is hard and times are tough. Tradition and place take prominent roles in the thinking and behavior of people in and from small towns across the country. Personal relationships continue to be prized over impersonal ones, although if one mentions the term *Gemeinschaft*, no doubt wary looks and puzzlement will ensue. Outsiders are still met with suspicion and doubt until they demonstrate that they are OK. And of course, attachment to family remains very strong—so strong, in fact, that it keeps people in their home communities even when the pastures may be greener elsewhere. This is rural as Mark Twain would readily recognize it.

Much as things stay the same, rural people have changed a lot. The effects of immigration trends are changing the diversity of rural communities, just as they affect the rest of society. As populations change, rural communities have begun to slowly adjust to new residents, even if begrudgingly and slowly. In addition, over the years as communications and mobility have improved, rural people have become a bit more cosmopolitan. Through improved transportation, it is common for country people to visit larger cities, whereas in the nineteenth and early twentieth century many never left the county of their birth. Television and the Internet bring vivid images of faraway places and different customs on a daily basis, and satellite transmission increases the range of programs from which people can learn. Through online and interactive video, rural residents in the twenty-first century can get a college education without venturing too far from home.

But the same influx of information that helped make rural people more world wise also helped change them. Images of life in the big city, different lifestyles, and consumer products have prompted some to question and abandon links to the past and traditions. These kinds of changes can produce generational gaps that produce tensions in families and communities.

With declines in the rural economy, people have been enticed to the city seeking a better or different life. But communities of country people have formed in the cities themselves, where lifestyles may be a bit different for them. Some urban migrants achieve what they set out to and succeed. But others trade a marginal rural life for a marginal city one. The latter group is one with which social workers particularly may come into contact. But because of their urban residence, social workers may not perceive how rough the fit is between clients' rural culture and their new urban home. Indeed, country city dwellers can easily become an invisible population, camouflaged in city neighborhoods.

Rural views have also tended to alter some as the influence of broader culture reached rural areas. Self-reliance and self-sufficiency may have come to mean something different to the younger generations of country people than they did to their parents and grandparents. To the modern generation, self-sufficiency generally means earning enough income to buy what you need. To their parents, it may have meant, at least in part, being able to make or provide for one's needs. For example, not many people make their own soap or their own clothes anymore, although those skills have not been entirely lost. Purchasing soap at the store may be easier, smell better, and be easier on the skin. But to older generations, providing their own fresh food, making their own clothes, and cutting wood for heat were a sign of self-sufficiency. And taking the easy way out and avoiding these tasks may appear to them as lazy. So there is a generation that has grown up valuing convenience and a better lifestyle. Rural people have adapted, although older generations fondly, even romantically, remember the traditions. Today, though, it is hard to imagine that people really enjoyed an evening trek to the outhouse in the dead of winter.

Some rural skills have been preserved in folk life centers and museums, and some people still practice those skills, but not on the scale that they did in the past. Some of this is done for instruction, just to pass skills and culture on to the younger generations—like blacksmithing, leather work, and so on. Parents and grandparents may teach young people hunting, fishing, tanning, cooking, and canning skills as much for enrichment as to carry on traditions.

But cultural influences go both ways. Rural people have influenced urban culture as well. It is not uncommon to see the large and expensive dually truck with four-wheel drive cruising the city streets as a status symbol rather than as working farm or ranch vehicle. Cowboy hats, boots, and bib-front overalls seen in the city are typically more for fashion than utility. And country style is marketable—from preserves to bacon and food recipes to art. City people often pay a premium to connect to a culture they have never experienced fully.

The truth is that in the twenty-first century rural folk have softened some, even in the strong belief in self-reliance. With the decline in traditional types of employment, government income-transfer programs have become an important source of support for rural people. Social Security, Medicare, Supplemental Security Income, Temporary Assistance for Needy Families, SNAP, Medicaid, and other services provide valuable supplemental income to rural people. Public social welfare programs constitute a more important part of the rural economy than they do in the cities, where there are more options for employment (Ginsberg, 2005). Indeed, while stereotypical views of public income support programs tend to focus on recipients as inner-city minorities, many rural families rely on these supports to help make ends meet. It is not so much that rural people embrace these programs; in fact, many oppose their very existence. Yet it is a reality that for some, receiving assistance is the price that they must pay to live in a place where they are comfortable and to be near supportive friends and family.

In the past, rural areas attracted new residents because the land offered a degree of independence, a livelihood, and perhaps a better life. That is not always the case today, as economic opportunities are often more rewarding in the city. Rural people still have and value their independence, but the land is not as economically rewarding as it once was. Land was once a symbol of wealth and prestige, and it remains so to many people. But rural America is home to many "landed poor" today, and it continues to be a source of independence and pride, if not a significant income. In the twenty-first century, redevelopment of rural communities is needed to energize the rural environment's most valuable resource: its people.

SOCIAL WORK IN RURAL PRACTICE

There is little doubt that the origins of modern social work in the United States began with societal concerns about large, often industrial cities (Daley & Avant, 2004; Ginsberg, 2011; NASW, 2012). Given the profession's primary focus on addressing the needs of urban communities, the development of the rural practice has received much less attention. As a result, in many ways the social work field has not always adequately stepped forward to address the needs of rural people and communities. Despite a renewed interest in rural social work in the twenty-first century, there is evidence that more needs to be done in terms of the development and promotion of rural practice. Take, for example, the NASW's 2012 "Rural Social Work" policy statement:

> Consequently, most social workers receive little content on rural social work in their professional education. This creates a major barrier to developing a social work labor force prepared to address the needs of rural clients and communities and poses a deficit for social workers practicing in rural areas. (p. 298)

The policy goes on to say that social work should support policies to attract and keep social workers in rural areas, develop ethical principles and applications for rural practice, recognize the importance of rural people and culturally competent practice, and promote social policy that benefits rural people and communities.

Indeed, more social workers with appropriate education and training are needed for rural work. In an ideal world rural positions should be made more attractive to provide services and meet the needs of country people. Despite the need for professional social workers, the US Bureau of Labor Statistics (2010) has indicated that there is less competition for social work positions in rural communities. Rural social work positions may be less desirable because salaries are lower than in urban areas and workers are less satisfied with the resources they have available to help clients (NASW Center for Health Workforce Studies & NASW, 2006). This combined with little emphasis in rural social work in education and fewer professional schools in rural areas do not make the outlook too promising on the surface. As with many other kinds of issues, the needs of rural people and communities, and the social workers who serve them, have become hidden by the demands of the masses from the city. It may be that the social work profession and rural social workers will have to become more active in advocacy efforts to promote rural social work in the future.

CONCLUSION

Social work with rural people and communities is an important field of practice that is often overlooked by the profession. In an increasingly urban society, it is easy to forget that about one in six people lives in the wide-open spaces of the country. While small towns and rural villages appear to have been passed by in society's drive to become modern and urbane, they still make important contributions to society. Without rural areas we would not have the energy we need to power our homes, the food on our table, the wood to build our houses, the ore that makes our steel, or the wonderful locations we enjoy for relaxation and recreation. Rural communities remain a bastion of values that we prize in society, like self-reliance, hard work, thrift, family, and church. And small communities have added materially to our culture through their arts, music, crafts, and literature.

We are fortunate that rurality has not been narrowly confined to the country but has spread throughout society to enrich us all. Over the years many rural people have migrated to the city in search of greener pastures, and in return they have added their culture to the melting pot. In cowboy boots, woodland plaids, humor, quilts, country music, and greens and grits, we find a bit of us all. There is a directness and honesty and sense of community in rural culture that some people feel has been lost in twenty-first-century living. Many of these things still reside in rural people.

Yet life in a rural community is often challenging. This means that social workers can be of help, but often they are not trained for rural work. There tend to be fewer resources and services available in rural areas than in cities, and typically there are not enough professionals to deliver them. Rural social work can be as challenging, if not more challenging, than equivalent work in a metropolitan area, yet rural social work positions tend to receive lower pay. Yet each professional social worker has a basic framework for rural practice, for the elements of good social work are present in either rural or urban practice. To quote a country analogy, "The difference between corn and cotton is the stooping" (Bowman, 1995, p. 46). In other words, the work is much the same in the country and in the city, but there is some adjustment that needs to be made.

There are indeed many life challenges for rural people and social workers in rural areas. But despite these challenges, small communities abound in strengths, and residents tend to value their lives there. They like the place, the lifestyle, and the sense of community and belonging that a rural area brings. Indeed, the biggest asset of any rural community is its people, who are resilient and feel a sense of connection to their neighbors. Small towns try to take care of their own, as people try to help one another deal with adversity, especially when times are tough.

However, there are times in rural areas when self-reliance, resilience, and community spirit are not enough to help everyone who may need assistance. This is where formal social welfare services try to assist, and social workers fill a vital role in helping people. Often, critical services are not close to those who need them, and the array of specialized services is limited, yet rural practitioners continue to find creative ways to empower people and help them meet their needs.

There is much promise and hope for rural communities and rural social work as the twenty-first century moves forward. Rural communities as a whole are not dying, being abandoned, or vanishing—as some people believe. Despite increased urbanization of the country, the population of small towns continues to grow. Many small towns in the country have found new ways to adapt and survive. Where family farms have declined as an economic force, wage work has helped supplement family income. Social welfare and health-care services are finding innovative ways to extend essential services to smaller and more remote communities. Technological innovations like mobile units, the Internet, and video links are accessible in more remote communities.

The social work profession has responded to the needs of rural communities as well. Over the past fifteen years the profession has expanded the literature and knowledge base considerably. More BSW and MSW programs are providing rural content in professional education than ever before. Although there are still not enough professional social workers to meet the needs of rural communities, there is hope for the future. Given both past and current trends, the field of rural practice appears to be an area open for growth.

Perhaps we have been too eager to write the obituary of small towns in this country; many are alive and well. We should remember that rural communities have a strong collective will to survive, even when times are tough—they are "tougher than a pine knot." And most rural people have not given up on the value of rural life, even when they have moved to the city. So rural people have not decided quite yet that it is "time to put the tools in the truck and head for the house." Social workers should be proud to work with people who have such motivation and resilience.

REFERENCES

Anderson, F. A., Salano, L., & Stein, B. L. (Eds.) (1975). *Mark Twain's notebooks and journals: Volume II (1877–1883)*. Berkeley, CA: University of California Press.

Bertaina, S. (2011). *Sustainable community development in rural communities*. Retrieved from http://www.arc.gov/noindex/programs/ardi

/2011TAWorkshops/WVWorkshop/EPA_ARDI_WV_Presentation _Community_Dev.pdf.

Bowman, B. (1995). *He's wetting on my leg, but it's warm and wet and feels good.* Lufkin, TX: Best of East Texas Publishers.

Brown, J. C. (1933). *The rural community and social casework.* New York, NY: Family Welfare Association of America.

Center for Rural Policy and Development. (2012). *2012 Minnesota Internet survey.* Retrieved from http://www.ruralmn.org/wp-content /uploads/2012/11/2012-broadband1.pdf

Daley, M., & Avant, F. (2004). Reconceptualizing the framework for practice. In T. L. Scales & C. L. Streeter (Eds.), *Rural social work: Building and sustaining community assets* (pp. 34–42). Belmont, CA: Thomson.

Dillman, D. A. (n.d.). *Dillman quotes.* Retrieved from http://www.search-quotes.com/quotation/Ironically%2C_rural_America_has_become _viewed_by_a_growing_number_of_Americans_as_having_a_higher _qual/237854/.

Economic Research Service, US Department of Agriculture. (2012). *US textile and apparel industries and rural America.* Retrieved from http://www.ers.usda.gov/topics/crops/cotton-wool/background/us -textile-and-apparel-industries-and-rural-america.aspx.

Ginsberg, L. H. (1976). *Social work in rural communities: A book of readings.* New York, NY: Council on Social Work Education.

Ginsberg, L. H. (2005). The overall context of rural practice. In L. H. Ginsberg (Ed.), *Social work in rural communities* (4th ed., pp. 4–7). Alexandria, VA: Council on Social Work Education.

Ginsberg, L. H. (2011). Introduction to basics of rural social work. In L. H. Ginsberg (Ed.), *Social work in rural communities* (5th ed., pp. 5–20). Alexandria, VA: Council on Social Work Education.

Hamrick, K. (2005, June 6). *Displacement of textile and apparel workers* [PowerPoint presentation]. Retrieved from http://www.farmfounda tion.org/news/articlefiles/229-Hamrick.pdf.

Harrington, M. (1981). *The other America.* New York, NY: Penguin Books.

Moore, R. M. (2001). *The hidden America.* Cranbury, NJ: Susquehanna University Press.

NASW Center for Health Workforce Studies & National Association of Social Workers. (2006, March). *Licensed social workers in the United States, 2004*. Retrieved from http://workforce.socialworkers.org/studies/chapter3_0806.pdf.

National Association of Social Workers. (2012). Rural social work. In *Social work speaks: National Association of Social Workers policy statements* (9th ed., pp. 296–300). Washington, DC: NASW Press.

Phrase Finder. (2013). *If it ain't broke, don't fix it*. Retrieved from http://www.phrases.org.uk/meanings/if-it-aint-broke-dont-fix-it.html.

Rural Development, US Department of Agriculture. (2013). *Rural energy development programs*. Retrieved from http://www.rurdev.usda.gov/Energy.html.

Swanson, M. (1980). The country life movement: An introduction. In E. E. Martinez-Brawley (Ed.), *Pioneer efforts in rural social welfare* (pp. 5–7). University Park, PA: Pennsylvania State University Press.

Thompson, R. L. (2007). Globalization and rural America. *Chicago Fed Letter*. Retrieved from http://www.chicagofed.org/digital_assets/publications/chicago_fed_letter/2007/cfljune2007_239.pdf.

US Bureau of Labor Statistics. (2010). *Social worker*. Retrieved from http://www.bls.gov/K12/help05.htm.

US Department of Agriculture. (n.d.). *Farm family income*. Retrieved from http://www.usda.gov/documents/FARM_FAMILY_INCOME.pdf.

VanWechel, T., Vachal, K., & Berwick, M. (2007). *Supply side basics: Niche agricultural marketing the logistics*. Retrieved from http://www.ams.usda.gov/AMSv1.0/getfile?dDocName=STELPRDC5064987.

Index

About the Author

MICHAEL R. DALEY, PHD, LCSW PIP, ACSW, is professor of social work at the University of South Alabama in Mobile. He was formerly director of the school of social work at Stephen F. Austin State University and social work program director at the University of South Alabama. Daley received his MSW from the University of Houston and his PhD in social welfare from the University of Wisconsin–Madison. He has been active in the rural social work field for more than twenty-five years, having published several articles and book chapters on the subject. He also served as editor of the journal *Contemporary Rural Social Work*. He has been involved in several professional organizations, including serving as president of the National Rural Social Work Caucus, the Association of Social Work Baccalaureate Program Directors, and the Texas Chapter of the National Association of Social Workers, and as chair of the NASW's National Ethics Committee. His research interests include rural social work, social work ethics, and the social work profession.